Caste in
Overseas Indian
Communities

Chandler Publications in
ANTHROPOLOGY and SOCIOLOGY
LEONARD BROOM, *Editor*

CONTRIBUTORS TO
Caste in Overseas Indian Communities

Burton Benedict, *London School of Economics*
Agehananda Bharati, *Syracuse University*
Colin Clarke, *University of Liverpool*
Chandra Jayawardena, *University of Sydney*
Hilda Kuper, *University of California, Los Angeles*
Adrian C. Mayer, *University of London*
H. S. Morris, *London School of Economics*
Arthur H. Niehoff, *George Washington University*
Barton M. Schwartz, *California State College, Los Angeles*
Philip Singer, *United Nations Secretariat*
Raymond T. Smith, *University of Chicago*
Johan D. Speckmann, *Leiden University*

Caste in Overseas Indian Communities

Edited by

Barton M. Schwartz

California State College, Los Angeles

CHANDLER PUBLISHING COMPANY

124 SPEAR STREET

SAN FRANCISCO, CALIFORNIA 94105

 Science Research Associates, Inc., 259 East Erie Street, Chicago, Illinois 60611
A Subsidiary of IBM   Distributors

To Clair

CONTENTS

SOUTH AFRICA

EAST AFRICA

TABLES

ILLUSTRATIONS

PREFACE

During the past few years, the study of overseas Indian communities has received widespread attention. While this particular field of study is not completely new, scholars are becoming increasingly aware of the potential significance involved in such investigations. They appear optimisic in their belief that this field of study is important not only for its particular value but also because it has the potential for answering, at least for refining, some of the unresolved critical questions posed by social scientists. Research already completed is indicative of the geographical scope, diverse interests, and wide range of problems involved. Field studies have been carried out in varying degrees of completeness in such geographically diverse areas as Mauritius, Guyana, Fiji, Trinidad, Surinam, Guadeloupe, Martinique, Uganda, Kenya, Tanganyika, Natal, British Columbia, Jamaica, the United States, and other regions too numerous to list completely. This research has resulted in the production of scholarly reports, professional articles, and books focusing upon marriage and the family, caste, ethnic interaction, legal systems and social control, magic and religion, social organization, social and cultural pluralism, population dynamics, differential fertility, migration, indenture systems, economic integration and exploitation, plantation systems, and sociocultural perpetuation and differential adaptation. These are some, but not all, of the more general topics intimately involved in the study of overseas Indian communities. While variation of this type is significant in and of itself, if only to demonstrate the relevant variables, additional importance is acquired when the results of such research are unified in some meaningful way. By bringing together the results of research on caste as it exists in overseas Indian communities, this book constitutes a concrete attempt to achieve unification of research dealing with a single problem. The research problem, caste, is the constant; history, environment, population, culture, and differential adaptation and perpetuation are the categorical variables. The articles that follow in this book explain the methods of analyses and report the results.

The idea for this book originally occurred in 1961. Since this time, some of the materials presented in certain articles have been published in different professional sources. This has been largely a function of the various and lengthy delays in having this book published. Following initial planning and discussion, individuals who had conducted research in Indian communities outside of India were approached as possible contributors. As with any book of this kind, not all individuals contacted have articles included in this volume, nor were all persons approached who had conducted research in overseas Indian communities. Hence, the book omits research from particular geographical regions, deals only lightly with others, and concentrates more directly on still others. Diverse reasons, not directly pertinent at this time, account for such omissions and inclusions. However, this volume *does include* analyses from each of the areas where majority or significant minority Indian populations reside. These inclusions speak for themselves.

Contributors were not requested to produce any particular type of report; they were not asked to focus on any specific aspect of caste; nor were they restricted in their method of analysis. The only requirement was that they report the results of their particular research dealing with caste in the communties in which they had conducted their research. Caste, therefore, provides not only the constant, but also the single unifying element for the book. While greater evenness might have been achieved through more precise specifications to the various contributors, these might have produced less realistic, even biased, results. Variation in methods of analyses, areas of concentration, data reported, and other aspects are as significant as the results of the research reported. Because of this commitment, I have attempted to remain as true as possible to the author's original manuscripts. This alternative, in my opinion, seems to be the most objective, the most realistic, and the most compatible with the general goals of scientific investigation.

The order in which the articles appear is only one of several possible alternatives. The articles may be rearranged for purposes of analysis or presentation by making use of particular criteria.

The *method of migration* of Indians to overseas communities may be used to divide the book into two main, but unequal, sections: (1) those populations that are historically characterized by indentured migration (Mauritius, Guyana, Trinidad, Surinam, Fiji, and South Africa) : and (2) those populations that have a history of "passenger" (nonindentured) migration (mainly South and East Africa). While existing data show that no absolute dichotomy between indentured and passenger migrants is possible (passenger Indians have migrated to "indentured areas" and indentured Indians have migrated to "passenger areas"), such a division can be used for comparative purposes in a meaningful way.

Chronology of migration is another of the alternatives that may be used. Thus migration to Mauritius commences in 1835, to British Guiana in 1838, to Trinidad in 1845, to South Africa in 1860, to Surinam in 1873, to Fiji in 1879, and to East Africa in 1896. While certain date discrepancies exist for the beginning and end of the specific migration from India to each of the geographical areas considered, these dates reflect the beginnings of the major migration periods.

The order of presentation may be revised in accordance with the *numerical dimensions of the Indian populations* for each of the societies. Majority or near-majority Indian populations occur in Mauritius, Guyana, Trinidad, Surinam, and Fiji, while numerically smaller populations occur in South and East Africa.

In addition, other criteria can be used in conjunction with or separate from those listed above. For example, the order of presentation may be revised only slightly to provide a *distinction between rural and urban populations*. Reports dealing with Mauritius, Guyana, Surinam, and Fiji, in addition to two of the articles from Trinidad (Schwartz and Niehoff), constitute the rural dimensions, while those reporting on South Africa, East Africa and "town" Trinidad (Clarke) provide the urban category. However, it must be recognized that some of the data reported for Surinam, Mauritius, and Guyana (Singer) apply to urban populations.

Still other criteria, such as *contact with India subsequent to migration, migration centers in India, proximity to India, and geographical unity* can be used to rearrange the existing order of presentation to advantage and without distortion.

Diacritical marks and italics, though originally included, have been largely omitted at the request of the publisher.

The book is a cooperative effort involving many individuals. Specifically, I would like to express my appreciation to each of the contributors for their genuine interest and sincere cooperation, as well as their extended patience during the preparation of this volume. I am also indebted to Professor Pedro Carrasco, who first suggested that I engage in research among Indians overseas. And I am indebted to Patsy Thompson for her assistance in indexing and in proofreading the manuscript.

I feel confident that all contributors to this volume join with me in expressing appreciation to each of the populations where research was carried out. Without the cooperation, interest, and hospitality of such populations, research of the type reported here would be near impossible. More candidly, "Let it be admitted . . . that the successful outcome of field research depends not only on an anthropologist's own skills, but also on the capabilities and interest of those who teach him their ways" (Casagrande 1960:x).[1]

BARTON M. SCHWARTZ, *Editor*

---

[1] I employ Joseph B. Casagrande's language from p. x of *In the Company of Man* which he edited in 1960 for Harper and Brothers.

THE CONTRIBUTORS

Burton Benedict received his Ph.D. from the University of London and is now Senior Lecturer in Social Anthropology at the London School of Economics. He has carried out extended anthropological research in Mauritius, Seychelles, Nyasaland, and London. Dr. Benedict is the author of numerous articles in leading anthropological journals. Among the books he has published are *Indians in a Plural Society*, *A Preliminary Survey of the Needs of Youth in Nyasaland*, and *People of the Seychelles*.

Agehananda Bharati is Associate Professor of Anthropology in the Department of Anthropology, Maxwell Graduate School of Public Affairs and Citizenship, Syracuse University. Trained at the University of Vienna and at the Advaita Ashrama in India, Professor Bharati, who publishes in four different languages, is author of an extensive list of articles, monographs, and books. In addition to continuous field work in India from 1948 to 1956, he has also carried out anthropological field research in Thailand and in East Africa. He has been guest lecturer as well as visiting scholar at universities throughout the world. Currently he is contributing editor to the journals *Universitas*, *Philosophischer Literaturanzeiger*, and *Folia Humanistica*. Professor Bharati's major books include *The Tantric Tradition* and *A Functional Analysis of Indian Thought and Its Social Margins*.

COLIN CLARKE is currently a Lecturer in the Department of Geography and Centre for Latin-American Studies, University of Liverpool, England. He was a Collins Exhibitioner at Jesus College, Oxford University between 1957 and 1960 and a postgraduate research student at Oxford from 1960 to 1963. He spent the major part of 1961 at the Institute of Social and Economic Research, University College of the West Indies, in research focusing on the social geography of Kingston, Jamaica. During 1964, in Trinidad, he pursued additional field work concerned with the East Indian and Negro communities.

CHANDRA JAYAWARDENA is Senior Lecturer in the Department of Anthropology, University of Sydney. He has carried out extensive field research in Guyana, Fiji, and in Northern Sumatra. In addition to articles published in professional journals, Dr. Jayawardena is also the author of the book *Conflict and Solidarity in a Guianese Plantation*.

HILDA KUPER is Professor of Anthropology, Department of Anthropology, University of California, Los Angeles. She received her Ph.D. from the London School of Economics and Political Science, University of London, and has held teaching posts at the University of Witwatersrand, University of North Carolina, and the University of Natal. She has held research posts at the National Council of Social Research, South Africa, and at Manchester University. Professor Kuper's field research has been undertaken in Swaziland, in Johannesburg, and in Durban. She has an extensive list of publications and is best known for her books *An African Aristocracy, The Uniform of Colour, The Swazi, Indian People in Natal, Bite of Hunger,* and *Urbanization and Migration in West Africa.*

ADRIAN C. MAYER is Professor of Indian Anthropology at the University of London. He has held the posts of Scholar and then Research Fellow, Australian National University; Lecturer, School of Oriental and African Studies, University of London; and Reader in Indian Anthropology, University of London. Professor Mayer has engaged in extensive field research in South India, Central India, Fiji, Vancouver, British Columbia, and West Pakistan. He is the author of *Land and Society in Malabar, Report on the East Indian Community in Vancouver, Caste and Kinship in Central India, Peasants in the Pacific,* and *Indians in Fiji.* Professor Mayer is at present Honorary Editor of *Man: Journal of the Royal Anthropological Institute.*

H. S. MORRIS is Lecturer in Anthropology at the London School of Economics and Political Science, University of London. He has previously been Solicitor of the Supreme Court of Justice of England and Research Officer of the Sarawak Government and the Colonial Social Science Research Council, as well as Senior Research Fellow at the Institute of East African Social Research, Makerere College, Kampala, Uganda. Dr. Morris received his Ph.D. from the University of London and has carried out field research in Sarawak, Thailand, and East Africa. He is the author of various articles and the book *Report on a Melanau Sago Producing Community in Sarawak.*

ARTHUR H. NIEHOFF received his Ph.D. from Columbia University and is now at the Human Resources Research Office, George Washington University. He has held positions in the Department of Anthropology of the Milwaukee Public Museum and at the University of Wisconsin, and has been Community Development Advisor for the Agency for International Development in Laos. Dr. Niehoff has carried out field research in India, Trinidad, and Laos. He has an extensive list of articles published in a variety of journals, and his monographs and books include *Factory Workers in India, East Indians in the West Indies, Cultural Reality and Technical Change* (with C. M. Arensberg), and *Introducing Social Change* (with C. M. Arensberg). In addition, Dr. Niehoff has produced a variety of lecture and teaching films including *Many Faces of India, Indian Journey, Trinidad: Melting Pot, Laos: Focus of Conflict,* and *Angkor Wat.*

BARTON M. SCHWARTZ received his Ph.D. in anthropology from the University of California, Los Angeles. He has held teaching positions at Washington State University and Lehigh University, and is now Associate Professor of Anthropology and Chairman of the Department, California State College at Los Angeles. Dr. Schwartz has carried out anthropological research in Trinidad, Fiji, Mauritius, and North America and has published articles in a variety of anthropological journals.

PHILIP SINGER received his Ph.D. in cultural anthropology from Syracuse University and is currently Social Affairs Officer with the United Nations Secretariat in New York City. He has held teaching positions at the Maxwell School of Citizenship and Public Affairs, Syracuse University and at the State University of New York, Albany. This article was written while he was Assistant Professor of Behavioral Sciences, Albany Medical College, Albany, New York, where he was instrumental in establishing the Cross-Cultural Clinical Clerkship between the Albany Medical College and the Georgetown Hospital, Guyana. He has done field work in India and Guyana and has published articles in both anthropological and psychiatric journals. The book *The Holy Men of India and Charisma* is in press.

RAYMOND T. SMITH is Professor of Anthropology at the University of Chicago. He received his Ph.D. from the University of Cambridge and has held teaching positions at the University of the West Indies, and at the University of Ghana. In addition, he has been Visiting Professor at the University of California, Berkeley (1957-1958) and at McGill University (1964-1965). Professor Smith has done research in Guyana, Jamaica, and Ghana. He has published numerous articles on a wide variety of subjects and is best known for his books *The Negro Family in British Guiana* and *British Guiana*.

JOHAN D. SPECKMANN is professor of methodology in the Department for Cultural Anthropology and the Sociology of Non-Western Peoples in the State University of Leiden (The Netherlands). He conducted research among East Indians in Surinam during the period 1959-1961 under the auspices of the Netherlands Foundation for the Advancement of Research in Surinam and the Netherlands Antilles (WOSUNA). He has published several papers on this subject and the book *Marriage and Kinship among the Indians in Surinam.* He also led a research team in Africa in connection with a social-economic survey in the Republic of Niger. He is at present in charge of a motivation research project on family-planning in Pakistan.

Caste in
Overseas Indian
Communities

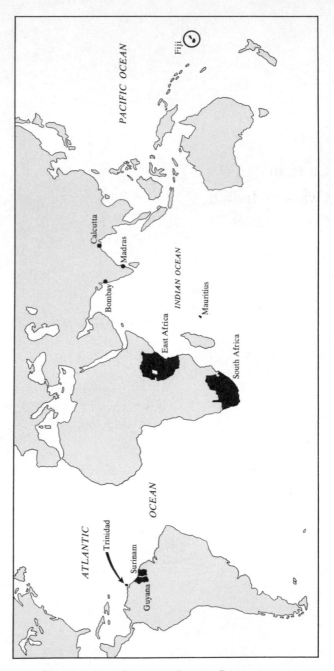

Locations of Overseas Indian Communities

Introduction

ADRIAN C. MAYER

The social scientist can approach the subject of caste in overseas Indian communities in several ways and at different levels of
generalization. (1) He can focus his study on caste as an organizing
principle of an overseas Indian community. To what extent are there
caste groups, and what part do these play in the various activities of
the community? (2) Or can he broaden the inquiry to embrace the
whole society, and ask whether caste is significant in the relations of
overseas Indians to members of other communities. (3) More generally still, he may compare caste in the overseas community with caste
in India, in order to see what significant differences exist in the institution. This comparative approach may lead to an attempt to assess the
degree to which "Indian Caste" has been retained after emigration,
or it may lead to an inquiry into the definition of caste itself. Should
the term be so defined that it applies to a wide variety of societies
over the world, or is it best restricted to the Indian institution? Here,
the overseas Indian communities may provide crucial borderline
cases in which some of the properties of Indian caste exist, but not all
of them.

The papers in this volume deal mainly with the first of these
approaches, though they also consider the second and third to a
lesser extent. Of the fourth little is said, though it may be of most

interest to readers who are neither Indianists nor students of the societies described. I shall consider each in turn. Limitations of space preclude a detailed critique of each paper and an assessment of its quality. This I leave to reviewers, and will focus only on the broader trends and problems with which the papers deal or upon which they touch.

Caste as the Organizing Principle of Community Structure among Overseas Indians

The view of most contributors is that castes do not form important units, nor are intercaste relations significant in the community structure of overseas Indians.

According to Smith and Jayawardena, for instance, within the Guyanese Indian community, economic, political, and juridic relations "are not structured on caste lines" (p. 88). Benedict writes that "caste is not a very important phenomenon in the social structure of Mauritius or even of the Indian section within it" (p. 40). For Trinidad, Niehoff reports that "caste is functionally a matter of little concern in this Hindu community" (p. 162), and Kuper concludes that in South Africa caste "does not necessarily operate as a clearly defined system of structured social relationships" (p. 244).

Morris, on the other hand, writes for Uganda that the "need for caste exclusiveness . . . was one of the most important structural principles in organizing Indian social life" (p. 276). Although the East African Indian community is different in origin and composition from the majority of the communities treated here, I do not think that these differences are the whole reason for the variation in emphasis. It also arises partly from the different uses of the term "caste" by the different writers. As Morris points out, the word has been given several sociological referents by Indianists. It is used for the fourfold division of Hindus into all-India categories (varna); for the named populations which comprise these varna and which are generally of regional extension (castes and subcastes); for the operating and usually endogamous groups which together comprise these named populations and which are of local extension (caste group and subcaste group); and for the associations recruited from caste or subcaste, and sometimes from varna, for social or political ends. When Morris says that caste is important in Uganda, he is referring both to the fact that Uganda Indians are divided into castes and varna, but more especially that these units are significant in terms of the fourth referent listed above; and when the other writers say that caste is not important, they are referring mainly to some or all of the first three referents, and in particular to the third. Let me expand this statement.

All contributors—including those reporting from East Africa —agree that local caste groups and subcaste groups do not exist, and give the same reasons for their disappearance. Not only were ritual purity and occupational specialization dealt mortal blows by the circumstances of immigration and initial settlement, but the immigrants came from many different localities of India and were unable to re-form the small-scale organization on which caste-group and subcaste-group behavior had been based. Because the hierarchical position and customs of groups within the named subcaste or caste population often differed from locality to locality in India, there could often be no agreement on single standards of behavior or status in the new country; nor could there be agreement on who had the authority to control behavior, since caste and subcaste leaders and councils had in India been recognized only by those in the same locality.

If the local groups no longer exist, what then of the named subcaste and caste populations? The picture presented by our writers is that these units do exist in the various overseas communities. They continue to exist partly because of an endogamy which keeps them separate; partly also because in an intercaste marriage the child belongs to the caste of one parent and the separate caste populations are maintained by this ascription.

There are widely varying degrees of endogamy in the different communities, however. For East Africa, Bharati states that intercaste marriages are very rare (p. 291) and implies that in some cases intersubcaste marriages are also exceptional. Benedict says that the "vast majority" of marriages in Mauritius are caste endogamous (p. 37), although he points out that intermarriages do occur, and Kuper says much the same thing (p. 253). Both authors make the important point, however, that the linguistic-cultural population may become the endogamous unit.[1] We have a detailed picture from Trinidad, where Clarke (p. 184) shows that exactly half the marriages, and

Schwartz (p. 127) that 55 per cent of the marriages in their multi-caste samples took place between castes. For Guyana, Smith and Jayawardena show that only some 25 per cent of the marriages in two samples are intracaste ones (p. 71). Here then, there seems to be a wide variation, running from East Africa to Guyana as extremes. But the absence of caste endogamy need not necessarily mean that castes do not remain separate populations. As long as the child is recognized as belonging to a caste, the units are maintained. In Guyana, the child belongs to the father's caste (Jayawardena 1963: 19), as he appears to do in Trinidad[2] and, so one assumes in accordance with Indian procedures, as he does in other communities.

At least as significant as the incidence of marriage outside the caste is the number of people who do not know to what caste they belong. In Guyana such people constituted 25 per cent of the sample (p. 65) ; for Trinidad, Clarke gives 13 per cent (p. 172)[3] and for Fiji Schwartz lists 16 per cent (p. 221). By contrast, less than 3 per cent of Benedict's sample did not know their caste (p. 32), and there would presumably be few in East Africa. Even the largest percentage forms only a clear minority and, I think, one can conclude on this evidence that named-caste populations do still exist. Whether they have any significance for the activities and structure of the community is quite another matter, of course.

---

[1]See also Bharati (p. 297) ; and Mayer (1961: 144 sqq.) for the place of the linguistic or "cultural" group in Fiji.

[2]All affiliations in Clarke's sample were patrilateral (p. 186) ; Schwartz's data are unclear on this point, since he says that a person's caste name often derives from "his parent's or his grandparent's caste name" (p. 144) but does not state whether matrilaterally or patrilaterally in cases of intercaste marriage. Niehoff indicates that a matrilateral affiliation is sometimes made (p. 162), though his suggestion that the patrilateral stress is the result of Western influence is surely misplaced (see for example Mayer 1960:24-28).

[3]Schwartz mentions "several individuals" who did not know their caste in his Trinidad village (p. 144) ; these people did not form part of his sample, however, in which all respondents were members of specific castes.

Another referent of caste is the varna category. In India, the main sociological significance of the varna is that it presents an all-India framework of reference, so that men coming from different local hierarchies and different linguistic regions can measure each other's approximate rank. Hence, the varna is in no sense a group, and its membership merely reflects the position in the system which a caste population or a local caste group is acknowledged to hold or asserts that it holds.

The functions of the varna fit well into the overseas situation, where people from different regions wish to find out about each other's approximate status; and they are made more important by the lack of any caste-group organization. Hence, there are indications that the varna has to some extent "replaced" the caste as the endogamous unit. Clarke, for example, shows that only 27 per cent of his sample married outside the varna as compared with the 50 per cent who married outside the caste (p. 186); Smith and Jayawardena state that a statistically significant number of their informants marry within caste categories (which are similar to varna) (p. 73); and Kuper quotes Rambiritch and van den Berghe's data to show a preponderant varna endogamy for South Africa (p. 253). Again, Benedict notes that intercaste marriages occur mainly within the "middle range" of castes, which may well approximate a varna (p. 37); and 53 per cent of Schwartz's Trinidad sample married inside the varna (p. 139). Moreover, although two-thirds of the people in a sample interviewed by Speckmann in Surinam (p. 210) said that they considered varna to be irrelevant in the choice of a marriage partner, we do not know how many intervarna marriages actually take place there—for the ideal and the actual patterns may frequently conflict. In Trinidad, for example, only 41 of the 94 people who thought that there should be freedom to marry outside the caste had actually done so (Clarke, p. 187).

Caste and varna are therefore named social units in these overseas Indian communities, insofar as they are defined to varying extents by endogamy and ascribed membership. To what extent do they have other qualities of Indian caste?

A major feature of Indian caste is the link between caste and hereditary occupation, which is the basis for an economic interdependence—or, some would say, an economic conflict—of castes. This link is almost completely absent in the overseas communities, by reason initially of the impact of an indenture system under which nearly everyone had the same occupation, and later by reason of the introduction of a cash economy in which there was little occupational specialization. True, Bharati (p. 290) notes that crafts such as carpentry, masonry, and cobbling are still restricted, to members of specific castes in East Africa, and Kuper says that although there is no general correlation of caste and occupation (p. 256), certain occupations are nevertheless performed mostly by specific castes and "this persistent association between [caste] and occupation contributes to the general awareness of caste" (p. 257). Most writers, however, stress that only one occupation still has any important caste connotation, that of the priesthood for the Brahmin. Even this is not a monopoly, because there are reform movements, such as the Arya Samaj, which explicitly throw open the conduct of ceremonies to non-Brahmins.[4] But the data suggest that Brahmins are still generally acknowledged as priests and have a consequent prestige which, however much weakened under new conditions, is important for the persistence of a caste ideology.

It would be wrong to ignore completely the wider connection of occupation and caste. The traditional occupational connotation of a caste name can, where it remains, to some extent influence the status of members whatever work they may be doing. To call someone a Chamar (Tanner) is a "blasphemy" in Trinidad, for instance (Clarke p. 179), and can lead to legal action in Mauritius (Benedict p. 36) ; again, Bharati notes that men of craft castes who have taken to other occupations avoid their caste mates, but can only succeed in being accepted as equals by members of higher castes in matters which do not involve rituals and marriage (p. 313). We can see, therefore, that occupation is important not so much in the literal sense of who is engaged in it, nor in the structural sense that there is an organically interdependent series of ascribed occupations, but rather in the sense that an occupation is hierarchically graded and

---

[4]See, however, Benedict's comment that sectarian lines are blurred in Mauritius, where Brahmins may be preferred officiants at Arya Samaj rites (p. 36).

thereby affects the status of the people belonging to the caste traditionally associated with it.

The discussion of occupation has brought us to another fundamental feature of Indian caste, that of the hierarchy of castes and
varna. It is clear from our authors that there is a notion of hierarchy,
though it is hard to say just how far this expresses itself in social
relationships, and specifically in caste relations. A fundamental feature of the Indian caste hierarchy is the relation between pure and
impure, which leads to a hierarchy of statuses based on pollution.
There is evidence that some of the traditional methods of showing
differences between such statuses still exist. Thus, there is some restricted residence of lower castes (Niehoff p. 156), some idea about
unclean occupations (Kuper p. 257) and some restricted commensality, for example that of Brahmin priests at rituals (Clarke p. 192),
of the Guyanese who told Singer that he would not eat in a low-
caste house (p. 104), and that of the restricted feeding of Valmikis
in East Africa.[5] As in India, the scale of purity rests on the polar
opposites of Brahmin and Untouchable, and the ranking of "middle
castes" is ambiguous. But neither pole is well defined in these communities, and all authors stress that the manifestations of ritual differences I have just mentioned are exceptional and unimportant in
the communities.

A more significant expression of hierarchy is found in the pattern
of hypergamous and hypogamous marriages. Where the child takes
the father's status, hypergamy gives offspring the status of the higher
parent, whereas hypogamy gives the reverse. If hierarchy of caste
status were important, then marriages should more often be hypergamous.

Hypergamous marriages are reported from several communities. Only in the more traditional East African situation is intercaste
hypergamy noted (Bharati p. 307) ; for the rest, it is intervarna
hypergamy, since the ranking inside the varna seems difficult to
determine and is apparently not made with any precision, if at all,
by informants. In Trinidad, Clarke's sample shows that 66 per cent

---

[5]Bharati (p. 289). Apart from this case "commensality is complete" says
Bharati, contrasting in terminology, though not I think in meaning, with his
earlier statement that "noncommensality is complete" (p. 284).

of intervarna marriages are hypergamous (p. 186);[6] but in the South African and Guyanese samples the proportions drop to 24 per cent and 44 per cent respectively (Kuper p. 253; Smith and Jayawardena pp. 71-73). Here, then, there is more hypogamous than hypergamous marriage. One is tempted to conclude that this denotes a lack of hierarchical caste considerations in matchmaking —and, indeed, several writers note that hypogamous unions concern mainly those low-caste husbands whose qualifications of wealth, occupation, or education overcome their caste status (Benedict p. 37 ; Rambiritch and van den Berghe quoted by Kuper p. 254). But the question then arises ; if there are no hierarchical caste considerations at all, why is there not an equal proportion of hypogamy and hypergamy? The high rate of hypogamy in South Africa and to a lesser extent in Guyana seems to imply that some factor other than wealth and education is present. This may be a notion of hierarchy, insofar as lower-caste men may wish to marry hypogamously to raise their status, but not wish their sisters to marry out of the varna. By marrying out themselves, but denying their women to another group, they are following a well-known technique of social climbing; but here hypogamy, rather than hypergamy, is the means, and it is the marriage which is important since the status of the children can fairly easily be changed if this is considered necessary. The data are slender on this point, and one would like to have correlations of the various types of marriage with the noncaste attributes (of wealth and the like) of the partners, as well as with the caste membership of off-spring.

The data presented in the book suggest, I think, that two of the main features of the "ideal" caste system can still be found in overseas Indian communities. There is still some separation of castes

---

[6]The other writers on Trinidad provide no numerical data, **Schwartz** in particular choosing to treat marriage solely in terms of exogamy without specifying whether this is hypergamous or hypogamous. The higher proportion of Sudra endogamy he notes (pp. 128 sqq.) may, however, stem from a tendency to Sudra hypergamy, but not hypogamy, similar to that shown in Clark's Table V (in which 6 Sudra women but only 1 Sudra man married out of the varna), which forces Sudra men to marry within their own varna. Again, Schwartz offers no data for Fiji, and it is impossible to extract hypergamy rates from his Table VIII because he does not specify the sex of the informants listed there.

and varna through endogamy and ascribed membership; and there is a notion of hierarchy, whether or not based on purity.[7] Neither of these features is analyzed out fully here, but both can be seen to exist. Yet caste is said not to be a significant social factor by most of our writers. Why?

I think that the answer can only be: because caste is not the primary basis for activities and relationships, except to some extent in marriage. Caste status is therefore generally only a reflection of a person's social status rather than a governing influence on it, status being derived instead from elements such as education, occupation and wealth, and political power. These have no *necessary* connection with caste in these communities (whatever may have been the connection in India), although they may have had historical connections, such as the fact that the higher castes were on the whole better educated at the time of indenture, and therefore were the first to assume community leadership (Smith and Jayawardena p. 56). What I have just said is, I think, what Benedict means when he calls caste a "prestige label" (p. 36) ; it is what Smith and Jayawardena mean by saying that an "idiom of caste" has persisted (p. 88) through which statements about Guyanese society are made, and which can be converted into a "bonus of esteem" (p. 89) ; it is what Kuper refers to when she says that the ideology of caste influences personal relationships (p. 244) and may be used as a justification for actions (p. 246) ; and it is what Schwartz means when he says that "caste itself does not exist" in Trinidad but that ideas of caste survive in certain social activities (p. 144). Clarke is more cautious, stating that "caste is a social attribute in its own right" (p. 182). But, though he shows that it is a dominant consideration in religious matters, he stresses that it can only add to or detract from the primary determinants of a Hindu's social status in secular affairs, which are occupation and wealth (p. 182). Moreover, in East Africa, where caste is said to be still important, it is shown that caste persists to a large extent because people will not be accepted when they return to India if they have not maintained caste rules, especially with re-

---

[7]Even mobility may be movement of an individual or family (not of a local group, as in India) into a higher caste or varna *within* the system and not necessarily a movement *out of* the system into a creolized noncaste world.

gard to marriage (Morris p. 276); and the linguistic and sectarian group has become important, rather than the caste.

The tendency is, therefore, to see caste and varna as validating social, economic, and political activities. Indeed, this secular aspect of caste is even more notable when we take into account the fourth sense in which the word caste is used—that of the association.

Associations in these overseas Indian communities are of various kinds, and are most often not caste-based at all. This statement would apply to the bodies described by Benedict, for instance, which are formed on linguistic and sectarian bases (p. 29) for public work in settlements. In Mauritius, the various party political groupings at local and national elections recruit people by being "political groupings using caste as a symbol, rather than . . . [by being] castes taking political action" (p. 40). For Trinidad, Clarke mentions a multicaste association whose main duty is to manage the local temple (p. 193); and in Guyana (Smith and Jayawardena p. 79) and South Africa (Kuper p. 259) there are a number of local associations which are not formed along caste lines. To say that these are not caste-based does not preclude some caste bias, insofar as their leadership tends to be in the hands of higher-caste members—who are at the same time upper-class men. The combined status indicates that political leadership may be more a class than a caste matter, though using the "bonus of esteem" which higher caste provides.

In East Africa alone there are a number of specifically caste associations including, for instance, the Lohana and Patel associations mentioned by Bharati (p. 303); and Morris analyzes the role played by these associations in the Uganda Indian community. Because this is composed almost entirely of traders, and because it numbers less than 1 per cent of the total population, Indians have from the start needed leaders who could intercede with the administration. At the start, there was no need for all Indians to band together, and because caste differences were maintained through the close continuing ties with India, leaders emerged who represented the various castes. Formal associations were required by law, and hence there grew up a series of associations which competed for the favor of the administration and for leadership of the community. The separation of castes thus occurred because of two factors—the

influence of India, and the particular economic and political structure and needs of the Uganda Indian community. Here indeed, as
Morris observes, "for most practical purposes the fact that a man
was a member of the Patidar caste . . . was more important to him
than being either a Hindu or a Muslim or even a member of the
Indian community" (p. 273). We can now understand the different
conclusions about the importance of caste drawn by Morris on the
one hand and by the other contributors on the other. The difference
stems partly from the position of the Indian community in the total
society, and it is to this subject that I now turn.

Caste in the Plural Society

The significance of caste for the Indian community's place in
the plural society has two aspects. First, to what extent are the plural
societies themselves caste societies, with the different ethnic communities occupying castelike positions? Second, to what extent are
caste differences within the Indian community reflected in relations
with other communities, and do these relations accentuate or influence caste differences inside the Indian community?

The first thing to note is that outsiders—Africans, Europeans,
and the like—do not usually recognize caste differences in thinking
about or in acting toward Indians (Morris p. 273; Clarke p. 197;
and others). This is, of course, similar to the Indian's undifferentiated classification of varna or kin groups, for example the definition cf "Cutchi" in East Africa (Bharati p. 297 sqq.). Insofar as the
communities think of each other as undifferentiated, it is perhaps
possible to see them as units in some sort of castelike system. Speckmann, for instance, sees the Indian population of Surinam as crystal-
lizing into one "national Indian caste" which is endogamous and
to which the previously caste-based "feelings of self worth" have
been shifted (pp. 211-212) and thereby implies a hierarchy of communities; and Kuper speculates briefly that it is South African society,
rather than its Indian component, which is castelike (p. 263). Only
Smith and Jayawardena treat the question in any detail, however.
They conclude that there was, in former times, something approach-
ing a caste hierarchy of communities. Each community formed an

endogamous population, but all were linked by the acknowledgment of a single value hierarchy, centered on physical and cultural "whiteness" (p. 84) and on the acceptance of British norms in place of Sanskritic ones; and each community had to some extent the separate but organically-linked economic function found in the ideal caste hierarchy. But the emergence of cross-cutting ties of common profession and class and common styles of life which can be summed up in the term "creolization," have blurred such a picture—though, as Smith and Jayawardena remark, creolization may go together with increased communal consciousness and competition (p. 81), a feature confirmed by Singer's account of militant Indianness (for example, p. 109). Studies in other communities might support this analysis, and assess the growing number of economic, social, and political cross-cutting ties in relation to the factors making for communal separation.[8]

As to the second question, several writers think that caste is not important in the external relations of the community. Benedict, for instance, states that "one could describe the social structure of the island without mentioning caste" (p. 40) and Clarke concludes that "[caste] does not help to define the social stratification of the town as a whole" (p. 196). Nevertheless, there are indications that caste may indeed be a factor in these wider social arenas. Clarke, for example, himself gives the case of a middle-caste man who is able to raise his status *inside* the community by running a religious organization and taking on high-caste sanskritized habits although he cannot himself become a Brahmin (pp. 194-195). This man's prestige stands in contrast to that of a low-caste man who is connected with a local socioreligious association. The latter's ability is apparently recognized by the public, which has elected him the association's chairman; but it is impossible for him to gain prestige in wider community affairs, which are dominated by upper-caste members, and he can validate and use his influence by activity only in the predominantly Negro political party which operates *outside* the Indian community (p. 193). In such ways, the links of the community with the outside may be influenced by caste; and, similarly, the presence of such outside agencies may make it easier for people affected by attitudes inside

[8]See, for instance, a similar analysis made for Fiji (Mayer 1963).

the Indian community to control activities inside that community.[9]

One external factor which may affect caste relations inside the community is the general atmosphere of interracial relations. Morris gives as a reason for the proliferation of caste associations in Uganda the fact that race relations were cordial, with the result that Indians did not have to unite to protect themselves, but could allow ambitious men to form their own followings (p. 277) ; and Singer suggests that a widening communal gulf in Guyana has resulted in an increased awareness of Indianness and Hinduness, though this is not on a caste basis (p. 109 sqq.). In this, Singer disagrees with Smith and Jayawardena's statement that attempts to make Hindu religious associations into political vehicles have been unsuccessful (p. 82) ; but both appear to agree that caste will not form part of any future model of behavior—be it Hindu, India, or Creole.

The picture of caste in the plural society, therefore, is similar to that drawn for its place inside the community. Just as it provides an idiom for differences of power and status (which are actually based on other things) between Indians, so can it also provide an idiom for such differences when they extend outside the community.[10] But caste itself does not appear to be a factor more important than this in the workings of these plural societies.

The Retention of Indian Caste

The only place where a structural link between caste in India and caste in the overseas communities occurs is East Africa, where, as Morris says, caste endogamy is maintained as an extension of the local caste hierarchies to which Uganda Indians frequently return. Beyond this instance, the idea of the retention of caste is considered by the contributors from two different angles.

One views caste primarily as a system of social relations; the

---

[9]Clarke's example may be compared with that given by Klass in which, again, an Indian was the supporter of the Negro party (Klass 1961: 222 sqq.) although this man was not of the Sudra varna. Neither situation is given with enough detail to enable us to assess it fully, however.

[10]See Crowley's remark that Indians "are using Indian culture *and often mythical caste* . . . as a club with which to beat contemptuous Creoles" (Crowley 1960: 853 ; my italics).

overseas social system is different, and though former caste names may be used in some of these new relations, this does not result in a caste system. Again, some of the ideas which lay behind caste relations in India (notions of hierarchy, for example) have been transposed to the new situation; and some of the relations (endogamy, for example) can also be found; but these, besides being greatly weakened, are now parts of another society and, rather than reforming a caste system, they allow interpretations of the new relations in caste terms. I have already discussed the basis for this view; from it can stem comparisons of the "strength" of these retentions in different places—difference between town and village or between one community and another with respect to rates of caste or varna endogamy or hypergamy.

The second approach is expressed by Singer, when he writes that to isolate cultural survivals is not enough. "The importance is not in the degree to which there is conformity to the 'original' structure . . . but whether the new cultural mosaic results in personalities which are more similar to those of the original culture than they are to the 'new' personality in the second country" (p. 101). Singer's thesis is that the personalities of Hindus in Guyana are sufficiently similar to those of the Hindus of India for him to be able to say that there is a Hindu identity in both countries. This identity contains as one of its elements the values which underlie caste relations in India. Caste, then, does not exist in Guyana if it is defined in terms of "specific characteristics, such as prohibitions on eating and social interaction, ascribed occupation, caste endogamy, limited mobility, and fear of ritual pollution" (p. 96), but it is retained in the transplanted Hindu identity which Singer delineates in his paper.

This Hindu identity is isolated along three lines. First, in both countries there is a concern with status and prestige—shown in India by the conflicts attending caste fission and in Guyana by eyepass disputes (p. 104). Second, there is a "remarkable similarity" between the "specific personality characteristics" of Hindus in the two countries (p. 105). And third, there is a conscious effort to make a Hindu identity through socioreligious organizations such as the Sanatan Dharma Maha Sabha; here, however, caste is not basic to the new Hindu "dharma" and such activities lie outside our topic.

This is an interesting approach, and one which calls for fuller treatment than Singer is able to give it here. As to the first point, I would like to see more discussion about the degree to which eye-pass conflicts are a specifically Hindu-based social feature, and the degree to which they can be explained in terms of the local social situation; for there are indications that they are primarily a function of the plantation social system and do not exist to anything like the same extent among Hindu clerical workers or rice farmers (Jayawardena 1963: 130). As to Singer's second point, I am not psychologically trained, and hesitate to comment on an analysis which lies outside my field. But I suggest that the social anthropologist would wish for more information about the six people to whom Rorschach protocols were administered, on the basis of which comparison is made with projective tests in India. Were these six people plantation workers, or white-collar workers, or rice farmers? If they came from all three categories, it is interesting that there were apparently no personality differences related to a differential concern with eye pass; if they came only from plantation workers, more data would be necessary before a Hindu identity for the whole population could be established. A social anthropologist would also like to see some discussion of the procedure adopted for the interpretation of the Rorschach protocols. These were made by an American psychologist who had little knowledge of Guyanese culture and no previous knowledge of Hindus (p. 107). Presumably, then, he interpreted the protocols in the same way as he would have interpreted the record of a European or an American subject. Yet this is a debatable procedure, as those who have followed it have stated.[11]

Clearly, it is extremely difficult to compare overseas Indians and Indian society on the basis of "specific characteristics" as a way of establishing degrees of retention. To compare present-day conditions, one has to take into account the social changes which have taken place in each country since the end of the indenture system some fifty years ago; yet it is difficult to compare or to take into account the societies at the time of the indenture system—which, incidentally, stretched for up to seventy-five years. Perhaps, then, the only way in which one can explore to what extent the old culture

---

[11] See the comments by Rosemary Gordon on her Rorschach interpretations in Carstairs 1957: 325.

has been retained, and to what extent something new has evolved, is through this kind of psychocultural analysis; but such an analysis, by considering caste in terms of feelings about status, without any of its "specific characteristics," makes it difficult for us to know where caste behavior and feelings stop and other aspects of status relationships begin. The difficulties involved in either type of approach may explain why most of our authors treat the overseas situation only.

I have reservations about some aspects of Singer's paper, but it is important because it links up with a major theme of the book— to what extent are social relations caste relations if people look upon them as such, when in form they may be quite different from "real" caste relations; and, conversely, to what extent are social relations caste relations when they have no connection in the informants' minds with caste but nevertheless correspond to "real" caste behavior. Such problems lead me to the last part of this introduction and a discussion of what we mean by "caste."

The Definition of Caste

The underlying theme of this book is: does caste exist in overseas Indian communities? This question is part of a wider problem discussed by Indianists. Should the term *caste* be used to define the Hindu phenomenon in India alone, or should it be used to cover institutions in other societies and in other religions? And, if the latter, should these be restricted to culturally "pan-Indian" societies (Leach 1960: 5) or should they include systems of closed stratification wherever these are found? The material in this book is related to this problem in two ways: (1) Which of the debated definitions of caste do authors choose, according to which they characterize the community they have studied as containing caste or not? (2) Can the material from overseas Indian communities help to resolve this discussion? It is possible that these pan-Indian communities provide important evidence both for the protagonists of the wider and more structural definition (for instance, Berreman, who defines caste simply as a "hierarchy of endogamous divisions in which membership is hereditary and permanent"—1960: 120) and for those who adhere to a culture-specific definition which takes into account the ideology and categorization of the people themselves (for instance, Dumont

1961, 1964) and which makes fundamental for caste the opposition of pure and impure.

A few authors openly choose the cultural definition. Kuper, for instance, favors a definition which takes ideology into account rather than one based on "universal cultural behavior" (p. 240): again, for Singer, some "peculiarities of Indian behavior in Guyana seem to be clarified" not by considering "caste as structure" but "as a reflection of a *particular* religiously based psychological constellation" (pp. 102-103 ; my italics).

Other contributors do not present the alternatives in this way, but take a definition of caste as it exists in India, which includes cultural elements. Speckmann, for example, sees Indian caste as based on the opposition of pure and impure (p. 204) ; Clarke bases his article on Hutton's definition, which says that intercaste relations are ritually determined (p. 167) ; Bharati sees commensality (a ritually based phenomenon) as part of the fundamental configuration of the "structure of Indian society" of which caste forms a part (p. 284) ; Niehoff includes "ritual cleanness [*sic*]" in the characteristics of caste which are "probably the most significant" (p. 151) ; and Schwartz, though not offering any comments on definitions, implicitly takes a cultural approach through Indian caste characteristics.

Some authors imply that there is a choice between seeing caste as a purely Indian phenomenon and as a more general institution. Thus, Benedict qualifies his definition of caste (which includes "an ideological religious basis") by saying that he is taking caste "as a strictly Indian phenomenon" (p. 21) ; and Smith and Jayawardena refer to the problem of definition, and conclude that their analysis shows that "it is doubtful whether the phenomena discussed here could be usefully thought of as castes, or as a caste system ... *whichever criteria* of caste are accepted" (p. 44; italics mine). Finally, Morris's analysis, based on the nature of Indian caste it is true, is made in structural terms and would, I think, be appropriate for a general comparative analysis of stratification systems.

We see, then, that most authors base their definition of caste on the Indian phenomenon. Their conclusion, as I have said, is that the Indian caste *system* no longer exists overseas, but that ideas about caste are still important to varying extents. However, these ideas are not simply "free floating" or attached to completely new institutions.

The degrees of caste and varna endogamy and hypergamy indicate that there is still some degree of caste division on traditional lines. This is not as systematic as before; there is little summation of roles; it is not exhaustive, for there are people who do not know what caste they belong to; and the divisions are not entirely closed to individual mobility. More important, the divisions are, in most communities, not functionally significant. The different opportunities in the political and economic spheres which men have according to their caste or varna membership form part of the new plural society, in which caste ideology may be important in providing a bonus of esteem or a symbol of organization, and in which there may still be "differences" between castes to which moral attributes are attached (Pocock 1957).

This picture can be compared to that described by Barth (1960) in which caste is said to exist in Pathan society in the form of certain structural features, rather than in the form of "particular features of the Hindu philosophical scheme" (1960: 145). It suggests that, within the pan-Indian sphere, there is a continuum of situations: at one end may be placed the Pathan pattern, in which the ideological elements of Hindu caste are at a minimum (for Barth says [1960: 140] that there is some notion of pollution even here) ; and at the other end are overseas Indian communities, in which caste's structural characteristics are of less importance than is a caste ideology which is then applied to relations within the new society.

The importance of this book is, I think, that it gives us data with which to consider in more detail the nature of such a continuum, and to see whether caste situations in India (which vary one from another) as well as situations outside the pan-Indian sphere can be arranged on the continuum. Readers will draw their own conclusions about the book's contribution to the general problem of the definition of caste; but it seems to support the view that the need to limit the definition of caste for broad comparative purposes suggests that Indian caste has features which are not necessarily found in other societies. On the one hand, then, a comparative approach to stratification, though sociologically valuable, should be distinguished from studies of the operation of caste in the Indian and pan-Indian context: and on the other, there are enough societies falling within the pan-Indian continuum to make a cultural definition of caste useful in comparative analysis.

REFERENCES

BARTH, F.
1960   "The system of stratification in Swat, North Pakistan." pp. 113-146 in *Aspects of caste in south India, Ceylon and north-west Pakistan,* E. R. Leach, ed. Cambridge: Cambridge University Press.

BERREMAN, G. D.
1960   "Caste in India and the United States." *American Journal of Sociology* 66:120-127.

CARSTAIRS, G. M.
1957   *The twice born.* London: Hogarth Press.

CROWLEY, DANIEL J.
1960   "Cultural assimilation in a multiracial society." pp. 850-854 in *Social and cultural pluralism in the Caribbean,* V. Rubin, ed. New York: New York Academy of Sciences.

DUMONT, L.
1961   "Caste, racism and 'stratification'." *Contributions to Indian Sociology* 5:20-43.

1964   *La civilisation indienne et nous.* Paris: Armand Colin.

JAYAWARDENA, CHANDRA
1963   *Conflict and solidarity in a Guianese plantation.* London: Athlone Press. (London School of Economics Monographs in Social Anthropology No. 25.)

KLASS, MORTON
1961   *East Indians in Trinidad.* New York: Columbia University Press.

LEACH, E. R.
1960   "Introduction: What should we mean by caste?" pp. 1-10 in *Aspects of Caste in south India, Ceylon and north-west Pakistan,* E. R. Leach, ed. Cambridge: Cambridge University Press.

MAYER, ADRIAN C.
1960   *Caste and kinship in central India.* Berkeley: University of California Press.

1961   *Peasants in the Pacific.* Berkeley: University of California Press.

1963   *Indians in Fiji.* London: Oxford University Press.

POCOCK, D. F.
1957   " 'Difference' in East Africa." *Southwestern Journal of Anthropology* 13:289-300.

MAURITIUS

Caste in Mauritius

Definitions and descriptions of caste have been legion. Indeed, by 1945 it was estimated there were over 5000 published works on the subject (Hutton 1951: ix), and the rate of production has certainly not decreased since. Taken as a strictly Indian phenomenon, caste possesses a number of characteristic features. These are (Ghurye 1950):

1. Membership by birth.
2. Endogamy.
3. A hierarchical ordering of castes.
4. Occupational specialization.
5. An ideological religious basis involving restrictions on social intercourse and commensality.
6. Some corporateness of the caste group at least on a local level.

Exceptions and modifications in some of these features can be found in various parts of India, particularly in the urban areas (Kapadia 1958: 119 ff.). What has happened to caste in overseas Indian communities? In this paper I shall examine caste as found among Indians in Mauritius, paying particular attention to the six features mentioned above. I shall trace briefly the history of Indians in Mauritius; the present position cannot be properly understood without it. There are few records of what has actually occurred to caste in Mauritius and to some extent this part of the article will be an exercise in what Bailey (1960: 63) has called "conjectural history." Next I shall look at caste as it existed during the period of my field work in 1955-1957. Last, I shall look at some recent manifestations of caste in the political field.

The History and Environment of the Indo-Mauritians

Mauritius is an island of 720 square miles located in the Indian Ocean some 500 miles east of Madagascar. Its population of over 750,000 is about 66 per cent of Indian origin, 28 per cent Creole of mixed African or Indian and European descent, 4 per cent of Chinese origin, and 2 per cent European, mostly of French descent.[1] Economically this British colony is almost entirely dependent on the production of sugar, which with its by-products accounts for 99 per cent of exports. Mauritius must import its basic foodstuffs and most of its manufactured goods. The greatest problem facing the island is overpopulation. Since the end of the Second World War the population has been increasing at the rate of more than 3 per cent per annum, owing largely to the eradication of malaria. If this rate continues, there may be well more than a million people in less than 20 years, and nearly three million by the end of the century (Titmuss 1961: 44).

The island had no indigenous inhabitants. It was first settled in the seventeenth century by the Dutch, who abondoned it after two unsuccessful attempts at creating permanent settlements. In the eighteenth century it was successfully colonized by the French, who introduced thousands of slaves from Madagascar and the African mainland. The British conquered the island in 1810, and after the abolition of slavery in 1835 began to introduce indentured laborers from India. Between 1835 and 1907, nearly 450,000 Indian immigrants were brought to Mauritius.[2] The composition of the population

---

[1] Percentages are based on the 1962 census. The figure for Europeans and Creoles are approximations; the census does not distinguish these categories.

[2] In the 1920's some 1200 more were introduced, but nearly all of these returned to India.

underwent a radical change. In 1835 Indians constituted only a minute proportion of the population; 26 years later, in 1861, two-thirds of the population was Indian, a proportion maintained to the present.

From what castes and areas did this vast body of Indians come? They were shipped to Mauritius through the ports of Calcutta, Madras, and Bombay. About 60 per cent came from Calcutta, 33 per cent from Madras, and 7 per cent from Bombay (Mauritius 1905: I-VI). These figures do not mean, however, that the emigrants were natives of these ports. Efforts were made to recruit laborers from country districts. A report by the Protector of Immigrants in 1861 lists 24 districts from which Calcutta emigrants came (Beyts 1861: 5). The same authority notes that emigrants embarking from Madras came chiefly from Tanjore and Trichinopoly in the south and Godovary in the north (1861: 13), while those embarking from Bombay came principally from the Deccan and Concan districts (1861: 13). On embarking from India and again on arrival at Mauritius, immigrants were entered on registers which listed their number, name, caste, stature, distinguishing marks, name of father or mother, district, subdistrict, and village. Of these registers, 91 or more volumes are preserved in Mauritius, listing the arrival of 431,557 immigrants between 1836 and 1924. Often the entries are incomplete, particularly as to place of origin. I took a small random sample of 1392 immigrants arriving between 1836 and 1903 which listed 289 places of origin. Not only was there a great diversity of immigrants coming from different parts of India, but within each area there was further diversity. Some immigrants indentured singly, but efforts were made to recruit laborers in groups under a sirdar (overseer) who knew and was known by his men.

Caste hierarchies tend to be local hierarchies in India. The diversity of places of origin means that only bits of any village or even of any subdistrict hierarchy emigrated to Mauritius. A caste (jati) bearing the same name may have different standing in different villages, as recent studies of the dominant caste have shown (for example, Mayer 1958). And in Mauritius we are not dealing with Indians from the same linguistic areas, but with Biharis, Bengalis, Tamils, Telugus, Marathis, and others; this diversity makes the possibility of any agreed over-all hierarchy unlikely except as to the four varna (Brahmin, Kshatriya, Vaishya, and Sudra), which have an all-India spread. The corporateness of any local caste group would not be likely to survive transplantation to Mauritius, not only because relatively few members of one caste came from a single village, but more importantly because conditions of work and livelihood in Mauritius were not conducive to the preservation of such groups.

The variety of places of origin listed in the immigration records is matched by the variety of castes listed. In my sample (Table I) I list 102 names, reputed to be caste names, though some clearly are not. This probably represents a minimal number, as agents in Madras and Bombay were less meticulous about listing caste than those in Calcutta. Emigrants from Madras were simply listed as Malabars, Gentoos (an obsolete word for Hindu, possibly a Telugu speaker), Muslims, or Christians. Those from Bombay were simply listed as Maratha, Muslim, or Christian.

TABLE I. NAMES AND PERCENTAGES OF CASTES FROM SAMPLE OF 1392 ENTRIES TAKEN FROM IMMIGRATION RECORDS

Name*	Per cent of Sample	Description
Abuss	.29	Possibly Muslim.
Bagdee	.86	A cultivating, fishing, and menial cast of central and western Bengal (Risley 1891 I:37).
Bahaleea	.07	A subcaste of the Dusads of Bihar, laborers (Risley 1891 I:45).
Bania	.50	A generic name applied to almost all trading castes throughout India.
Bausfore	.57	Possibly Bansphor, a subcaste of mat and basket makers of Bihar (Risley 1891 I:60).
Bhayloo	.07	Unable to trace.
Bhoomiz	.57	Possibly Bhumij, a western Bengal tribe related to the Mundas (Risley 1891 I:116-117).
Bhoomy	.50	Possibly Bhumia, a name applied wholesale to landholders in Chota Nagpur, Bengal, Orissa, and Bihar. Their status varies greatly in different areas, being particularly low in Bihar (Russell 1916 II:305, 307). Also an alternative name for Bhuiya.
Bhooyea	3.23	Usually Bhuiya, a caste of landless workers in Bihar but a military caste in Orissa (Risley 1891 I:112-113).

*Caste names are spelled as found in the immigration records.

Name	Per cent of Sample	Description
Bhowaury	1.08	Possibly Bauri, a cultivating caste of western Bengal (Risley 1891 I:78).
Bhoyta	.50	Possibly Bhuta, a subcaste of Gonds in Betul.
Bhur	.50	Possibly Bhar, a small caste of cultivators and personal servants of western Bengal and Chota Nagpur.
Bim	.07	Possibly Bin or Bind, a large agricultural, fishing, and hunting caste of Bihar and Upper India (Risley 1891 I:136).
Bowose	.07	Unable to trace.
Brahmin	.29	Priestly caste found all over India.
Cahar	.86	Usually spelled Kahar, a large cultivating and personal-service caste of Bihar (Risley 1891 I:370).
Camatte	.29	Possibly Kamati, a cultivating caste of Bihar (Risley 1891 I:393).
Camdoo	.50	Possibly Kandu, a grain-parching caste of Bihar and Bengal (Risley 1891 I:414).
Carimdoo	.07	Unable to trace.
Chacal	.07	Possibly Chakla, a synonym for Dhobi (Russell 1916 I:353).
Chamar	11.58	Caste of tanners and menial laborers of north India (Russell 1916 II:403).
Chasa	.07	The chief cultivating caste of Orissa (Russell 1916 II:424).
Christian	1.36	Often listed as a caste.
Coodusy	.14	Unable to trace.
Coombee	.50	Possibly Kunbi, a subcaste of landowners and cultivators (Russell 1916 I:381).
Coomhar	.29	Usually spelled Kumhar, a caste of potters of Bengal, Bihar, and Orissa (Risley 1891 I:517).
Coormee	3.74	Usually spelled Kurmi, a very large cultivating caste of Upper India (Risley 1891 I:528).
Culowar	.07	Possibly Kalwar, a liquor-selling, distilling, and trading caste of Bihar (Risley 1891 I:385).
Cundoo	.22	Possibly either Kandu (see Camdoo above) or a title used by a number of castes in Bengal (Risley 1891 I:527).
Curvary	.29	Unable to trace.
Descauldee	.07	Unable to trace.
Deswaree	.07	Possibly Deswali, a former criminal caste now cultivators (Russell 1916 I:358, IV:240).

(continued)

Name	Per cent of Sample	Description
Dhamoo	.14	Possibly Damu, a subsection of a pastoral caste in Bihar (Risley 1891 I:212).
Dhobi	.29	A caste of professional washermen from Bihar (Risley 1891 I:229).
Dhoonyea	.29	Possibly Dhunia, a caste of cotton corders (Risley 1891 I:237).
Dusad	4.74	A cultivating caste of Bihar and Chota Nagpur; also serve as watchmen and messengers (Risley 1891 I:252).
Dusowar	.07	Possibly Deswar, a subcaste of the Kalwars of Bihar (Risley 1891 I:217).
Ganrary	.29	Possibly Ganreri, a shepherd, goatherd, and blanket-weaving caste of Bihar (Risley 1891 I:271).
Gentoo	6.75	A Hindu in south India; a Telugu speaker (O.E.D. IV:121).
Ghutwar	.50	Possibly Ghatwar,• a synonym for Bhuiya (which see).
Gore	.57	Possibly Goar or Goria, a subcaste of the Ahir, a pastoral caste of Bihar (Risley 1891 I:282).
Gorilb	.07	Unable to trace.
Gowalla	2.30	Possibly Goala, a large pastoral caste of Bengal (Risley 1891 I:282).
Gungok	.07	Unable to trace.
Gunjhoo	.14	A subcaste of liquor sellers and distillers in Bengal and Bihar (Risley 1891 I:269, II:275).
Gurryeth	.29	Possibly Gorait, a caste of musicians, comb makers, and cotton corders of Bengal (Risley 1891 I:297).
Hajam	.50	The barber caste of Bihar.
Jautee	.14	Possibly Jati, the Hindu word for "caste," or a subcaste of the Gowallas (Risley 1891 I:344).
Jugee	.07	Possibly Jugi, a weaving caste of eastern Bengal (Risley 1891 I:355) or a subcaste of Chamars (Russell 1916 I:369).
Kamma	.14	A large cultivating caste of Madras (Russell 1916 I:372).
Kapooloo	.29	Possibly Kapali, a cultivating and weaving caste of eastern Bengal (Risley I:421).
Karee	.29	Possibly Khari, a title of the Murha caste of laborers of Jubbulpore (Russell 1916 I:378, IV:252).
Kaumar	.50	Possibly Kamar, a metal-working caste of Bengal and Bihar (Risley 1891 I:388).
Kauyeth	.14	Possibly Kayasth, a caste of scribes from the Central Provinces (Russell 1916 II:404).

Name	Per cent of Sample	Description
Kawoor	.14	Possibly Kaur, a caste of cultivators of Chota Nagpur (Risley 1891 I:435).
Khoyra	1.08	A title of the Bagdee caste (which see).
Koybut	.29	Possibly Koput, a division of Gonds in Chota Nagpur (Risley 1891 I:506).
Koyrie	.50	A large cultivating caste of Bihar and Chota Nagpur (Risley 1891 I:500).
Koysie	.14	Unable to trace.
Kunjar	.07	Unable to trace.
Kuttree	.07	Possibly Kuti, a subdivision of Muslims in eastern Bengal (Risley 1891 I:539).
Lohar	.14	The blacksmith caste of Bihar, Chota Nagpur, and western Bengal (Risley 1891 II:22).
Mahratta	3.09	A native of the area where Mahratta is spoken; also the military caste of south India (Russell 1916 IV:198).
Malabar	16.74	A native of the Tamil-speaking areas of south India.
Mauja	.07	A Muslim title for a religious specialist.
Maujhee	.07	A Muslim title for a religious specialist.
Medari	.29	A Telugu caste of bamboo workers and mat makers (Russell 1916 I:390).
Moodi	.07	Usually Mudi, a title of the Binds and Bagis; a petty shopkeeper (Risley 1891 II:100).
Moonda	1.08	Usually Munda, a large tribe of Chota Nagpur which has spread to the Upper Provinces and Central India (Russell 1916 I:392).
Moosohoo	.07	Possibly Musahar, a cultivating caste of Bihar (Risley 1891 II:113).
Morsula	.07	Unable to trace.
Moyra	.50	Usually Moira, a confectioner caste of Bengal which now has many occupations (Risley 1891 II:84).
Mulye	.07	Unable to trace.
Muslim	16.88	Often listed as a caste.
Naroot	.07	Unable to trace.
Nauput	.07	Possibly Napit, the barber caste of Bengal (Risley 1891 II:124).
Nayanamsam	.29	Unable to trace.
Nayar	.14	A large warrior caste of the Malabar coast.
Noonia	.29	Usually Nunia, a cultivating caste of Bihar and Upper India (Risley 1891 II:135).
Nunduth	.07	Unable to trace.
Pariah	.57	Largest of the lower castes of south India.
Pasee	.50	Usually Pasi, a caste of toddy tappers of Bihar (Risley 1891 II:166).

(continued)

Name	Per cent of Sample	Description
Purwaree	1.01	Unable to trace.
Rajawa	.36	Possibly Rajwar, a cultivating caste of Bihar, western Bengal, and Chota Nagpur (Risley 1891 II:192).
Rajpoor	.07	Possibly a local group of Brahmins in the Parganas (Risley 1891 II:184).
Rajput	2.80	A large heterogeneous warrior and landholding caste of north India (Risley 1891 II: 184).
Saswoo	.07	Unable to trace.
Sauntal	.07	Possibly Santal, a large non-Hindu tribe of western Bengal, north Orissa, and Bhogalpur (Risley 1891 II:224).
Sautat	.36	Possibly a variant of Santal.
Sohar	.14	Possibly Sonar, a caste of goldsmiths of Bihar (Risley 1891 II:236).
Sonar	.50	See Sohar above.
Sookumbhee	.36	Unable to trace.
Soolumtelhe	.29	Unable to trace.
Soonee	.07	Usually Sunni, one of the major divisions of Islam.
Sudgope	.14	Unable to trace.
Tailee	.57	Usually Teli, a caste of oil pressers and sellers of north India (Russell 1916 IV:542).
Tantee	.14	Usually Tanti, a weaver caste of Bihar and Bengal (Risley 1891 II:295).
Tatara	.07	Possibly Tatwa, a weaving caste of Bihar (Risley 1891 II:305).
Telegu	.86	Telugu speakers from southern India.
Vannia	.36	Possibly Bania (which see).
Vellalen	.14	Possibly Vellala, the large cultivating caste of the Tamil country (Russell 1916 I:146).
Wodda	.14	Possibly Waddar, a Telugu caste of laborers (Russell 1916 I:417).
Total	99.89	(.11 error due to rounding off)

Even though castes among the immigrants cannot be placed in a strict hierarchy, it can be seen that a very wide range was represented from Brahmins and Rajputs (Kshatriyas), through the occupational castes to the very lowest castes (such as Chamars and Dusads). The largest percentages in my sample, apart from generic designations such as Muslim, Malabar, and Gentoo, come from these lowest castes and from various agricultural and cultivating castes. Thirty castes in my sample are represented by only a single individual (indicated by .07 per cent).

The systems under which Indians were indentured to work in Mauritius varied greatly throughout the years of immigration (Benedict 1961: 22-23). On the estates they were housed in barracks or in rows of cubicles made of thatch which had been slave quarters. Little attention was paid to the caste, religion, or linguistic group of the immigrants. Muslim might be housed with Hindu, or Brahmin with Chamar, or Tamil with Marathi. Under such conditions restrictions on social intercourse and commensality were difficult if not impossible to maintain. Indeed, conditions in ships bringing Indians to Mauritius must have dealt an early blow to such restrictions. Caste groupings lost their corporateness, though the immigrants formed socioreligious associations where the *Ramayana* was recited and religious rites were performed (Benedict 1961: 135 ff). Muslims, Tamils, Telugus, and northern Hindus tended to form separate associations, but how far such associations were limited to members of a single caste is not known. A relatively numerous caste, such as the Chamars, may have been able to form its own association, but several castes with only a few members each would probably have had to combine in a single association. Though there were separate socioreligious associations for northern Hindus, Tamils, Telugus, and Muslims, during the period of my field work, I found none organized around a single caste.

The family basis of caste was also lacking in the early years of immigration. Between 1834 and 1842 only a little over 1 per cent of Indian immigrants were women. The planters expected women to work in the fields as slave women had done, but this was stated to be "contraire aux usages et aux idées des Indiens" (Challaye 1844: 13). Disorders over women arose on estates and the Mauritius government fixed the ratio of females to males to be imported from 1853 onward (Mauritius 1905: Appx. III-VI). Under Mauritian law, marriage contracted in India was not recognized unless the parties swore to their union before the Protector of Immigrants, who gave them certificates of which duplicates are still preserved in the archives. I examined a sample of 356 marriage certificates dating from 1847 to 1903. All but four of these unions were endogamous as to caste. The four intercaste marriages comprised three cases of hypergamy (two Brahmins married a Rajput and Bagdee respectively; a Kumhar married two Munda wives), and possibly one of the hypogamy (a Kauyeth married a Kurmi). It appears that caste endogamy was imported with women. Endogamy has remained the most persistent feature of caste in Mauritius.

As the list of castes from my sample shows, many immigrants came from castes whose traditional occupation was not agricultural labor. Planters and estate managers complained that the immigrants they received were not laborers, and some Brahmins refused to work in the fields (Frere and Williamson 1875: 247 ff.). Yet under indenture Indians could engage in few occupations other than agricultural laborer.

Conditions of immigration and indenture probably affected the six features of caste in the following ways:

1. Membership by birth could have been preserved.
2. Endogamy could have been preserved.
3. The hierarchial ordering of castes could have been maintained as an idea, but was difficult or impossible to put into practice, both because of the lack of Indian villages or communities and because of the wide variety of places from which immigrants came.
4. Occupational specialization must have disappeared except in certain ceremonial contexts.
5. The religious ideology behind caste could have been maintained, but restrictions on social intercourse and commensality must have been very difficult if not impossible to preserve.
6. Castes could not form corporate groups, except possibly for some of the larger castes in the form of socioreligious associations.

Most important of all, Indians in Mauritius were not part of an Indian society with interdependent occupational castes organized on a village level. Instead, they formed the laboring section of a colonial society with a plantation economy and a culture which was largely French. Under such conditions it was impossible to maintain caste structure in the same form found in India. Indian immigrants were subject to strict laws concerning their indenture and their movement throughout the island (Benedict 1961: 22 f.). There were no village or caste panchayats (councils). Though attempts were made by Indians to settle disputes within the estate camp and later within the village by means of the socioreligious associations; major disputes brought action by the police and magistrates of the colony.

As soon as they were able, at the end of their indenture periods, Indians left the estate camps to settle in villages. They also began to acquire plots of land for growing vegetables, raising livestock, and growing sugar cane. Some became hawkers or shopkeepers. The more successful began to educate their children for entry into the professions and the civil service.[3] The Indians acquired freedom of movement and of settlement and the opportunity to engage in a wide variety of occupations. What happened to caste under these conditions?

Caste as Observed in the Period 1955-1957

During 21 months of field work in Mauritius between 1955 and 1957, I took sociological censuses of two villages in different parts of the island, an estate camp and a section of the principal town, Port Louis—covering in all 9169 persons of whom 6897 (75 per cent) were of Indian descent. Their castes are set out in Table II. If we compare this with Table I we can see that the number of caste names represented has diminished by about two-thirds. It is dangerous to make comparisons about the relative numbers of various castes at present in Mauritius, as my censuses do not represent a random sample of the whole island but an intensive investigation of four areas. Nevertheless, certain features are worth noting. The percentages of Muslims, Tamils (Malabars) and Telugus (Gentoos) have remained high, leading to the hypothesis that there was little assimilation of these groups into the numerically dominant northern Hindus. Muslim-Hindu marriages are exceedingly rare; I heard of only a single instance during my stay in Mauritius. Marriages between northern Hindus and southern Hindus (Tamil or Telugu) are also rare though there are a few instances, notably among some of the Western-educated elite of the towns. Tamil-Telugu marriages occasionally occur. Among Tamils and Telugus there appear to be very few caste distinctions. As already noted, the immigration records rarely mention caste

---

[3]For a discussion of the economic and political rise of the Indians in Mauritius, see Benedict, 1961: 24-31.

TABLE II. NAMES AND PERCENTAGES OF CASTES FROM FOUR SETTLEMENTS

Caste Name*	Per Cent of Total Indian Population in Settlement			
	Beaumont	La Vallée	Estate Camp	Town
Ahir	.8	3.7	2.5	1.4
Barhai	—	.7	—	—
Bhooyar (Bhooyea)	.6	—	—	1.7
Bin (Bim)	2.2	—	.3	—
Brahmin	4.8	1.6	—	11.2
Chamar	19.1	.1	.3	.7
Dhobi	.4	—	1.2	.3
Dom	—	1.4	—	—
Dusad	8.1	2.8	12.5	.7
Ganrary	3.4	—	1.8	—
Gosai	—	—	—	1.2
Hajjam	.4	—	—	—
Halwai	2.2	—	5.2	.2
Kahar (Cahar)	.2	3.9	.3	.1
Kaite	—	1.3	—	.1
Koiri (Koyrie)	3.7	2.7	—	—
Kshatriya (Rajput)	2.2	4.9	2.8	19.3
Kumhar (Coomhar)	.2	—	—	—
Kurmi (Coormee)	10.9	.7	—	.6
Lohar	.8	—	—	—
Mahaton	—	—	—	.6
Marathi (Mahratta)	—	—	.3	1.9
Mayram	—	—	—	.3
Muslim	10.8	57.9	4.3	26.6
Nunia (Noonia)	.8	—	—	—
Passy (Pasee)	.8	—	—	—
Rajphur (Rajpoor)	.1	—	—	—
Ravidas (Chamar)	—	—	13.9	—
Rujwar (Rajawa)	.5	—	3.3	—
Sudra	.6	.2	—	—
Takoor	1.5	.2	—	—
Tamil (Malabar)	9.1	15.3	36.4	23.2
Telugu (Gentoo)	13.6	.5	11.5	3.1
Vaish	1.1	1.6	—	4.2
Unknown N. Hindu	1.1	.5	3.4	2.6
	100.0	100.0	100.0	100.0
Total Indian population	2693	1987	671	1546

*The spelling as found in Table I appears in parentheses.

for southern Hindus but use the blanket terms, Malabar and Gentoo. Most Tamils whom I questioned about caste agreed that it had all but disappeared. Some claimed it had been strong in earlier days, and that the lowest castes had not been allowed in the temples. Most said there were no Tamil Brahmins in Mauritius, though one claimed there were two. A Tamil temple priest could name 15 Tamil castes. A Tamil postman could name nine. My censuses in one village and in the estate camp revealed only four Tamil castes—Naiker, Parien, Pariachi, and Pallen. Tamils today do not stress caste differences among themselves but do stress their differences as a whole from northern Hindus.

I have not included Christians in Table II. Intermarriage between Christians of Indian origin and Christians of African or mixed origin has been frequent and there seems no valid basis for distinguishing Indo-Mauritian Christians. One suspects that in the 1952 census Christians bearing Indian surnames have been listed as Indian Christians, whereas Indo-Mauritian women married to men with French surnames have been listed as belonging to the general population. The 1962 census does not distinguish Indo-Mauritian Christians.

While one informant was able to name five Telugu castes, Telugus claimed that caste distinctions were virtually nonexistent in Mauritius, and that castes were no longer endogamous categories. I acquired no census data on Telugu castes. Few Marathis appear in my sample. It appears that the Marathi population is concentrated in a few areas and seems to be losing its distinctiveness by blending with the northern Hindus. Intermarriages do occur and the Marathis make use of northern Hindu temples (Mauritius 1956: 5).[4] As with the Tamils, the Telugus and Marathis are not concerned with internal caste differences but with their differences from the numerically superior northern Hindus.

An examination of northern Hindu castes as listed in Table II shows that most of the castes listed were found in the sample taken from the immigration records (Table I). It also shows significant differences in the caste composition of the four communities.

Beaumont is predominately a village of northern Hindus, and is characterized by the greatest variety of castes. Indeed, the distribution among various castes is not unlike that in the immigration sample (Table I), with high percentages of Chamars, Dusads, and Kurmis.

---

[4]I have no information on Marathi castes in Mauritius.

La Vallée, with its predominately Muslim population, shows fewer castes. The percentages of the very lowest castes (Chamar, Dusad, Sudra, Dhobi) are smaller than in Beaumont. One low caste, the Dom, is represented in La Vallée but not in Beaumont, but the total percentage of low castes is 28.2 in Beaumont and only 4.5 in La Vallée. At the other end of the hierarchy there is a smaller percentage of Brahmins but a larger percentage of Kshatriyas (Rajputs) than at Beaumont. In the middle range of castes the Kurmi, which comprise over 10 per cent of Beaumont, are barely represented in La Vallée, whereas the Kahar are more strongly represented in La Vallée. Other castes are to be found in Beaumont but not in La Vallée and vice versa. These differences would seem to indicate that certain castes are to be found concentrated in particular villages. Observations in other villages lend support to this hypothesis.

The estate camp is located near Beaumont and all castes except Marathi occurring in it are also found in Beaumont. The apparent significant exception, Ravidas, is another name for Chamar. It will be noted that the estate camp has the highest percentage of lowest castes (Chamar, Dhobi, Dusad, Ravidas) of any settlement, though it is only slightly higher than Beaumont. At the other extreme, it has no Brahmins. This pattern is in part a reflection of the low social status of living in estate camps (Benedict 1961: 54-55).

The town shows a marked contrast to the other settlements. It has by far the highest percentages of Brahmins and Kshatriyas of any settlement and by far the lowest percentage of the lowest castes. Does this patern mean that only the highest castes moved to the towns or does it indicate that people who moved to town changed their caste status? Though I do not have the histories of all high-caste town dwellers, I have evidence (direct in two cases and indirect in half a dozen others) that changes in caste have taken place. The Kshatriya would appear to be the favored caste into which to claim membership. It is easier to gain acceptance as a Kshatriya than as a Brahmin since the role is less exacting. Kshatriyas are not expected to perform rituals for others or to maintain rigid dietary and ritual restrictions as are Brahmins. The chances of acceptance and of finding suitable marriage partners are greater among Kshatriyas than among the smaller number of more exclusive Brahmins.

High caste is prestigeful, but it is very difficult for a villager or an estate-camp dweller to change his caste. He and his antecedents are well known in such small communities and attempts to change caste will be greeted with ridicule and with refusal by higher-caste individuals to accept him. He will find the greatest difficulty in acquiring a wife from the caste to which he aspires. A move to town, however, removes or at least modifies some of these disabilities. There is greater anonymity; relationships are partial and less intense. A man's caste status is more apt to be taken at his own evaluation of it.

An instance of an attempt at caste mobility was that of a low-caste teacher who aspired to Kshatriya status. He added the Kshatriya suffix *singh* to his name and attempted to arrange a marriage with a Kshatriya girl in a distant town. The girl's family refused to receive him. He then arranged a marriage with a girl whose father was a Kshatriya but whose mother was a Chamar. She was the daughter of the second marriage for both parents, each of whom had been married endogamously before. The teacher had a civil marriage performed in a village which was neither his own nor that of the girl. Among Indians in Mauritius, religious marriage usually precedes civil marriage, often by years (Benedict 1961: 92 ff.) ; and religious marriage, though it is not legal, is considered the validating rite. The civil marriage can be performed before a Civil Status Officer in his office with only two witnesses. A religious marriage is performed before all the kinsmen and friends of both parties. The teacher thus presented the girl's kinsmen with a *fait accompli* in the form of the civil marriage. He did not, however, attempt to live with his wife until after the religious marriage which took place some weeks later. Before the religious marriage he arranged to have the ceremony of the assumption of the sacred thread (janeo) performed for him. This is the the mark of the "twice born" higher castes, but no Brahmin priest (pandit) from his own village would perform it for him. He had to import a priest from a village some distance away. He was severely criticized in his own village, and the ceremony was boycotted by most villagers. When the religious marriage ceremony was eventually performed in the bride's village, very few of the bridegroom's villagers attended. Eventually he moved with his bride to Port Louis.

Examples such as this one show that high caste is a label of prestige value among some Indo-Mauritian Hindus. Conversely, the imputation of low-caste status can be taken as an insult, in the past even leading to legal action. At a marriage dinner two men turned out a third, calling him a Chamar. He sued and the two men were fined 15 rupees each, plus costs, because of the intent to hurt the feelings of the man turned out (Sawarath v. Soomaroo; Mauritius Reports 1928: 4-8).

Many low-caste Hindus in Mauritius joined the Arya Samaj movement. This was a reformist Hindu movement founded in India by Swami Dyanand Sarasvati (1824-1883). It reached Mauritius in 1913 (Mauritius 1956: 6). Its doctrines include the abolition of caste and the simplification of Hindu ritual. The distinction between Sanatan (orthodox) and Arya Samaj becomes blurred in practice. An Arya Samaji wedding is simpler and hence less expensive and may be favored over a Sanatani one. One Brahmin priest performed both sorts of ceremonies, and many people clearly preferred to have a Brahmin perform Arya Samaji wedding rites. Most Hindus are not strict adherents of either the Sanatan or the Arya Samaj, and the mothers, wives, and daughters of even the staunchest Arya Samajis attend Sanatani temples and participate in Sanatani ceremonies. The rejection of the caste name Chamar in favor of Ravidas (son of the sun) is another example of the desire to eschew low-caste status. Some low-caste individuals have adopted the dietary restrictions of the higher castes.

It should be emphasized that all these efforts are on an individual level. As castes are not corporate groups in Mauritius there is no attempt for a whole caste to raise its status collectively as reported by Cohn (1955) for the Chamars of Madhopur. The caste hierarchy, insofar as it exists in Mauritius, is not a hierarchy of corporate groups or of occupational groups, but a hierarchy of prestige labels valued at the upper end, disvalued at the lower end, and largely ignored in the middle. Brahmins, especially those who practice their hereditary priestly occupation, are frequently addressed by other Hindus as "maraz," a corruption of "maharajah." Kshatriyas may be addressed as "babuji." Both these are terms of respect. In both villages in which I lived questions about the qualities which gave a man importance in the community elicited the reply "high caste" among such other attributes as wealth and education. This prestige is based not only on Hindu religious values, but on such local traditions as the Brahmins being the teachers and the only lettered men among the Indian immigrants who kept Hindu culture and values alive in Mauritius, and the Kshatriyas carrying to Mauritius the ideals of honor of the aristocratic Rajputs.

Stevenson (1954) has pointed out that it is important to distinguish between caste in a ritual sphere and caste in a secular context. It is on ritual occasions and on such occasions only that the vestiges of the pollution concept can be seen in Mauritius. At a ceremony for protecting a village from disease there were separate ceremonies for high and low castes (Benedict 1961: 132 ff.). At weddings and other religious ceremonies every respect is shown the officiating Brahmin. He must eat first and is served food on a banana leaf in a special place apart, lest he become polluted. But such restrictions apply only on ritual occasions defined as such. On secular occasions there are no restrictions on interdining and no notion of pollution or untouchability. Again it is only in the ritual sphere that there is any occupational specialization along caste lines. Priests among orthodox (Sanatani) Hindus are Brahmins by caste, though not all Brahmins are priests, and among Arya Samajis there are no caste qualifications for being a priest. The barber who assists the Brahmin priest in many rituals is usually a barber by caste, but there are many more barbers in Mauritius who are not barbers by caste. They tend to stick to hairdressing, though a few have learned the rituals of assisting the Brahmin. Hindus avoid such polluting occupations as butchering and shoemaking, but this is not a matter of caste but of the Hindu religion as a whole. In a similar way Muslims, though they may be butchers, will not slaughter pigs nor deal in pork products. In secular life caste has no relevance to occupation.

Of the traditional features of caste, endogamy has been the most persistent. It is cited as an ideal by most Indo-Mauritians and the vast majority of marriages are endogamous as to caste. Yet nonendogamous unions occur, particularly in the middle range of castes. Unions between Kurmis and Koiris, for example, are no longer thought to be very exceptional. Among the Western-educated elites of the towns, education and wealth may be more important considerations than caste in arranging a marriage. There are several instances of male and female teachers of different castes marrying. There are also cases of wealthy individuals of low-caste origin marrying themselves or their sons to high-caste girls from poor families. Hindus occasionally marry into other ethnic groups. A few who have gone abroad to study have returned with English or French wives. Some have married Creoles in Mauritius. This sometimes brings about a change in religion and community. One is told that this kind of change was a means of upward social mobility in the past, but it is difficult to estimate its extent. Notices in the newspapers such as the following probably indicate a change of community as well as a change of name:

> Notice is hereby given that 'Lutchmee Parsad Lokman' has applied to His Excellency the Governor in Executive Council for leave to change his name and surname into that of 'Marc Vitrie'.... (*Advance*, 3 September, 1957)

Caste in Indo-Mauritian Politics

Caste labels have become political symbols in some circumstances in Mauritius, though at the time of my fieldwork there were no caste associations with political aims, as have been reported in India (Bailey 1963: 128 ff.). In some villages there have been factions along caste lines struggling for control of village councils. Yet the caste component of such factions is reinforced by common kinship on the one hand and territorial alignments on the other (Benedict 1957). In one village, high and low castes lived at different ends of the village. The high castes adhered to orthodox (Sanatani) practices. The low castes joined the Arya Samaj in great numbers. Disputes about the location of a new school, the appointment of a village librarian, and the running of the village council itself tended to be symbolized in terms of high caste versus low caste.

The ethnic composition of a village is significant in determining whether caste becomes an important symbol of alignment. The village above was almost entirely inhabited by northern Hindus. In Beaumont, which is 67 per cent Hindu, there are seven separate Hindu socioreligious associations (Baitkas) around which factions may form. Distinctions between northern and southern Hindus, Sanatanis and Arya Samajis, or high and low castes may become foci of factions. In La Vallée, on the other hand, Hindus constitute only 37 per cent of the population. La Vallée has only two socioreligious associations, a

Sanatani and an Arya Samaji, and northern and southern Hindus share a temple. Here the distinctions between Hindus and Muslims are of major importance in factional disputes, and divisions in the Hindu community, including those of caste, are submerged in a political context (Benedict 1957).

In 1963, before the most recent elections in Mauritius, there were attempts to rally the lower castes on an island-wide basis. "Les Vaishs, les Soudras et les Ravidas s'élevent contre la politique discriminatoire du Parti au Pouvoir," proclaimed the headlines of an article in one newspaper (*Le Citoyen*, 7 August 1963). Speakers, reported in this and other papers, attacked the Brahmins and the Kshatriyas, claiming they had oppressed the lower castes and monopolized positions of power and wealth. Other Hindu papers replied. Passages from my own book on Mauritius were cited in evidence.

It is difficult to estimate the political importance of such outbursts. No Hindu politician ever publicly defends caste, but the issue may be politically important in some areas of the island. Mauritius is divided into 40 single-member constituencies. In an island one-tenth the size of Wales or of New Jersey, this means that each constituency is very small, and ambitious politicians use caste or ethnic labels in attempts to rally local support. Mauritius is scheduled to become independent in 1967. A new constitution will provide for twenty three-member constituencies, each voter having three votes. In addition there will be eight Specially Elected Members returned from among the unsuccessful candidates who have made the best showing in the election. The first four of these go to the "best losers," irrespective of party, of whichever communities in the island are underrepresented in the legislature. The remaining four will be allocated on the basis of both party and community. There is no suggestion that "community" shall be interpreted to mean caste. It refers to the main ethnic and religious groups in the island—the Hindus, Muslims, general population (Europeans and Creoles), and Chinese. Mauritius is a plural or multiracial society. The struggle for political power involves ethnic, linguistic, religious, and other interest groups. In this struggle the question of communal representation periodically arises. So far, the British Government and the leading political party have resisted communal representation, but should the idea gain ground the definition of communities on the basis of caste would be a possibility. Even without this development, certain politicians have seen the possibilities of attracting support on a caste basis.

Summary

Let us return once more to the six features of caste outlined at the beginning of this paper.

1.   Membership in a caste is still chiefly a matter of birth, but all that is really acquired is a caste name, not membership in a corporate caste group. We have seen that such caste names can be changed by individuals who are socially and physically mobile.

2.   Castes are still endogamous categories, though the number of castes appears to have diminished. Also, intercaste marriages between castes of similar status in the middle range of castes seem to be increasing.

3.   Caste is still a hierarchy, but it is a hierarchy of status symbols rather than of groups. It is most clearly defined at the upper and lower ends.

4.   Occupational specialization according to caste has entirely disappeared except for a few occupations concerned with Hindu ritual.

5.   Except for a very few conservative Hindus, there are no defenders of caste on a religious basis. Hindus in Mauritius approve of the official abolition of caste in India. Most consider that caste is rapidly dying out in Mauritius and do not consider it to be essential to Hinduism. In secular life there are no restrictions on social intercourse or commensality between members of different castes. Such restrictions appear symbolically only in ritual contexts.

6.   There are no corporate caste groups in Mauritius though there have been attempts by politicians to organize political groupings on the basis of caste. Such groupings might be effective during elections, but they should be seen as political groupings using caste as a symbol rather than as castes taking political action.

Caste is not a very important phenomenon in the social structure of Mauritius or even of the Indian section within it. One could describe the social structure of the island without mentioning caste. Caste survives in Mauritius not as a structural principle but as a cultural category.

REFERENCES

BAILEY, F. G.
1960   *Tribe, caste and nation.* Manchester: Manchester University Press.
1963   *Politics and social change.* Berkeley: University of California Press.

BENEDICT, B.
1957   "Factionalism in Mauritian villages." *British Journal of Sociology* VIII:4:328-342.
1961   *Indians in a plural society.* London: H.M.S.O.

BEYTS, H. N. D.
1861   *Report on his mission to India.* Port Louis.

CHALLAYE, C.-A. DE
1844   *Mémoire sur l'émigration des indiens et sur le travail libre dans les colonies de Maurice et de Bourbon.* Extrait des Annales Maritimes et Coloniales. Paris.

COHN, B. S.
1955   "The changing status of a depressed caste." pp. 53-77 in *Village India,* McKim Marriott, ed. American Anthropological Association Memoir No. 83.

FRERE, W. E., and V. A. WILLIAMSON
1875   *Report of the Royal Commissioners appointed to enquire into the treatment of immigrants in Mauritius.* London: William Clowes and Sons.

GHURYE, G. S.
1950   *Caste and class in India.* Bombay: Popular Book Depot.

HUTTON, J. H.
1951   *Caste in India.* 2d ed. London: Oxford University Press. [1st ed., 1946; 3d ed., 1961; 4th ed., 1963]

KAPADIA, K. M.
1958   *Marriage and family in India.* 2d ed. Oxford: Oxford University Press.

MAURITIUS
1905   *Precis showing the different phases through which immigration to Mauritius from the East Indies has passed before it assumed its present form.* Port Louis.
1928   *Mauritius reports.* Port Louis.
1953   *Census of 1952 of Mauritius and its dependencies.* 3 parts. Port Louis.
1956   *Report of the commission appointed to examine the possibility subsidizing religions which are not being subsidized at present in Mauritius.* Sessional Paper No. 9. Port Louis.

1963   *1962 Population census of Mauritius and its dependencies.* 2 vols. Port Louis.

MAYER, ADRIAN C.
1958   "The dominant caste in a region of central India." *Southwestern Journal of Anthropology* 14:4:407-427.

OXFORD UNIVERSITY PRESS
n.d.   *The Oxford English dictionary.*

RISLEY, H. H.
1891   *The tribes and castes of Bengal.* 2 vols. Calcutta: Bengal Secretariat Press.

RUSSELL, R. V., and BAHADUR HIRA LAL RAI
1916   *The tribes and castes of the Central Provinces of India.* 4 vols. London: Macmillan and Company.

STEVENSON, H. N. C.
1954   "Status evaluation in the Hindu caste system." *Journal of the Royal Anthropological Institute of Great Britian and Ireland* 84:45-65.

TITMUSS, R. M., and B. ABEL-SMITH
1961   *Social policies and population growth in Mauritius.* London: Methuen.

GUYANA

Caste and Social Status among the Indians of Guyana[1]

RAYMOND T. SMITH

AND CHANDRA JAYAWARDENA

More than half the population of Guyana is descended from immigrants from India; the rest is made up of persons of African, Chinese, Portuguese, and Amerindian descent, and a large number of persons of racially mixed origin.[2] The East Indians (henceforth referred to as Indians) recognize themselves, and are recognized, as a differentiated group within the society of Guyana. They retain a

---

[1] This paper is based mainly on fieldwork carried out between 1956 and 1958 by Smith in a rice-growing village in Demerara and in Georgetown, and by Jayawardena in two plantations in Berbice. Since then Smith has revisited Guyana several times.

[2] At the census of 1960 the population was enumerated as follows: East Indian—267,840 (48 per cent); African—183,980 (33 per cent); Amerindian—25,450 (4.5 per cent); Mixed—67,189 (12 per cent); Chinese—4,074 (0.7 per cent); White—3,218 (0.6 per cent); Other (mainly Portuguese)—8,348 (1.5 per cent); Syrian and Lebanese—69; Not Stated—238. Total—569,406.

considerable amount of Indian culture, including religious belief and practice, but absorption into a new social system marked by sharp ethnic differentiation has profoundly changed the meaning and content of "Indian culture" in the new setting.

One of the most striking features of this process has been the disintegration of the caste system. Changes in this institution have been so extensive that the caste system as it is known in India cannot be said to persist even in a modified form. Castes are no longer endogamous units defined in terms of meaningful functions—ritual, economic or political.

The problem of "What should we mean by caste?" has been set out adequately by Leach (1960). The main problem is to decide whether the term shall be used solely to refer to the social institution peculiar to Hindu India, or whether we may use it to indicate any extreme form of social stratification. Leach prefers to retain the term as a descriptive label for aspects of Indian society, while other contributors to his symposium favor a wider use of the term. It is not part of our task to settle this terminological question, although the question of what is a variant and what is a different form becomes particularly acute when discussing the social institutions of overseas Indians.

It is our argument that, whichever criteria of caste are accepted, it is doubtful whether the phenomena discussed here could be usefully thought of as castes or as a caste system. However, in order not to prejudge the issue, we retain the term until the data have been presented.

Although the caste system was not re-created in the colony of British Guiana, some elements of it retain a place in Hindu social life; but their meaning and functions have changed radically. One object of this paper is to show that caste survives as an ascribed attribute of individuals which is relevant only within a limited set of activities and contexts. Even such limited significance shows that there is some continuity of cultural values from India; it would be surprising if there were not, considering the fact that the majority of Guyanese Indians are Hindus. But in the operative system of social stratification and differentiation, factors such as income, education and occupation, or of ethnicity are far more important than Hindu castes. Within the Indian community castes do not form operative groups comparable to jati groups. Many writers have suggested that systems of sharp ethnic differentiation constitute caste systems. The colonial society of British Guiana certainly had many castelike features, but to call these "caste" confuses the issue and obscures important differences at the level of culture, including values.

Patterns of Settlement

The Indians were imported as laborers for the plantations, all of which are situated on the narrow low-lying coastal strip. Since the early part of the last century these plantations have concentrated on sugar production; they have grown in size and diminished in number; and their ownership has been consolidated. All are now controlled by two companies. This process has been dictated mainly by the demands of efficiency and economy, but the result is that in Guyana cane is grown on large plantations with hired labor; unlike Fiji and Mauritius, Guyana has hardly any small farmers. Therefore, even after the indenture system was abolished, Indians in the sugar industry remained wage workers. Today almost 20 per cent of the total population of Guyana reside in plantations, and the great majority of these are Indians. Most tasks in cane cultivation are carried out manually, although considerable progress has been made in mechanization and in the application of modern scientific methods. Schemes of technical training have been organized and sugar workers have been encouraged to build their own houses through loans and grants. But the sugar worker still is an employee in a large industrial-agricultural concern, and even when he grows some rice on a plot provided by management or obtained through his own initiative he is primarily a member of the rural proletariat rather than a peasant.[3]

Since the first decade of the twentieth century, the majority of Indians have lived outside the plantations. Indentured immigration was started partly to make good the loss of labor resulting from the partial withdrawal of the emancipated Negro slave from plantation labor and partly to defeat the Negroes' demands for higher wages.

---

[3]For an account of plantation life, see Jayawardena 1963.

After emancipation most of the Negroes had gone to live in the villages where they grew crops such as cassava, plantains, and other vegetables for their own use and for sale, and from where they could work for wages on the plantation if they so desired. The indentured laborers provided a core labor force which could be depended on to carry out the essential tasks, and which could be paid very low wages. The planters were not anxious to see the immigrants return to India after the trouble and expense of importing them. So they encouraged those who had completed their indentures to settle in villages close to the plantations, where their labor would still be available. Some Indians settled quite independently, becoming farmers, shopkeepers, or hucksters. Official land-settlement schemes were not very successful before the early twentieth century, mainly because they were not economically remunerative (Nath 1950). There was no movement of Indians from plantations to economically independent villages comparable to that which had been made by Negroes. The Negro villages were established as communities focused upon a church, and with the positive intention of escape from the plantations. Indians rarely established villages in this way. Indian villages either developed out of collections of rice farmers (rice became profitable with the growth of an export market during the first twenty years of this century), or they were the residue of abandoned sugar plantations.[4] There was rarely any conscious attempt to recreate a specifically Indian mode of village life on the Guyanese Coast. Sometimes Muslims congregated in small settlements in an informal way, but even this practice was not a marked feature. A few settlements grew upon land bought by individual landlords and rented to rice farmers. The most famous of these settlements was McDoom village on the east bank of the Demerara river, where the proprietor Mr. McDoom made strenuous efforts to create a model village community on his lands.

Since 1900, rice cultivation has come to be the basic economic activity in the villages. Negroes as well as Indians are engaged in rice cultivation although rice is often spoken of as an "Indian" crop.[5] Rice

---

[4]An abandoned sugar plantation which had been converted into a Government Land Settlement at the end of the First World War was studied by Smith in 1956. Some features of that community are described in Smith and Jayawardena (1959).

[5]See Smith 1956 for a discussion of rice farming in Negro communities.

is a small-farmer's crop, average holdings being between 5 and 10 acres. A good deal of machinery is now being used even by small farmers (Smith 1957; O'Loughlin 1958). Whatever type of community Indian farmers live in, they share a basically similar pattern of life which arises partly because of economic similarities and partly out of the "Indian" mode of life they have developed. The term "Indian" is used here to distinguish this mode of life from that of other Guyanese rather than to refer to a pattern of life identical with that of a villager in India.

Although it is possible to refer to "Negro" or "Indian" villages, there were, until recently, very few communities which were not ethnically mixed. In a few, the numbers of Indians and Negroes were almost equal. The extent of interpenetration of ethnic groups was demonstrated rather tragically during the first half of 1964 when political conflict resulted in killing, beating, rape, and arson. Indians living in predominantly Negro villages and Negroes in Indian villages in the affected areas tended to move out, so that there was considerable displacement and virtual segregation for the first time in Guyanese history. Not all the country was affected and in some mixed villages Negroes and Indians joined to form vigilante committees to prevent violence.

The extent of urban migration and social mobility among the Indians should be mentioned here, although these will be dealt with more fully below. The urbanization of Indians began during the nineteenth century. There was first a drift to town of Indian beggars, hucksters, and unskilled laborers. At the other end of the scale a small number, who were usually the children of drivers, interpreters, priests, and house servants of white planters, managed to acquire a higher education and move into prestigious occupations such as dispensing, medicine, or law. Their number was very small until well into the twentieth century. In between these two extremes, an increasing number of moderately well-to-do Indians, who had made their money in such diverse ways as farming, shopkeeping, moneylending, or clerical occupations, began to buy houses or open shops in Georgetown. Since 1945 the movement of Indians to Georgetown has grown as more have acquired higher education and are entering urban occupations. At the census of 1960 Indians constituted 22 per cent of the total population of Greater Georgetown.

The Period of Immigration

The Indians who came to British Guiana were almost all brought to work as indentured laborers on the sugar plantations. They were recruited from a wide area of India, and before embarkation the recruits were registered; their personal characteristics, including caste affiliation, were recorded.

An analysis of a random sample from immigration registers shows that the great majority of immigrants were from northeastern India: Uttar Pradesh, 70.3 per cent; Bihar, 15.3 per cent; and Bengal, 1.4 per cent. Most of the remainder came from Rajputana, 3.1 per cent; and south India, 4.4 per cent (Smith 1959). The sample, which records 95 castes, shows that most of the larger castes of northeastern India were represented. However, this representation was not proportionate: several factors influenced the selection of recruits.

One was official policy. The original policy was to import the "hill coolies" of northern India, who had the reputation of being hardy and docile agricultural laborers (Nath 1950). But these were difficult to obtain and recruiters were therefore instructed to enlist emigrants from the "agricultural castes" because agricultural experience was mistakenly equated with agricultural caste. There was therefore a bias against those whose caste occupations were not agricultural. Castes whose occupations were cultivation and herding thus comprised about 36 per cent of the Hindu immigrants, while Brahmin and trading castes were each less than 2 per cent and artisan castes were 8.7 per cent. However, about 11 per cent were Kshatriya, Thakur, and Rajput.

Another factor was the likelihood that low castes found in emigration an escape from their depressed situation. Thus 22.6 per cent of the immigrants consisted of menial castes, of which three-quarters were Chamar, Dusad, and Pasi. The proportion of these castes among the immigrants was several times their proportion in northeastern India (Crooke 1896 I:cxlvii). Further, nearly half the artisans were weavers (Kori), who were frequently outcastes and were, in India, beginning to be thrown out of work by machine-made imports.

For the purposes of studying change, one can assume that the emigrants were the carriers of an "Indian culture," bearing in mind the major caste, religious, and regional differences. All had been involved in "caste society," and had some contact with the central elements of Hinduism or Islam.[6] Many of them had been displaced from a traditional way of life by the advent of British economic enterprise and administration. Others were misfits in their villages, and had signed indentures as a convenient means of escape. In some sense the Indians who embarked upon the immigrant ships may have been among the first products of the breakdown of the traditional caste system in India itself.

Influence of Plantation Life

Without going into details of the history of Indian immigration into the West Indies, it is important to mention certain general features of the historical experience of Indians in the colony of British Guiana. Throughout Guyanese history, the plantation has been a basic social as well as economic complex. In the first days of coastal settlement, plantations were almost self-contained units and, although a wider society grew up around them, they continued to be relatively self-sufficient and socially isolated. Apart from the British and the Amerindians, every ethnic group in Guyana has passed through a phase of plantation labor, so that the plantation has stamped its imprint upon all Guyanese. From the middle of the eighteenth century until 1917, the plantations received recruits from Africa, from the West Indian islands, from Madeira, from China, and from India. They even received a few from Germany, Ireland, England, and Malta in the 1830's.

Techniques of induction were developed which corresponded very closely to those described by Goffman (1961) as being typical of "total institutions." The Indians who arrived in British Guiana had already begun their induction process: they had been numbered, issued with standard clothing, and had their eating habits reorganized in accordance with administrative requirements. Their prior social experience, including caste, was largely ignored.

Immigration and the indenture system destroyed the demo-

---

[6]We are not concerned with Muslims as a special group here, although they have become an important element in present-day Guyana, and will be mentioned where appropriate.

graphic basis of caste group structure. Some castes were represented in too small numbers to persist as endogamous units. In addition, there was a severe imbalance in the sex ratio which was only partly restored in later decades by the imposition of a quota of females on every ship-load. The following figures indicate the acute shortage of women during the indenture period (Nath 1950: 208-209):

WOMEN PER 100 MALES AMONG IMMIGRANTS AND ON PLANTATIONS

Among Immigrants		Among Plantation Residents	
Year	Women	Year	Women
1838	3	1875	45
1848	25	1885	54
1858	38	1895	59
1868	38	1905	67
		1915	69

Scarcity of women resulted in intense competition for the few available and made the maintenance of caste endogamy most difficult. Marriage was very brittle and both men and women generally married several times. It was common for a unit of mother and children to pass successively through the households of two or three males before the children were adult.

During this period there were many intercaste marriages, the children of such unions being ascribed to the father's caste. According to a contemporary observer (Bronkhurst 1883: 286-287):

A woman of low caste may be taken in a kind of marriage by a high caste Hindu, but a high caste or respectable woman will not be given in marriage to a man who is a Chamar (cobbler) or any other inferior caste. All such temporary marriages hold good whilst they are in Demerara, but when they arrive in India there is an end to such marriages. The woman goes one way and the man another.

Intercaste marriages among those who did not return became the established pattern. Judging from present evidence, in time, hypogamy became as frequent as hypergamy.

Conditions in the ships during the long voyage to the West Indies had made caste avoidances impossible. Absence of segregation was perpetuated in the plantations, where the laborers were housed in barracks partitioned into rooms, one to a family. Here members of different castes lived in close proximity, sharing the same water supply, latrines, and sometimes even kitchens.

If these traumatic, but temporary, experiences were the only ones, it is conceivable that the caste system could have been reconstituted at a later period when conditions were more propitious. However, there were other less direct but more pervasive and persistent influences which destroyed the caste system beyond reconstitution. Officials of the Government of India, sent out to report on the condition of the Indians, noted these changes. In 1893 Comins noted (p. 79) :

> Caste is not only modified, but its laws and restrictions are practically ignored after the immigrants leave Calcutta.

In 1925 K. M. Singh commented (p. 13) :

> Indian customs undergo considerable change in the Colonies. For instance, among Hindus in British Guiana there are no depressed classes, caste restrictions in terms of marriage as well as food are practically non-existent, and there is no purdah.

The deeper influences underlying this change were connected with the fact that the expectations, rights, and duties of the new world in which the immigrants found themselves were quite alien to those of the way of life in which caste was a dominant factor.

For instance, the division of labor in the plantation was based on economic and technological practices which belonged to a culture quite foreign to that in which caste was embedded (Jayawardena 1963: 29-36). It was administered by managers who were not concerned with the preservation of traditional Indian ways. The assignment of immigrants to jobs in the factory and the field bore no relation to their caste statuses, taboos, and specializations. The type of occupational specialization which was the economic basis of the Indian caste system was not found in the plantation. Men of different castes performed the same jobs, worked in the same gangs under the direction of an overseer, and were paid at the same rate. Consumer goods required by laborers were purchased at the plantation store. There was no place for jajman relations in the economic organization of the plantation.

Similarly, the political system of the plantation bore no relation to the caste system. Decisions were made by a European manager and executed by European overseers, each of whom was assisted by one or more drivers selected by management from among the laborers. These decisions had to be obeyed by all laborers, regardless of caste. The laborers had no authority to make any important decisions even in nonlabor activities. Most plantations had courts presided over by management officials, where policies concerning social life were laid down and enforced, and where public and private disputes between laborers were settled. Matters handled by the manager's court ranged from disputes between Hindus and Muslims to complaints of wives against husbands, and the composition of households. Laborers were not permitted to form associations to regulate any important matters relating to their economic and political interests. Although there was sporadic community-wide organization of action (strongly disapproved by managements) in the fields of religion and labor disputes, there were no panchayats or caste councils. In later decades managers permitted and helped in the formation of religious associations which they closely supervised.

The plantation managers' interest in controlling all aspects of social life within their domains stemmed from their responsibilities to maintain an orderly and disciplined labor force. Their attitudes to caste derived from this major concern. Some managers regarded the lower castes as better laborers. Comins reported such a classification which distinguished Kurmi, Ahir, Chamar, Dusad, and Dom as "best laborers"; Kshatriya, Jat, and Kahar as "good laborers"; and Brahmin, Bania, and Sonar as "worthless". High-caste coolies were suspected of being ringleaders in strikes, and their influence was regarded as "pernicious" (Comins 1893: 79).

The caste hierarchy received no support from the structure of authority of the plantation. Managers dispensed rewards, privileges, and favors in accordance with work, loyalty, and obedience, irrespective of caste. They had little sympathy for, and enough power to destroy, a parallel hiararchy of power and prestige which could interfere with their freedom to deploy the labor force, or which could cause friction among the laborers. Authority based on caste had little prospect of persisting outside the sphere of labor either, since managers could and did intervene in any matter which directly or indirectly affected discipline. Thus a laborer who resented the attempts of high castes to assert their superiority could complain to management of provocation and annoyance.

Managers were, in principle, indifferent to the preservation of traditional Indian institutions. Yet, although their main guide as to whether to permit a given practice was its effect on labor discipline, there was often a latitude of decision where their own cultural attitudes came into play. If the attitudes of senior and experienced managers of the 1950's may be taken as indications of those of their predecessors, it is possible to indicate some aspects of the culture of the immigrants, against which nonconformists could win managerial sympathy. Spirit possession ("playing jumby") and sorcery ("obeah") were strongly disapproved. To a lesser degree the complete authority of husband over wife, and of mother-in-law over resident daughter-in-law were disfavored by managers. Similarly, managers regarded claims of caste superiority with suspicion and skepticism. While there was some appreciation of the "martial" Kshatriya, there was also a sentiment that an individual's rewards should depend on his worth in this life as a hardworking, obedient, and thrifty laborer. Although most managers were tolerant of religious customs and treated Brahmin priests with some deference, they were also inclined to suspect an element of charlatanry in the Brahmin's invocations and predictions.

At the same time, managers may have been influenced by caste in selecting drivers. Since one of the main qualifications of candidates for this office was ability to discipline the gang, there was a bias in favor of Kshatriya and Brahmin. On the other hand, the derivation of leadership qualities from caste was only a presumption which was likely to be overridden by such considerations as personality, efficiency, and reliability. Among the famous and powerful drivers recalled by older men, Brahmins and Kshatriya figure prominently; but there were also Kurmi, Lohar, Kewat, and Teli. At present, drivers are derived from all castes, including Chamar, Bhar, and Dusad.

In short, the immigrants were resocialized into the role system of the plantation. This change did not mean that they lost all memory of Indian culture and of the roles appropriate to life in an Indian village, any more than the inmates of a prison or mental hospital or a concentration camp forget what life is like on the outside. Many indentured laborers returned to India upon completion of their period of service and were absorbed back into Indian society; some took back considerable sums of money which they had saved.[7] Those who stayed in British Guiana were not "completely stripped of their culture"— a phrase which has caused some difficulty and given rise to bitter argument when applied to the New World Negro. They continued to practice many customs that they had brought from India, and since their numbers were being constantly augmented by new arrivals, Indian languages continued to be used by many. But they were involved in a different social system and their culture had to be adapted accordingly.

At the level of colonial political structure, officials often felt that the Indians ought to be left alone and not assimilated into Guianese society lest they became "spoilt" like the Negroes. By the end of the nineteenth century the Negroes, the Portuguese, and the Colored intelligentsia secured constitutional reforms which gave them control over the legislature after more than three decades of struggle against planter domination. The Governor and the planting interest retained control of the Executive Council, and the idea was very generally prevalent that the Indians regarded the British administration and the planters as their guardians and protectors against Negro domination. Contrariwise, it was also pointed out to the intelligentsia that demands for a widened franchise would lead to the "uncivilized" Indians obtaining a large measure of control. It therefore suited the planters to encourage Indians to retain or revive such elements of Indian culture as did not interfere with the running of the plantation. This attitude was not uniform; some planters encouraged Christian missions working with the Indians and tried to persuade laborers to send their children to school; but the majority seem to have preferred to keep their laborers illiterate and tractable by discouraging assimilation to Creole ways.

---

[7]Out of the 238,960 persons who came to British Guiana from India between 1838 and 1917, the majority remained in the colony or died there. Between 1843 and 1949 official repatriation schemes returned 75,547 persons to India. It should be noted that many repatriates found it extremely difficult to readjust to life in India and re-engaged for work in the sugar colonies.

Challenges to the Legitimacy of Caste

The norms of the caste system were also undermined by doubts concerning the legitimacy of claims to high-caste status. These arose partly through the realization that the high castes, who had already transgressed by crossing the seas, were also not observing the prescribed taboos, and partly out of the practice of changing caste.

PASSING

It is believed that some immigrants assumed high-caste status when they arrived in British Guiana. The phrases "ship Brahmin" and "ship Kshatriya" express this skepticism. Since the immigrants arrived as individuals rather than as kin groups or village sections, local communities in British Guiana were composed of immigrants from different districts of India. There was no reliable means of ascertaining claims to high caste. Passing sometimes took the form of assuming surnames such as Sharma or Tiwari (Brahmin) and Singh (Kshatriya). Those who dared do so, even if their contemporaries disbelieved them, had only to weather some sneering and gossip which decreased with the passage of time. There was no organization with the authority to sift claims, nor was there a consensus on such matters so that spurious claims could be concertedly ignored. Some argued that they, or their parents, assumed a low caste in order to be accepted as immigrants. A high rate of residential mobility among plantation laborers enabled some to establish their claims. Eventually, whatever doubts were entertained in one generation were forgotten in the next.

Doubts concerning caste also arose from the instability of marriage and family life. Children were often brought up by step-parents or maternal kin. Many adults of today know little about their parents, not to mention their castes. Others have assumed the castes of those who fostered them. Family instability produced a background of genealogical uncertainty in the histories of many individuals who could, if they wished, change their castes. The relatively large number of Brahmins and Kshatriya today tempts one to stress the fact of passing. On the other hand, it should be noted that the actual proportion of Kshatriya among the immigrants was larger than might be expected from immigration policy. Furthermore, it is possible that, during the period of the scarcity of women, Brahmins and Kshatriya had better chances of obtaining wives, and so of procreating their kind, than did lower castes.

It is unlikely that passing occurs to any significant extent today, if only for the reason that little is to be gained from it. Though many prominent leaders in national organizations are of high caste, it is reasonable to suppose that the first Indians to obtain higher education were the children of drivers, interpreters, and Brahmin priests, so that a selective factor has been at work. There is also the probability that persons who were of higher caste felt greater self-confidence and were more oriented toward social success and the performance of leadership roles.

But, whatever the speculations about the past, the actual extent to which these factors prevailed cannot be accurately assessed today. What is important is that they are believed to have occurred. This undermines the legitimacy of the claim to superiority of the local high castes, for such doubts can be raised to question their status. Thus it is sometimes said that "There are no 'real' Brahmins (or Kshatriya) in Guyana today."

RELIGIOUS INFLUENCE

The majority of Indians in Guyana claim to be orthodox Hindus. In 1960 there were 187,432 Hindus out of a total Indian population of 267,840. A small number of these belong to Hindu reform movements such as the American Aryan League. These movements are influential but do not have a large membership. Muslims numbered 49,297, and although this group includes a handful of Negroes and other non-Indians, it is remarkable that in Guyana Islam is thought of as an "Indian" religion. The conversion of Indian immigrants to Christianity was begun during the nineteenth century but was never very successful.

Merely to enumerate the religious affiliation of Indians, without examining what these categories mean, can be very misleading. It is particularly so in the case of Hinduism, which in India was a congeries of various beliefs and practices tied to a whole way of life. Reform Hinduism such as that represented by the Arya Samaj, or the American Aryan League as it is called in Guyana, is more easily definable since it has become an open church with a formal doctrine.

Although it incorporates many elements of the Indian religious tradition, it is imbued with values which derive more from Europe than from ancient India. "Orthodox" Hinduism in Guyana is partly a collection of bits of traditional belief and rite, and partly a formal organization which came into being in response to attacks by reform Hindus. As in India itself, a Sanatan Dharm Maha Sabha was formed in self-defense against attacks from the Arya Samaj and, as in the case of the parent organization, the doctrines of this body represent a retreat from some orthodox outposts to more defensible positions. In Guyana these are relatively recent developments, dating from the late twenties and early thirties of this century.[8]

These various religious developments have reinforced challenges to the legitimacy of caste. The ritual distinctions which formed a basis of the caste system were totally discarded. Caste rites were dismissed as superstition, and there are no more caste priests. Life-cycle rites have been standardized, and all castes perform the same marriage and funeral ceremonies, which are conducted by Brahmin priests regardless of the castes of their clients. Brahmin priests do not serve only the twice-born castes. The investiture of the sacred thread (janeu) is a relatively rare ceremony, and is held mainly in Brahmin families. All castes participate freely in puja, holy readings, services in the temple, and public festivals.

The only expression of caste in orthodox religious activities is the privileged position of Brahmins, who alone have the right to perform the main rites. The Guyana Pandits' Council, which is closely allied to the Guyana Sanatan Dharm Maha Sabha, recommends priests to the Government for appointment as marriage officers. The Pandits' Council will never recommend anyone but a Brahmin priest, nor would any Sanatan branch appoint a non-Brahmin as a priest to a community temple.

Brahmins who do not practice as priests are, for the most part, classed as other laymen, although on occasion they too may receive *dakshina* as a token "feeding of Brahmins." In *yag* (reading and exposition of the scriptures by several pandits) there is a special

---

[8]For an account of developments in Hinduism in British Guiana, see Jayawardena 1966.

enclosure for Brahmins. But this area is occupied by practicing priests, and a Brahmin who did not consider himself adept in ritual and scripture would hesitate to join them.

Guyanese Hindus have been receptive to reformist ideas which reject the caste system. While actual converts to Arya Samaj are relatively few, its views on caste and Brahmins have gained wide currency. In Guyana the American Aryan League attacks the whole concept of hereditary priestly status, accuses the Brahmins of fraud, and condemns such things as idol worship. According to the reformists, the four varna were meant to indicate levels of spiritual achievement attained by an individual during his lifetime. Their views are aptly summarized by the slogan, "One is a Brahmin not by birth but by deeds." The Arya Samaj argue that any member of the Samaj with the requisite piety and technical knowledge can act as a priest. The Government recognizes priests of this sect so that in the society at large they are not distinguished from orthodox Brahmin priests.

Even within the Sanatan movement there are dissidents such as the Bharat Sevashram Sangh who sympathize with Arya Samaj views about the privileges of Brahmins. A case in point is that of a dispute which arose in a village temple in 1956. A small group of men (who were influential in the village and relatively prosperous) started a branch of the Bharat Sevashram Sangh. At first they obtained permission to carry out their special ceremonies in the temple in the absence of the Brahmin priest, but were later denied the concession. Consequently they acquired a small "church" of their own in which they carried out rituals, sometimes inviting a friendly Brahmin priest from a neighboring village, but managing quite well on their own most of the time.

Attitudes to Caste

The majority of Hindus are able to tell an inquirer which "caste" they belong to. But this dimension of their social personality is very small, and is of relatively little significance in most cases. In the local idiom the usual word for caste is "nation," a term which also means race, tribe, or ethnic group: thus, Black nation (Negroes), White nation, Indian nation, Fula nation (Muslims). Brahmins are "high nation" and Chamars are "low nation," and in the idea system of

Guyanese Indians these two groups represent the poles of the caste hierarchy.

Attitudes toward caste vary little among the different sections of the Indian population. Some high-caste families may seek to preserve their exclusiveness in various ways, but the common attitude is expressed in such comments as "Nation is ol' time story," or "Nation dead-out now." This view is in part an assessment of the significance of caste in social life and in part a condemnation of caste as a reactionary and disruptive force. Many assert that "Nation cause the downfall of the India people," meaning that disunity bred by caste led to the foreign domination of India.

In 1958, for example, a visiting dignitary from India was widely applauded for his forthright condemnation of caste as the cause of India's "backwardness," even though his pronouncements drew a mild protest from the Pandits' Council. Insistence on caste rank is regarded as a kind of snobbishness derived from an outmoded past. Most people feel that caste consciousness contradicts the progressiveness and modernity felt to be necessary if Indians are to prosper in modern Guyana.

CASTE HIERARCHY

With their absorption into Guyanese society, Indians have adopted Guyanese criteria for the evaluation of social status. In comparison with income, occupation, education, race, and style of life, caste is recognized to be irrelevant in the many important fields where Hindus interact with other groups. In such fields, performance determines the social career of the individual Hindu, as it does those of individuals of other ethnic or religious groups; Hindus are accorded a high social status if they possess the qualities and achievements valued in the wider multiethnic society. Non-Indians have little knowledge of Indian cultural traditions and are insensitive to gradations of caste.

High-caste individuals may speak in private of the unethical and boorish manners of the low castes. They may refer to the past, when their forefathers refused to treat low castes as equals. The sons of high-caste families may be invested with the sacred thread, especially if the father is religious. But the holding of such a ceremony depends on whether the father is wealthy enough or cares enough about the added prestige it will bring him. The incentive to publicize high ritual status in this way is limited by the fact that, although being twice-born in itself has value, alone it does not confer a special status on the individual. Outside the sphere of influence of Indian tradition, there is no appreciation of this dimension of the Hindu's social personality, for here the important characteristics are, as was mentioned earlier, race, occupation and education.

Furthermore, in the plantations the caste hierarchy is contrary to the egalitarian ethic which informs most social relations between laborers (Jayawardena 1963). A person who parades his caste superiority offends notions of proper conduct. In a typical reaction, a man who boasted "Me a Kshatriya; me got warrior blood," was knocked into a ditch by an Ahir who taunted him with the query, "Where you warrior blood now?" Much of this attitude also prevails in the villages, though there is more room for differentiation based on individual ownership of property.

Brahmin priests themselves are aware that they work in a milieu unfavorable to claims of superiority. Criticism of their alleged venality and chicanery is not uncommon; they are said to have "fooled the people" in the past, kept them in ignorance, and battened on *dakshina*. Brahmin priests restrict their expectations to ritual contexts and, when they finish a ceremony, rejoin the other guests to eat and smoke as equal members of the fraternity of Indians. The honorific title of *Maraj* is accorded only to those Brahmins who lead a respectable life, especially to priests. Addressed to a Brahmin who patently does not do so, the title carries ironic connotations. Conversely, it may be said of a pious man that although he is not a Brahmin, "he lead the life of Brahmin." The traditional respect due to a Brahmin is awarded mainly to those who regularly or occasionally act as priests.

The behavior of the Hindus of Guyana has become sanskritized by processes similar to those that have occurred in India, and has been described by such writers as Srinivas (1952) and Cohn (1955). As the status divisions between jati groups had no significance in the context of Guyana, so cultural and ritual differences between people of different castes lost their meaning, and gradually the concept of a Hindu status hierarchy came to be polarized in terms of a contrast between Brahminical or Sanskritic patterns on the one hand, and Untouchable patterns on the other. The Brahmin and the Chamar came to represent two ends of a scale of status valid only within the Indian subgroup of Guyanese society, and even then not to all its members, particularly the growing number of Muslims. With the abandonment by low castes of distinctive rites and the standardization of ceremonies, the Untouchable end of the ritual scale has also lost all significance and differences are marked only by degrees of Sanskritization.

The upwardly mobile Indian will often adopt a more Sanskritic mode of life or become a Christian or Muslim and so leave the Hindu system of status evaluation altogether. The upwardly mobile person of Brahmin or Kshatriya origin may begin to lay more stress upon his ritual standing and become more orthodox. But, if the upward movement continues, eventually every Indian also becomes more creolized. This does not mean that he ceases to stress his "Indianness," but he enters a new social domain where it takes on new significance and where caste has little meaning. Of course, the coincidence of high secular (class) status and high ritual status may be valuable in claiming representational roles, but neither is necessarily linked to the other. Indians may attribute to a high-ranking person the characteristics of Brahminical behavior, whatever his caste. Thus Dr. Jagan is often said to be a "pure sannyasi" because, according to Indian villagers, he neither drinks nor smokes and eats only vegetable food.

POLLUTION

The notion of pollution has become so restricted that, with a few gradually disappearing exceptions, it no longer serves to classify castes. The only concepts of pollution which are important are those involving life-cycle events such as birth and death. The avoidances and ablutions prescribed for these periods are carried out by all but the nominal Hindus.

Although the Chamars are regarded as being at the other end of the scale from the Brahmin, from the point of view of behavior they can hardly be distinguished from other non-Brahmins. People say that in the past Chamar families reared pigs and conducted pig sacrifices. However, pigs were gradually replaced by goats and, in time, all animal sacrifice was abandoned under the mounting criticism that such practices were barbarous and superstitious. A very few families still rear pigs for sale, and they are said to be Chamar, but the vast majority of Chamars have long since abandoned this practice.

In general, the same views on what is clean and what is polluting are accepted and adhered to by all castes. Pollution is a matter not of what a given caste may or may not do, but of what a "good Hindu" may or may not do. All Hindus are inclined to avoid such occupations as shoemaking, clothes washing, or butchering. Eating pork and beef is forbidden to all, and this taboo is generally obeyed in rural areas, although it is said that some break it surreptitiously. "Taking life" (as in hunting and fishing) and eating meat are avoided only by "good Hindus," and are engaged in by all castes without loss of caste prestige. With the exception of Brahmin priests, and those "leading the sadhu life," all castes drink alcohol; and a Brahmin who owns a rum shop suffers no loss of esteem.

COMMENSALITY

There are no restrictions on commensality on public occasions. At weddings and religious ceremonies guests sit down together at meals prepared by their host regardless of his caste. Persons of higher *class* are often fed separately, and Brahmin priests may be included with them. Attendance at such gatherings, especially in plantations, is an obligatory public affirmation of ties of kinship, neighborhood, or friendship with the host. A refusal to participate is an unfriendly snobbish act likely to provoke a quarrel at some later date. In such quarrels, arising out of behavior suspected of asserting superiority, the insult, "You dirty Chamar bitch!" may be heard. But this has no reference to the caste of the person abused, who may be a Chamar, a Brahmin, or of any other caste.

Although there are no restrictions in public, occasionally restrictions operate in private. While the latitude of choice in inviting guests to a public feast, or in attending one, is limited, individuals are relatively free to decide whom they will invite to private dinners in their homes, or with whom to share food if visiting at mealtimes. In this respect there are a few well-to-do high-caste families who express a reluctance to entertain low castes. But, although this avoidance refers to the caste system, it is an expression of status snobbery rather than caste avoidance in the traditional sense. Brahmin priests, who may depend for a living on the three or four ceremonies they perform each week, eat at the homes of clients, regardless of caste. They, as well as individuals in respected positions, such as professionals, overseers, drivers, teachers, and clerks, both high-caste and low, are prized as guests by humble laborers and farmers. The notables do not usually reciprocate by inviting their lower-class hosts.

This phenomenon is not a persistence of caste restrictions on commensality, for in the traditional situation the high castes offer food to the lower but refrain from accepting it. The situation described is a reversal of orthodox caste practice, and represents the exclusiveness and gains of a high status which is not of the caste type.[9] In the cases observed, such discrimination was practised when low caste was compounded by low status on other grounds, and not when low caste was associated with high socioeconomic status. The appeal to caste provides a justification for maintaining social distance in a different type of social stratification.

Restrictions on commensality resembling those of caste occur sporadically, not between castes but between Hindus and Muslims when they choose to emphasize religious differences concerning food taboos. Hindus may object that the utensils used for cooking mutton have been previously used for beef; and Muslims may avoid eating at Hindu homes because the animal has not been killed in the prescribed manner. However, these restrictions are almost never practised by whole groups and are not usually emphasized even by the orthodox. When invoked, such objections are counters in disputes of wider dimensions which have little relation to differences of religious belief.

ENDOGAMY

There is no prohibition of marriage between castes and inter-marriage occurs more often than not. Children are ascribed the father's caste. However, caste may be taken into account and balanced against other factors such as income and education when a spouse is chosen. High-caste parents who prefer high-caste spouses for their children are particularly likely to do so.

One factor which governs the realization of this preference is the

---

[9]Leach 1960 and Gould 1964 emphasize the fact that advantages and disabilities in a caste system are characteristically balanced between the component units of the system.

availability of spouses of the appropriate caste. Young people of a marriageable age, and of the right caste, may not be available in the district or within the network of contacts through which marriages are arranged. Scarcity is partly solved by selecting someone of similar or approximate caste rank. A Brahmin father, for example, may choose a Kshatriya husband for his daughter and feel satisfied that he has kept up his prestige. This practice may also be found among castes which are numerically small.

The education and occupation of the bridegroom and the financial circumstances and social standing of his family are as important as caste (Smith and Jayawardena 1959). A high-caste father may prefer a low-caste bridegroom with good prospects to a high-caste one with no future. A Brahmin priest thus married his daughter to a Chamar. Conversely, Brahmin youths make economically advantageous marriages with low-caste girls.

High-caste status thus can be exchanged for other types of reward and prestige. Where these other benefits are not pronounced, marriages tend to be contracted within the caste or between castes of approximate rank. What is avoided, if feasible, is not marriage outside the caste but too great a disparity between castes. However, marriages of high castes with low castes occur even when there are no social advantages, when romantic attachment and personal choice figure prominently in the selection of a spouse.

Caste in the Plantations

The fact that caste is not a basic determinant of social status within the Indian community can be illustrated with reference to the internal organization of local communities. In this section we present quantitative data showing the relation of caste to other social characteristics of the Hindu population of two plantation communities: Blairmont, West Coast Berbice; and Port Mourant, Corentyne, both in the county of Berbice. We do not have corresponding figures for the villages, but consider that they would be similar in essential respects to those presented here, except that there would be a higher proportion of persons professing ignorance of caste origin. In the succeeding section we discuss some aspects of a rice-growing village in order to show the way in which a local elite is related to the system of social stratification in the country as a whole. Social stratification in plantations has been analyzed elsewhere (Jayawardena 1963: Chapter 3).

The statistics presented here were collected in the course of a general social survey by asking the heads of households to name their castes and those of their dependents.[10] Where possible, information was also collected about the castes of the mothers and of the spouses of married siblings and spouses. It is, however, unwise to place too much reliance on these figures, and the following words of caution are in place.

Because caste influences an individual's position in the community only marginally, there was little public consensus concerning caste status that would enable a check to be made on personal statements. It is unlikely that more than a few lied grossly about their castes, but minor mistakes and distortions may have passed unnoticed.

Nearly a quarter of the household heads in Blairmont, and a smaller proportion in Port Mourant, stated that they did not know what their caste was. These numbers were reduced after consultation with Brahmin priests who had conducted many of the marriages in the locality, with old men who knew the histories of many of the families in their neighborhood, and with kinsmen.[11] Judging from these indirect sources of information, the proportion of people who did not know what their caste was, and who were reputed to be low caste, was not markedly high. Those whose caste was ascertained indirectly represented the whole range, excluding Brahmin and Kshatriya. In the following tables they are classified according to the castes attributed them by reliable sources. There is no means of deciding whether claimed lack of knowledge was due to ignorance, principles, or de-

---

[10]The statistics presented here were obtained through a survey which, in Blairmont, aimed at a total coverage but succeeded in covering 94 per cent of the Indian households; the rest consists of incompleted schedules, those absent during the period of the survey, and two refusals. The statistics for Port Mourant are based on a sample of 205 households which constitutes about a fifth of the households in the plantation. For various reasons it was not practicable to obtain a random sample. However, the sample was stratified according to area of residence, religion, race, and occupation, the proportions of which were ascertained from records and inquiries.

[11]It was more difficult to obtain indirect information about the castes of married women since most of them came from outside the plantation.

liberate concealment.[12] To the extent that it was the first, it should be remembered that the categories in which some are classified are meaningless to them.

Except among the high castes, the usual attitude was that questions concerning caste raked up aspects of tradition which were better buried and forgotten. In some cases there was doubt and speculation, and replies were informed guesses. Some interpreted their caste according to present circumstances, evaluating field labor as "Vaisya." There were a few who derived their castes from affinal connections. The son of a Chamar priest of the Siva Narayani sect gave his caste as Gossai because of his father's profession. Where such inaccuracies were perceived (and there can be no assurance that they always were), further questions were asked in order to arrive at the ancestral caste.

Of some importance in this connection are the two castes "Bengali" and "Madras" which indicate regional origin. The "caste system" of the Guyanese Indians is derived from Uttar Pradesh, and Indians from other regions seem to have been regarded as undifferentiated "nations." Persons of the "Madras nation" recognize that they were traditionally divided into castes, but very few know what these are, and other Indians do not care. Yet the Madras Indians retain some cultural peculiarities which set them off from the North Indians. By contrast, whose who call themselves "Bengali" are completely identified with the North Indians, and their separate "nation" is revealed only in answer to specific questions concerning caste.

In the survey of Blairmont 34 caste names were collected and in Port Mourant 25. The number of married persons in each caste is listed in Appendix A. For convenience of tabulation the castes are classified into five categories:

I. High Castes (comprising Brahmin and Kshatriya)
II. Middle Castes (comprising Gossai, Ahir, Kurmi, Bania, Mali, Gadariya, Teli, Boojwa, Halwai, Murau, Nonia, Sonar, Lodh, Lala, Kalpa, Nao, as well as "Vaisya" and "Bengali")
III. Low Castes (comprising Chamar, Kahar, Kewat, Bhar, Pasi, Dusad, Kori, Dhobi, Bhuiyar, Musahar, Dom, Kalwar, Katik, as well as "Sudra")

---

[12]A few Arya Samajists maintained that since caste was "wrong," questions about it deserved no answer.

IV. "Madras"

V. "Do Not Know"

The rank order of the first three is derived from the views of knowledgeable residents. There were a few discrepancies concerning the place of Nao, Kahar, and Kewat; in these cases the more general view is followed. The Madras are regarded as a different sort of Indian people and are not included in the same hierarchy as the others.

Tables Ia and Ib compare caste with occupational status which is the basis of social stratification in the plantation. Junior Staff (clerks, drivers, and foremen), Skilled Laborers (electricians, mechanics, welders, panboilers, tractor operators, and the like), and Unskilled Laborers (canecutters, shovelmen, forkmen, weeders, mule boys, and the like) may be arranged in a descending order of income and prestige. In Blairmont (Table Ia) a proportionately greater number from the High Castes is found among the Junior Staff, probably because of the tendency in the past to select drivers from the higher castes. Yet there is no consistent pattern of association between caste rank and occupational status. For example, while the percentage from the Low Castes among the Junior Staff is lower than that from

TABLE Ia. CASTE AND OCCUPATIONAL STATUS : BLAIRMONT*

Caste		Junior Staff	Skilled Laborers	Unskilled Laborers	Total
High	No.	13	12	38	63
	%	20.63	19.05	60.32	100.00
Middle	No.	15	12	90	117
	%	12.82	10.26	76.92	100.00
Low	No.	9	14	62	85
	%	10.59	16.47	72.94	100.00
"Madras"	No.	1	3	5	9
	%	11.11	33.33	55.56	100.00
Do Not Know	No.	4	10	23	37
	%	10.81	27.03	62.16	100.00
	No.	42	51	218	311
	%	13.50	16.40	70.10	100.00

Total $\chi^2 = 9.54$; d.f. $= 8$; $p > 0.20$

*Excluding those not employed in the plantation, and those under 21 years.

TABLE 1*b*. CASTE AND OCCUPATIONAL STATUS: PORT MOURANT*

Caste		*Junior Staff*	*Skilled Laborers*	*Unskilled Laborers*	*Total*
High	No.	1	3	22	26
	%	3.85	11.54	84.62	100.00
Middle	No.	0	3	65	68
	%	0.00	4.41	95.59	100.00
Low	No.	2	11	65	78
	%	2.56	14.10	83.33	99.99
"Madras"	No.	3	2	23	28
	%	10.71	7.14	82.14	100.00
Do Not Know	No.	1	1	14	16
	%	6.25	6.25	87.50	100.00
	No.	7	20	189	216
	%	3.24	9.26	87.50	100.00

$Total \chi^2 = 7.38$; d.f. $= 8$; $p > 0.30$

*Excluding those not employed in the plantation, and those under 21 years.

the Middle Castes, it is also lower among the Unskilled Laborers. The highest percentages of Skilled Laborers are found in the categories "Madras" and "Do Not Know." The absence of any association between the occupational hierarchy and caste is more marked in Port Mourant (Table Ib), where the Low Castes have the highest percentage of Skilled Laborers. The distribution of frequencies in each table is not statistically significant.

Tables IIa and IIb compare caste with degree of education. In Blairmont, the High Castes have a higher percentage of persons with more than five years schooling than do the Low Castes. While this difference may reflect a greater readiness among members of the High Castes to avail themselves of educational facilities, again there is no consistent association between caste rank and education. The percentage of those without education is higher among the High Castes than among the Middle Castes or "Do Not Know." The last show the highest ratio of those with more than five years of school. A greater percentage of Low Castes than of Middle Castes have been to secondary school. The slight tendency of High Castes to be better represented in the higher occupations may reflect the correlation between education and occupation. Yet the over-all inconsistency between caste rank and educational attainment shows that, at least

TABLE II*a*. CASTE AND EDUCATION : BLAIRMONT*

Caste		No Education	1-4 Years	5-6 Years	Secondary School	Totals
High	No.	15	25	22	6	68
	%	22.06	36.76	32.35	8.82	100.00
Middle	No.	23	64	29	3	119
	%	19.33	53.78	24.37	2.52	100.00
Low	No.	28	37	18	3	86
	%	32.56	43.02	20.93	3.49	100.00
"Madras"	No.	4	1	5	1	11
	%	36.36	9.09	45.45	9.09	100.00
Do Not Know	No.	6	15	15	1	37
	%	16.22	40.54	40.54	2.70	100.00
	No.	76	142	89	14	321
	%	23.68	44.24	27.73	4.36	100.00

$Total \chi^2 = 16.34$; d.f. $= 12$; $p > 0.10$
*Excluding those under 21 years.

TABLE II*b*. CASTE AND EDUCATION : PORT MOURANT*

Caste		No Education	1-4 Years	5-6 Years	Secondary School	Totals
High	No.	7	19	8	1	35
	%	20.00	54.29	22.86	2.86	100.00
Middle	No.	24	36	27	0	87
	%	27.59	41.38	31.03	0.00	100.00
Low	No.	24	42	24	2	92
	%	26.09	45.65	26.09	2.17	100.00
"Madras"	No.	10	12	7	2	31
	%	32.26	38.71	22.58	6.45	100.00
Do Not Know	No.	4	5	10	1	20
	%	20.00	25.00	50.00	5.00	100.00
	No.	69	114	76	6	265
	%	26.04	43.02	28.68	2.26	100.00

$Total \chi^2 = 7.75$; d.f. $= 12$; $p > 0.80$
*Excluding those under 21 years.

in recent times, Low Castes have also used educational facilities. This trend is illustrated clearly in Port Mourant (Table IIb), where the percentage of those with more than five years of school is higher among the Low Castes than among the High Castes. The degree of association between caste and education is, if at all, extremely low in Blairmont, and none in Port Mourant.

Tables IIIa and IIIb throw some light on the discussion of passing. They show that a relatively high percentage of High Castes were born beyond a ten-mile radius of the plantation: in Blairmont 26.86 per cent of the High Castes as compared with 15.51 per cent of the

TABLE IIIa. CASTE AND PLACE OF BIRTH: BLAIRMONT*

Caste		Born in Plantation	Born within Radius of Ten Miles	Born beyond Radius of Ten Miles	Totals
High	No.	30	19	18	67
	%	44.78	28.36	26.87	100.00
Others	No.	169	38	38	245
	%	68.98	15.51	15.51	100.00
	No.	199	57	56	312
	%	63.78	18.27	17.95	100.00

$Total \chi^2 = 11.71$; d.f. $= 2$; $p < 0.01$

*Excluding those under 21 years and those born in India.

TABLE IIIb. CASTE AND PLACE OF BIRTH: PORT MOURANT*

Caste		Born in Plantation	Born within Radius of Ten Miles	Born beyond Radius of Ten Miles	Totals
High	No.	26	1	6	33
	%	78.79	3.03	18.18	100.00
Others	No.	201	13	9	223
	%	90.13	5.83	4.04	100.00
	No.	227	14	15	256
	%	88.67	5.47	5.86	100.00

$Total \chi^2 = 7.86$; d.f. $= 2$; $p < 0.05$

*Excluding those under 21 years and those born in India.

others and, in Port Mourant, 18.18 per cent as compared with 4.03 per cent. This contrast suggests the possibility that several of those who migrated from one district to another successfully claimed a high caste. In the past (before about 1939), communications were poor, so that a ten-mile radius defined the area within which the plantation community could maintain regular contacts with other plantation and village communities. It would have been difficult to verify the castes of strangers coming from beyond this range.

Although caste influences marriage, the frequency of marriage within the caste is very low. This supports the view that "nation is ol' time story." In Table IV the castes with five or more married males are listed, and the percentage of intracaste marriage is indicated. The figures for females are comparable.

TABLE IV. PER CENT OF MARRIAGES INTRACASTE

Caste	Total Married Males	Per Cent of Marriages Intracaste
BLAIRMONT:		
Kshatriya	36	27.77
Ahir	34	32.35
Chamar	32	21.87
Brahmin	25	36.00
Bengali	21	9.52
Kahar	14	0.00
Kurmi	12	0.00
Kewat	11	0.00
Bhar	10	20.00
Madras	8	25.00
Lohar	6	0.00
Gossai	5	0.00
Gadariya	5	0.00
Teli	5	20.00
All	224	22.01
PORT MOURANT:		
Chamar	49	38.77
Madras	26	23.07
Kshatriya	22	18.18
Ahir	22	27.27
Gadariya	12	0.00
Kurmi	11	27.27
Bhar	10	10.00
Brahmin	9	55.55
Kahar	7	14.28
Nao	6	16.66
Nonia	5	40.00
All	179	31.92

These figures suggest that the degree of intracaste marriage is partly associated with caste rank; thus the higher frequencies tend to be associated with the top (Brahmin and Kshatriya) and bottom (Chamar) of the hierarchy. On the other hand, the size of each caste also appears to be relevant, in that such castes as Ahir and Madras have relatively high rates of intracaste marriage. Whatever the reasons for variations between the castes, it is clear that neither statistically nor normatively is caste among the Guianese Indians an endogamous unit.

Nevertheless, despite the absence of sanctions against intercaste marriage, as well as the fact that most members of each caste marry outside it, caste rank influences the selection of spouses indirectly. Since the small numbers in many castes make it impracticable for them to practice endogamy, in Tables Va and Vb the data on the castes of husbands and their wives are arranged according to the five categories described above. This procedure takes into account the possibility that numerically small castes may regard some others as acceptable alternatives.[13] These two tables show that, excluding the category "Do Not Know," most marriages in both plantations

TABLE Va. CASTE AND MARRIAGE: BLAIRMONT*

Husband Caste		High	Middle	Low	Madras	Do Not Know	Totals
				Wife Caste			
High	No.	31	15	9	0	5	60
	%	51.67	25.00	15.00	0.00	8.33	100.00
Middle	No.	23	35	23	4	16	101
	%	22.77	34.65	22.77	3.96	15.84	100.00
Low	No.	18	18	23	5	16	80
	%	22.50	22.50	28.75	6.25	20.00	100.00
Madras	No.	0	2	1	2	1	6
	%	0.00	33.33	16.67	33.33	16.67	100.00
Do Not Know	No.	4	3	1	0	14	22
	%	18.18	13.64	4.54	0.00	63.64	100.00
	No.	76	73	57	11	52	269
	%	28.25	27.14	21.19	4.09	19.33	100.00

$Total \chi^2 = 54.73$; d.f. $= 16$; $p < 0.001$

*The following categories of persons are excluded: those widowed or separated at the time of survey; those Hindus whose spouse's father was not a Hindu; Christians who gave "Christian" as their caste.

---

[13]Although this is not a generally expressed opinion, a couple of informants suggested this.

TABLE V*b*. CASTE AND MARRIAGE: PORT MOURANT*

Husband Caste		High	Middle	Low	Madras	Do Not Know	Totals
				Wife Caste			
High	No.	11	6	6	4	3	30
	%	36.67	20.00	20.00	13.33	10.00	100.00
Middle	No.	14	30	13	6	5	68
	%	20.59	44.12	19.12	8.82	7.35	100.00
Low	No.	5	14	33	6	17	75
	%	6.67	18.67	44.00	8.00	22.67	100.00
Madras	No.	2	5	5	6	6	24
	%	8.33	20.83	20.83	25.00	25.00	100.00
Do Not Know	No.	0	2	2	4	7	15
	%	0.00	13.33	13.33	26.67	46.67	100.00
	No.	32	57	59	26	38	212
	%	15.09	26.89	27.83	12.26	17.92	100.00

Total $\chi^2 = 47.93$; d.f. $= 16$; $p < 0.001$

*The following categories of persons are excluded: those widowed or separated at the time of survey; those Hindus whose spouse's father was not a Hindu; and Christians who gave "Christian" as their caste.

occur outside the caste categories. On the other hand, the selection of spouses in relation to these categories is not random. There is a statistically significant tendency toward marriage within the category, even though it does not represent the majority of marriages. The figures support the observation that, although caste is not usually a key factor in the choice of a spouse, an attempt is made to avoid great disparities of caste rank.

Tables VI, VIIa, VIIb, VIIIa, and VIIIb throw light on factors

TABLE VI. CASTE CATEGORY AND MARRIAGE IN THE TWO PLANTATIONS

		Blairmont	Port Mourant	Totals
Marriage within Caste Category	No.	91	80	171
	%	43.54	48.19	45.60
Marriage outside Caste Category	No.	118	86	204
	%	56.46	51.81	54.40
	No.	209	166	375
	%	100.00	100.00	100.00

Total $\chi^2 = 0.63$; d.f. $= 1$; $p > 0.30$

that influence the tendency to marry within the caste or with castes of approximate rank. While Table VI shows that there is a similar tendency in both plantations, Tables VIIa and VIIb and Tables VIIIa and VIIIb suggest that the factors influencing it differ. Table VIIa shows that in Blairmont marriage within the category is associated with the first marriage and, conversely, marriage outside the category is associated with subsequent marriages.

Among rural Hindus, a girl's first marriage is normally to a bachelor. The agreement to marry is made between the parents or guardians of the bride and groom, and the wedding is conducted by a Brahmin priest according to customary Hindu rites (Smith and Jayawardena 1958)—"under the bamboo," to use the Creole expression. In this elaborate and costly ceremony, which is one of the main public events in the life of rural Indians, large numbers of guests from

TABLE VIIa. CASTE CATEGORY AND ORDER OF MARRIAGE: BLAIRMONT—FEMALES

		First Marriage	Subsequent Marriage	Totals
Marriage within	No.	78	13	91
Caste Category	%	49.68	25.00	43.54
Marriage outside	No.	79	39	118
Caste Category	%	50.32	75.00	56.46
	No.	157	52	209
	%	100.00	100.00	100.00

$Total \chi^2 = 8.69$; d.f. $= 1$; $p = < 0.01$

TABLE VIIb. CASTE CATEGORY AND ORDER OF MARRIAGE: PORT MOURANT—FEMALES

		First Marriage	Subsequent Marriage	Totals
Marriage within	No.	73	7	80
Caste Category	%	48.67	43.75	48.19
Marriage outside	No.	77	9	86
Caste Category	%	51.33	56.25	51.81
	No.	150	16	166
	%	100.00	100.00	100.00

$Total \chi^2 = 0.00$; d.f. $= 1$; $p > 0.99$

TABLE VIIIA. EDUCATION AND MARRIAGE ACCORDING TO CASTE CATEGORY:
BLAIRMONT—MALES

		Marriage within Caste Category	Marriage outside Caste Category	Totals
No Education	No.	21	31	52
	%	40.38	59.62	100.00
1-4 Years	No.	42	62	104
	%	40.38	59.62	100.00
Over 4 Years	No.	28	25	53
	%	52.83	47.17	100.00
	No.	91	118	209
	%	43.54	56.46	100.00

$Total \chi^2 = 1.90$; d.f. $= 2$; $p > 0.30$

TABLE VIIIB. EDUCATION AND MARRIAGE ACCORDING TO CASTE CATEGORY:
PORT MOURANT—MALES

		Marriage within Caste Category	Marriage outside Caste Category	Totals
No Education	No.	32	13	45
	%	71.11	28.89	100.00
1-4 Years	No.	34	43	77
	%	44.16	55.84	100.00
Over 4 Years	No.	13	31	44
	%	29.55	70.45	100.00
	No.	79	87	166
	%	47.59	52.41	100.00

$Total \chi^2 = 14.34$; d.f. $= 2$; $p < 0.01$

the local communities of both fathers are feasted, first in the home of one and then in the home of the other. Wedding ceremonies are the most prominent expression of Indian cultural distinctiveness in the multiethnic society. They provide a means whereby an individual demonstrates his membership and prestige within the local Indian community. It is in this exhibition of "Indian culture" that most surviving minutiae of the traditional culture, many of them meaningless and slightly incongruous to the performers, are preserved and reenacted. The tendency to avoid marked disparities is linked to such wedding customs. The concern to do things the customary way entails some attention to traditional avoidances. The influence of caste on marriage thus persists as a peripheral part of the complex of "Indian culture" of which the bamboo wedding is a central item. But the persistence takes the form of avoiding great disparities of caste rather than of caste endogamy. And even this, as the figures attest, is a dispensable part of the cultural tradition.

According to Hindu custom, a woman marrying a second time is not entitled to a traditional ceremony; a man may, but usually does not, go through one a second time.[14] Second and subsequent marriages are therefore informal, and any ceremonial recognition is marked by a private puja. In contrast to the first marriage, which is a transaction made in public between the parents and expresses their social position and interest, a second marriage is an individual decision made by the contracting persons in private, even though friends and relatives may have arranged the introduction. Individuals are relatively free to choose their second spouses on the basis of personal likes and assessments; they are not influenced by considerations of caste.

The frequency of caste-ignored marriage is therefore related to the frequency of remarriage. In Port Mourant, however, although marriages are bedeviled by the same tensions as in Blairmont, there are processes of mediation and resolution, lacking in the other plantation, which result in a lower incidence of separation and remarriage (Jayawardena 1960). The question then arises as to what factors operate in Port Mourant to produce a similar proportion of marriage outside the caste categories, despite the lower incidence of remarriage.

Tables VIIb and VIIIb illustrate the situation in Port Mourant. The first shows that the frequency of marriage outside the caste categories is not related to remarriage. The second shows that the degree of education of the husband covaries with disregard for caste in the choice of a spouse. Thus the majority of those without education have married within the caste category, while the majority of those with five or more years of education have married outside it. By contrast, in Blairmont, degree of education is not significantly associated with marriage outside the caste category.

The difference between the plantations may be explained partly by the more creolized and prosperous character of Port Mourant and

---

[14]Second marriages can only occur when the first has been dissolved by death, divorce or separation.

of the Corentyne district in general.[15] In comparison with the Indians of Port Mourant, those of Blairmont may be described as relatively more conservative and closer to the immigrant coolies of the indenture period. The Indians of Blairmont praise Port Mourant as a "bright," progressive, and modern place. Trends of change incipient in Blairmont may be observed at a later stage in Port Mourant. Parental choice of a spouse is more limited by the wishes of children in Port Mourant. In Blairmont, where deference to tradition is greater, customary avoidance, as marked by the absence of free intermarriage, exercises a stronger influence. Other factors such as wealth and occupation being equal, traditional distinctions receive more attention in Blairmont, so that marriage regardless of caste occurs mostly in second marriages which are made away from the glare of ceremonial publicity.

In both plantations, however, traditional restraints are strong enough to make marriage outside the Hindu community (with the exception of marriage with Indian Christians) relatively rare, though the incidence of this is somewhat higher in Port Mourant. Such marriages follow a pattern similar to intercaste marriages in Blairmont: they are mainly subsequent marriages which are transactions occurring outside the arena of Indian public celebrations. In Blairmont, out of 9 marriages of Hindus with Muslims or Negroes, 6 are subsequent marriages, and in Port Mourant 8 out of 12 are subsequent marriages. Out of the first marriages of this type in both plantations, 5 followed elopements.

Caste and Social Stratification in the Villages

The village on which this section is based has a population of about 2,700 people, is administered as a Land Settlement by the central government and is less than ten miles from the capital, Georgetown. It is therefore not a "typical" village, and is probably less conservatively "Indian" than some other predominantly Indian communities of rice farmers. On the other hand, it is known as a center of organizations concerned with the expression of Indian identity and

---

[15]The two plantations are compared along these lines in Smith and Jayawardena 1959, and Jayawardena 1963.

culture in the context of Guyanese society as a whole. There is no strongly corporate community identity expressed through a local government organ which could provide a vehicle for local leadership. The government of the community is paternalistic, being formally in the hands of the Land Settlement Department. There is a locally elected Advisory Committee, and membership of that committee is carefully arranged by the residents to include all the major racial and religious groups: Negroes, Muslims, orthodox Hindus and reform Hindus.

Within the community, division is a more marked feature than unity. The community developed directly out of abandoned sugar plantations between 1908 and 1912, after which resident laborers gradually changed over to rice cultivation and stock raising. Some cane is still grown for sale to nearby factories but it is of minor importance. There are divisions within the community in terms of geographical section, in terms of wealth and education, and in terms of factional division. There were approximately 150 Negroes in the village in 1956, many of them descendants of Barbadian immigrants who had been resident laborers in the days of sugar. Relations between Negroes and Indians were very good at that time, with no sign of conflict, despite the fact that the Negroes tended to keep to themselves and looked to nearby Negro communities for most of their social life. Negro teachers at the local government-run primary school mostly lived outside the community or on its periphery and were not involved in community affairs outside the school. All the village children attended school, where they were taught in accordance with standard Guyanese curricula by both Negro and Indian teachers.

This particular village had the largest number of Muslims of any Guyanese rural community—approximately 700. All constituted one Jamaat of the orthodox Sunnatwal sect, which was a closely knit body with a full complement of officers, a mosque, and a small school where Urdu and Arabic were taught outside normal school hours. Muslims are not residentially segregated, and while their local community is closely knit, Muslims participate in many local organizations which cut across religious affiliation, while in the country as a whole they identify themselves as Indians vis-à-vis other ethnic groups. This identification was clearly shown in the general election of December 1964, when a party was formed to appeal to the collective feelings of Muslims and to win their votes away from the dominant People's Progressive Party. That new party received only 1,194 votes, while the total number of Muslim voters was probably near 20,000.

The Hindus are divided into three groups: the Arya Samaj, the Bharat Sevashram Sangh, and the residue of persons claiming to be orthodox Sanatanists. The most active Hindu group is the Arya Samaj, whose members use religion as a positive weapon in the fight for respectability and prestige. All three Hindu groups have some measure of organization similar to that described for the Muslims. That is, all have committees of management, and all run schools for instructing children in Hindi and religion outside normal school hours. The Sanatan group also has a temple and an official Brahmin priest, while the two reform groups tend to take on additional tasks for the benefit of their members: some own collections of cooking utensils, plates, and cups which can be used at weddings or on other ritual occasions; some have burial funds; the Muslims run a Scout troop. We may regard these organizations as vertical segmental divisions of the village population since they contain members of varying status. They are in no way ranked in prestige, nor does every villager belong to one of them. The Sanatan group is the least organized, since any Hindu who is not a member of one of the reform groups will claim to be a Sanatanist, even if he hardly practices his religion. A few Indians are Christians—either members of churches outside the village or attending one of the two very small churches within it —though being Christian does not mean that they are not also Hindu.

So far as the horizontal status divisions within the community are concerned, one can distinguish at least four levels. At the bottom are the majority of villagers who are small farmers and who sometimes work for wages in the plantations or the Public Works Department. Most of the Negroes are casual workers rather than farmers, while a few are skilled tradesmen. Among Indian villagers there are some skilled workers such as carpenters, tinsmiths, and tailors, but almost all grow rice as well. Rising just above the ordinary level, but not yet distinguished in any clear way from it, are farmers who have rather bigger acreages and therefore more income, men who have small shops or run a taxi, perhaps a goldsmith or a man who has a herd of cattle or goats. These men are apt to speak with a more authoritative voice in village or religious-group affairs; many of them are found as faction leaders in religious groups, and many get elected to committees of various kinds. Above them are the men of more than average wealth, such as large storekeepers, rice-mill owners and farmers, or men with secondary education who have been absorbed back into the village economy, usually through the inheritance of a family business. There is, finally, a group of residents who are quite different. In 1956 this stratum was composed of individuals who were more highly educated and who held positions outside the village, such as civil servants, teachers, lawyers' clerks, salesmen, plantation technicians, agricultural officers, and so on. This stratum is particularly important because it constitutes a link between the village and the wider society of a kind that would not be found in many smaller Indian villages.

There is no direct correlation between caste origin and any of the status divisions mentioned here. The socioeconomic system of the village is thus not made up of a collection of jati groups between which there is both separation and interdependence. There are hardly any traditional occupations which are of significance, except those of barber and priest, and a few specialized trades such as goldsmith.

Within the three lower strata, religion and Indian custom tend to be very important. For the lowest status group, religion is full of magical elements. Its members carry out domestic rituals to achieve good luck or wealth or health, or to give thanks for good fortune. In the case of Hindus, their religious beliefs and ideas are taken from oral tradition and from popular Hindu works such as the *Ramayana,* and even Muslims of this stratum manage to inject many magical features into Islam. In addition to formal religious beliefs and practice, use is made of obeah men, or of special healing practitioners who use magical means; some Brahmin priests provide such services as a sideline. Life-cycle rites are also observed, together with the magical precautions associated with them. Members of the Hindu reform movements are drawn mainly from the next two higher levels. Here there is generally a much greater awareness of religious doctrine and a tendency to be dissatisfied with orthodox Brahminical teaching based on popular sources. Since these persons are generally oriented to achievement of some kind, even if it is only within the social-status system of the local community, they either seek to adhere more closely to Sanskritic norms within the Sanatan group, or become actively opposed to orthodox Hinduism through the reform movements. If they are of higher caste origin, then it is likely that they will stay within the Sanatan body. Among this group, religion becomes quite literally a means of arguing about status and prestige, and the reform movements tend to be divided into factions for this very reason.

The highest status group in the village is not directly involved in these activities and conflicts. Although its members are bound to the village through ties of kinship and neighborhood, and may patronize local religious and other organizations, their main ties of social intercourse are either with people of similar status within the village or with friends outside. More choices are open to such individuals in expressing their social standing, though some features are obligatory. For example, all these persons will be distinguished in terms of dress and speech. Whereas the majority of villagers normally wear open-necked shirts and trousers only, or perhaps the distinctive Indian smock worn over the trousers, the village elite will normally wear in addition ties and jackets when they go to work. Similarly, they will speak "better English." Almost all will adopt a more "Creole" style of life in such things as home furnishings, eating habits, drinking, and entertaining. But beyond this, they may react to higher status in various ways. Some tend to drop Indian ways altogether, may marry non-Indians and move to Georgetown. If one does marry an Indian she is usually of a similar social status, and the couple may acquire non-Indian friends, go to dances, and engage in other "Creole" ways. Alternatively, such persons may become quite involved in religious organizations at a wider level than the village. They may acquire positions in the urban Hindu or Muslim organizations and, while they become more "Creole" in many aspects of their daily lives, they may simultaneously become more militantly "Indian." Or they may drift away from religion, while at the same time remaining self-consciously Indian, and perhaps become involved in Indian social and political organizations. But whatever happens, these individuals tend to move into a world which is multiracial, where there is opportunity to become more creolized, but also more opportunity to ascribe the jealousies, frustrations, and failures of a competitive world to race and racial discrimination. This aspect is discussed more fully below.

We have seen that the domain within which religion and adherence to traditional Indian customs is most important is that of the village. But at the same time, the members of the higher status groups in the village achieve their position not on account of caste origin, but because of their economic or educational standing. The position of Brahmin priests is interesting in this respect. Most are of lower-class origin and have little formal education, so that they are unable to acquire the kind of status in the wider society that most Christian ministers acquire. There is no regular training procedure for Hindu priests, and their sons rarely become priests themselves if they have been to secondary school. The result is that Brahmin priests have prestige of a very limited kind. Most are no match for an educated and vocal person of low-caste origin when it comes to decision making, even within the religious organizations. Many Brahmin priests manage to rise within the local hierarchy to at least the second and third level because many manage to acquire more land. But they cannot become part of the village elite without the formal education and occupational prestige that are basic to its membership.

Indian Organizations at the National Level

It has already been indicated that there are national organizations of one kind or another that are specifically Indian. The Guyana Sanatan Dharm Maha Sabha is one such organization, as is its affiliate the Guyana Pandits' Council. Apart from these religious organizations, there is the Guyana East Indian Association, which was formed in 1919 with more specifically political aims. Leadership in many of these organizations has often devolved on persons of high caste, and this tendency may be taken as an indication of the persistence of caste prestige. Yet, though we do not wish to minimize the relevance of caste as one factor in the selection of leaders in these organizations, it needs to be pointed out that in the vast majority of cases the persons concerned are also of high status on the occupational scale. Furthermore, the educated elite of Indians has assumed positions of leadership whatever their castes and, it might be added, irrespective of religion. Prominent Indians have been Muslims and Christians as well as Hindus. It is also a striking fact that the Hindu religious organizations have not become vehicles for the expression of political ambition, even though attempts have been made to make them such. Dr.

Jagan, for instance, is the acknowledged leader of the vast majority of Indians in Guyana. He has no formal religious affiliation, is not of high-caste birth, and is married to a white American.

Caste in the Total Society

The discussion so far has showed that "caste" is not a useful concept for understanding the internal organization of the Indian community in Guyana. We have seen that Indians are involved in a wider system of social relations which is multiracial and multicultural, and that this involvement affects every aspect of their lives. What are the main features of that wider system, and does it present any features which are castelike? One of the difficulties of analysis here is that the system has been constantly undergoing rapid change, partly because of the changing composition of the population since about 1840. In order to simplify matters, it is convenient to present a rather static model of what we term the "colonial society," and then indicate what processes modified that system.

Colonial society, as defined here, grew up around the plantation, and at first included only the planters, a few free persons of color, and some white artisans. After emancipation the old nonslave society was extended to incorporate the ex-slaves as peaceful citizens. The focus of these new developments was upon integration, law, and order, and they were based upon the common recognition of the superiority of British culture and of the dominant position in the society of British people. While there was no ordering of the society into legally defined ethnic groups, there was an implicit assumption that the various groups in the society were different in recognizable ways. The basic units of the system were initially the British, the Africans (as they are still often termed), and the intermediate group of Colored. As immigration proceeded after 1840, the Indians, Portuguese and Chinese were added.[16] The Amerindians were always peripheral, being regarded as childlike creatures of the forest, even though they had

---

[16]The recognized divisions in the society varied from time to time, and sometimes according to the interests of the observer. For example, one writer distinguished between "Creoles, Barbadians and Orientals" as constituent parts of the labor force on plantations.

previously been used for the unchildlike task of capturing or killing runaway slaves.

As in the case of the Hindu caste system, these groups came to be integrated into one social system, through their common recognition of the differences between themselves, and their common recognition of the superiority of the white group and its style of life. Just as Hindus in India recognized the superiority of the Sanskritic culture practiced by the Brahmins, so Guyanese came to accept the idea of the superiority of English culture. In traditional India there was a common recognition of certain key elements of the religious tradition, despite the separation of castes and their divergent styles of life. Similarly, in Guyana, all groups accepted a basic minimum of English culture. Language came to be universally English, despite class variations in dialect; the progressive adoption of a Creole culture was also an integrating factor. However, so far as the model of "colonial society" is concerned, the really significant basis of integration was that all groups accepted the value of whiteness, even though they recognized that they were not white and could not be white themselves. In making such an assertion we do not mean to neglect the fact that the British as the dominant political and economic group ensured compliance partly by coercion. Coercion often took the form of naked force, especially in the plantations. But even in the latter communities there were mechanisms at work leading to the passive acceptance of a subordinate role by the slaves and indentured laborers: mechanisms analogous to those found in concentration camps, for example (Cohen 1953). Both slaves and indentured laborers fought back, and Guyanese history is punctuated by investigations into riots and disturbances in plantations. But these protests were sporadic and uncoordinated until the middle of this century.

The ranking of ethnic groups in the social system of colonial society was by reference to whiteness; but whiteness had two dimensions. Color and physical characteristics were one important dimension of the definition of whiteness, and on this basis Indians tended to rank higher than Negroes because of their lighter color, straight hair, and more "European" features, as did the Portuguese and the Chinese. The other dimension of whiteness was cultural, and on this basis the Negroes ranked higher than Indians because they were Christian, more educated as a group, with a larger proportion of their number in white-collar occupations, and in general more anglicized in their style of life. While it is broadly true that both Negroes and Indians accepted the superiority of the English, each looked down on the other. The Indian looked down on the Negro because he was black, and the Negro looked down on the Indian because he was "uncivilized," each judging the other in terms of one aspect of "whiteness."

To some extent this system of social relations has remained operative, but other developments have modified it. The most important have been the emergence of what we call—for lack of a better term— a national "middle class," and the development of lower-class organizations which transcended ethnic divisions. A Creole intelligentsia emerged during the nineteenth century, composed of persons who had moved into prestigious occupations through education. With the growth of colonial society, there was an increase in the number of positions available for teachers, lawyers, clergymen, doctors, and civil servants. At first these positions were filled by Englishmen (as the managerial positions in plantations continue to be filled), but it became increasingly difficult to persuade Englishmen to come out to the colony to fill the lower ranks. Consequently a limited degree of social mobility developed for educated local people. Teachers were recruited through the pupil-teacher system, and civil servants through the few secondary schools originally started for Europeans but which gradually broadened their intake. Other semiprofessional occupations, such as dispensing, soon became open to persons of lower class.

By the end of the nineteenth century there were enough persons of Portuguese, Negro, Colored, Chinese, and even a few of Indian origin to constitute a radical political group, its members expressing their dissatisfaction with planter domination and demanding a greater share in the political life of the country on the grounds of their cultural qualifications. Although the urban middle class remained to a large extent fragmented into ethnic associational divisions of one kind or another, and while color remained almost as important a determinant of status as occupation or education, there was at least the overt recognition of values laying stress upon achievement, although achievement was still measured and expressed in terms of anglicization. Nonetheless, a break had been made away from development toward a "caste system" in which each group has special rights and in which endogamy is enforced. The white group continued to be mainly endogamous, but intermarriage between other groups became common.

We accept as a useful means of distinguishing caste from other types of stratification Leach's (1960) argument that

> For me, caste *as distinct from either social class or social grade* manifests itself in the external relations between caste groupings. These relations stem from the fact that *every* caste, not merely the upper elite, has special "privileges." Furthermore, these external relations have a very special quality since, ideally, they exclude kinship links of all kinds.

Empirically, a caste system of this type has never been found in Guyana, although the formal features of the ideal type of colonial society bore some resemblances to it. To a limited extent it was accepted that each ethnic group had special occupational characteristics: Europeans were top administrators and managers; Africans were civil servants, teachers, policemen, nurses, and part-time cane cutters; Indians were resident plantation laborers and rice farmers; Portuguese were shopkeepers, spirit merchants, and salesmen; Chinese were storekeepers and traders; the Colored were civil servants, clerks, and professionals. However, this occupational expectation was never more than a rough conception of the social system. There was never any formal allocation of privileges or of hereditary rights to such positions, and certain key avenues of social mobility such as teaching, law, medicine, and dentistry remained wide open to anyone who could acquire the qualifications. The civil service too remained formally open to appointment on the basis of merit, and commerce to individual initiative. During the nineteenth century it was the Portuguese who availed themselves of these opportunities and were the most important radical element which led the assault upon the whole conception of the Englishman's exclusive rights.

At the lower-class level, the development of solidarities cutting across racial divisions was much less evident. We have already remarked upon cooperation and multiethnic representation at the local community level. Despite the tendency for local communities to be predominantly either Indian or Negro by reason of the histories of their establishment, there was never any residential segregation. Inter-marriage between Indians and other races has been infrequent though not unknown by any means; it has been common between Negroes, Portuguese, and Chinese. Trade-union development in the early 1920's united both Indians and Negroes in a common struggle for better wages and working conditions. But unionism decayed sub-sequently and, in the 1930's, tended to be replaced by the develop-ment of ethnic movements such as the League of Coloured Peoples and the East Indian Association. Even the unions, though formally representing all races, tended to organize mainly within racial divi-sions: for example, the British Guiana Labour Union among the Negroes and the Man Power Citizens' Association among the Indians. After the reforms introduced on the recommendations of the West India Royal Commission of 1938, there was a fresh growth of political parties and trade unions. The first election to be held under universal adult suffrage in 1953 produced the remarkable victory of the Peo-ples' Progressive Party, which was at that time the vehicle for both Negro and Indian radical sentiments, and focused a good deal of middle-class resentment against British domination. The subsequent disintegration of that party into two sections, based on separate Negro and Indian electoral support, is a complex matter than cannot be discussed here.

From one point of view, recent politics in Guyana represent a revival of some features of the colonial-society model. With the British vacating political power, the question of succession has arisen. If the old P.P.P., with its broad multiracial electoral base, had been permitted to inherit that power smoothly instead of being expelled from office on charges of "communist subversion," then it is pos-sible that it could have built up an institutional framework which transcended race at the political level. But at present, although the two parties that have emerged from the old P.P.P. have each main-tained a multiracial leadership, the average voter regards them as vehicles for the expression of racial solidarity. However, it is signif-icant that both parties profess to represent national rather than racial interests and are, therefore, committed to programs, and policies which they claim will advance the welfare of all sections. Whether they will have this actual outcome is another question.

Conclusions

It may be argued that the definition of "caste" adopted here is unduly narrow, and that this narrow definition permits the conclusion that caste is not found in Guyana. Perhaps a great deal depends upon one's initial approach: those who start with a primary interest in the structure of society, rather than in culture, are led toward the analysis of economic, political, and juridical relations. In Guyana, it is clear that such relations within the Indian community are not structured along caste lines. Nor do we consider it justified to suggest that a caste system exists within the total society in which the Indians constitute one caste. The similarities between a multiethnic society and a caste society are only partial; they are suggestive but can be misleading.

The "caste system" among the Hindus of Guyana is not a set of groups "which are at once specialised, hierarchised and separated (in matters of marriage, food, physical contact) in relation to each other" (Dumont 1961). The "castes" are not parts of a system of inter-dependent relationships, political, economic or ritual (Leach 1960). They cannot even be described as social groups.

Culturally speaking, it is clear that some of the idiom of caste has persisted. In any Guyanese village where there are Indians caste is discussed. Most are able to provide some sort of answer if asked the question, "What is your caste?" When marriages are arranged, caste may become pertinent. But when these bits of consciousness of Indian tradition are translated into action they amount to very little. If they were crucial, it would not be possible for the castes of many to be unknown to others. In the village described above, the majority of people dismissed any discussion of an individual's caste as being un-important, though it was recognized that a Brahmin would prefer a Brahmin for a son-in-law, and oppose the marriage of his daughter to a *poor* person of low caste.

Caste is no longer a principle of social structure but a source of prestige on which some individuals can draw in limited areas of social life. This statement applies especially to Brahmins, who can still claim their traditional monopoly of priestcraft and the respect at-tached to it. For laymen, caste becomes a factor to be considered in arranging a traditional Hindu marriage, and even in this it is only one of several considerations.

Outside the context of traditional ceremonies, caste is ancillary to such major determinants of social status as occupation, wealth, and style of life, which are as much the basis of prestige in the Indian subgroup as they are in the wider society. There is, of course, an aura of prestige about being born of a high caste, analogous to the English concept of "gentle birth"; and similarly, a low caste carries connotations of humble origins. While the high caste alone means little, it can add to the prestige achieved in other fields. Thus a Brahmin teacher, clerk, or driver may be treated with more respect than a Chamar in those positions. However, this bonus of esteem, unlike the case of "gentle birth," is not derived from observed characteristics of the individual such as speech or deportment, nor from personality traits, but from the historical association of Brahmins with holiness and Kshatriya with imperiousness.

One point which emerges from this discussion is that items of culture change their meaning in situations which are quite different from those in which they developed. We are familiar with the contemporary relics of feudal culture in modern Britain, for example, but no one would make the mistake of equating a modern baron or knight with his medieval counterpart. Similarly, although some Indians may clothe their leaders in traditional dignity, and refer to the late Dr. J. B. Singh as an "Indian prince" because of his Kshatriya origin, or refer to Dr. Jagan as a "pure Sanyasi" because of his supposed behavior, it is clearly understood that these are symbolic statements about the positions and respect these men had in Guyanese society, positions which they achieved through education and their performance as leaders in the national political scene.

APPENDIX A. CASTE COMPOSITION OF THE MARRIED POPULATION*

Caste	Blairmont			Port Mourant		
	Males	Females	Total	Males	Females	Total
Brahmin	27	38	65	9	15	24
Kshatriya	38	48	86	23	23	46
Gossai	6	5	11	3	3	6
Ahir	37	47	84	23	26	49
Kurmi	13	8	21	11	11	22
Bania	3	4	7	4	2	6
Mali	4	2	6	2	2	4
Gadariya	5	1	6	13	5	18

(continued on next page)

(continued from preceding page)

Caste	Blairmont			Port Mourant		
	Males	Females	Total	Males	Females	Total
Teli	5	7	12	3	5	8
Boojwa	2	0	2	0	0	0
Halwai	1	0	1	0	0	0
Lohar	7	1	8	0	1	1
Lodh	0	0	0	0	1	1
Murau	2	4	6	3	2	5
Nonia	1	3	4	7	7	14
Sonar	2	1	3	4	1	5
Kalpa	0	0	0	1	0	1
Lala	1	0	1	0	0	0
Nao	0	1	1	6	1	7
"Vaisya"	2	2	4	0	0	0
"Bengali"	23	12	35	0	0	0
Chamar	35	36	71	54	49	103
Kahar	14	9	23	7	6	13
Kewat	11	9	20	0	0	0
Bhar	11	8	19	10	5	15
Pasi	3	3	6	5	6	11
Bhuiyar	2	1	3	0	0	0
Dusad	3	2	5	4	7	11
Kori	1	2	3	2	2	4
Musahar	1	4	5	0	0	0
Dhobi	3	1	4	1	1	2
Dom	0	2	2	0	0	0
Kalwar	0	1	1	0	0	0
Katik	0	2	2	0	0	0
"Sudra"	1	0	1	1	2	3
"Madras"	9	12	21	28	39	67
Do Not Know	22	61	83	16	38	54
Total	295	337	632	240	260	500

*Including those divorced, separated, and widowed.

REFERENCES

Bronkhurst, H. V. P.
1883   *The colony of British Guiana and its labouring population.* London: T. Woolmer.

Cohen, E. A.
1953   *Human behaviour in the concentration camp.* New York: W. W. Norton and Co.

Cohn, B. S.
1955   "The changing status of a depressed caste." pp. 53-77 in *Village India,* McKim Marriott, ed. Chicago: University of Chicago Press.

COMINS, D. W. D.
1893   *Notes on emigration from India to British Guiana.* Calcutta: Bengal Secretariat Press.

CROOKE, W.
1896   *The tribes and castes of the North-Western Provinces and Oudh.* 4 Vols. Calcutta: Office of the Superintendent of Government Printing.

DALTON, H. G.
1855   *The history of British Guiana.* London: Longman, Brown, Green, and Longmans.

DUMONT, L.
1961   "Caste, racism and 'stratification.' Reflections of a social anthropologist." *Contributions to Indian Sociology* 5:20-43.

GOFFMAN, E.
1961   *Asylums.* New York: Doubleday & Co.

GOULD, H. A.
1964   "A jajmani system of North India: Its structure, magnitude, and meaning." *Ethnology* III: 1:12-41.

JAYAWARDENA, CHANDRA
1960   "Marital stability in two Guianese sugar estate communities." *Social and Economic Studies* 9:1:76-101.

1963   *Conflict and solidarity in a Guianese plantation.* London: London School of Economics Monographs in Social Anthropology No. 25.

1966   "Religious belief and social change." *Comparative Studies in Society and History* 8:2.

LEACH, E. R.
1960   "Introduction: What should we mean by caste?" pp. 1-10 in *Aspects of caste in South India, Ceylon and North-Western Pakistan,* E. R. Leach, ed. Cambridge: Cambridge University Press.

NATH, D.
1950   *A history of Indians in British Guiana.* London: Thomas Nelson & Sons.

O'LOUGHLIN, C.
1958   "The rice sector in the economy of British Guiana." *Social and Economic Studies* 7:2:115-143.

SINGH, K. M.
1925   *Report on a deputation to British Guiana.* Calcutta.

SMITH, RAYMOND T.
1956   *The Negro family in British Guiana.* London: Routledge and Kegan Paul.

92   R. T. SMITH AND CHANDRA JAYAWARDENA

SMITH, RAYMOND T.
1957   "Rice production in an East Indian community in British Guiana."
       Social and Economic Studies 6:4:502-522.

1959   "Some social characteristics of Indian immigrants to British
       Guiana." *Population Studies* 13:1:34-39.

SMITH, RAYMOND T., and CHANDRA JAYAWARDENA
1958   "Hindu marriage customs in British Guiana." *Social and Economic
       Studies* 7:2:178-194.

1959   "Marriage and family among the East Indians of British Guiana."
       Social and Economic Studies 8:4:321-376.

SRINIVAS, M. N.
1952   *Religion and Society among the Coorgs of South India.* Oxford:
       Clarendon Press.

GUYANA

Caste and Identity in Guyana[1]

PHILIP SINGER

Like the ten tribes of the ancient Israelites, the overseas Indians scattered throughout Africa, the Pacific, the Caribbean, and North and South America could have been expected to be absorbed and so become "lost." However, although acculturation has gone on apace, apostasy does not yet seem to have been part of the process for the overseas Indian. Like the prophets of Judah with their phylacteries and the Torah, the cosmopolitan missionary sadhus come to their own selves in Guyana with their saffron robes, rudraksha beads, Gita and "message." In place of the Ten Commandments, there is the Sanatan Dharma—the "eternal way."

The riddle of the persistence of the Jew has been the subject of countless books and articles without any apparent end or resolution. A similar literary productivity may be expected in relation to the overseas Indians. A special "Session on Overseas Indians" held dur-

[1]Research for this paper was partially supported in 1964 by Research Grant MH08221-01 from the National Institutes of Mental Health, United States Public Health Service, Department of Health, Education, and Welfare. Before independence on May, 1966, Guyana was known as British Guiana. Some references in this paper will refer to British Guiana. The views expressed here are those of the author and do not necessarily reflect those of the United Nations.

ing the 1963 Meetings of the Association for Asian Studies in Phila-
delphia was perhaps one of the earliest signs of the growing interest
in this field. This book is another.

The concern with caste is natural, for caste has always been
linked with the idea of Hinduism. The central importance of caste to
Hinduism has been stressed by Srinivas (1956: 495; my italics) :

> . . . classless and casteless society . . . might mean the disappearance of
> Hinduism altogether. To the question whether the threat to religion
> from westernization is not common to all countries in the world and not
> something peculiar to Hinduism, the answer is that Christianity and
> Islam are probably better equipped to withstand westernization be-
> cause they have a strong organization whereas Hinduism lacks all
> organization excluding the caste system. *If and when caste disappears,
> Hinduism will also disappear.*

In this paper I shall be concerned only with the Hindu Indian
in Guyana.[2] As far as Guyana is concerned there seems to be agreement by all contemporary observers that caste, if it exists at all, does
so in a most vestigial or attenuated form. There is the beginning of
disagreement as to whether Hinduism, or a Hindu identity, exists.

The identification between Hinduism and caste has been so
complete that even the efforts of those scholars (influenced by Robert
Redfield and Milton Singer) trying to think afresh about Indian
civilization maintain their loci in caste (Marriott 1955). Nor is it
sufficient to assert, and largely let it go at that, that cultural and
social identity has been maintained in India because of "the richness
of Indian culture and the flexibility of its social structure . . ." (M.
Singer, 1955: 108).

W. Norman Brown (1961), Sanskritist and specialist on India,
is also concerned with the question of the "cultural continuity," the
"vitalizing element," the "special character and vitality" in Indian
civilization. He rejects a definition of continuity and identity through
the method of cataloguing such reappearing cultural items as the
sacred cow, the joint family, or caste.[3] Instead, he suggests that the

---

[2]Smith (1962: 120) notes that the 1946 British Guiana Census reported
118,095 Hindus and 29,281 Muslims.

[3]Even though Brown will not settle for caste, Brown does note that
"With two millenia of development it is still the basic feature of Hindu social
structure" (1961: 430).

investigator must turn for an answer "into the field of values and attitudes, and thus to the basis of behavior patterns" (1961: 431). But values and attitudes are intangibles. We make them tangible, if we are scholars or politicians, according to our own selective scholasticism or brand of politics. Thus, inevitably, values and attitudes are fleshed out by the cataloguing of cultural items and traits, or self-fulfilling political prophecies. Generally, scholars confine their polemics and even their *ad hominem* attacks to the low-circulation journals in the subculture of scholars. Politicians, because they are concerned with the basis of behavior patterns, may often find their polemics writ large in riots. The riots have been particularly prominent recently in Guyana and seem to be a continuing thread in Caribbean history.

Thus, Indian-civilization specialists, when they turn their attention to the study of overseas Indian communities, are likely to see continuity and persistence, although there may be differences as to what constitutes the "vitalizing element" (Bharati 1964; Horowitz 1963; Klass 1961). Other specialists, with other points of view, will see other things (Furley 1965).

Here, I shall be concerned with pointing up those items of cultural behavior, values, and attitudes among the East Indians in Guyana, which seem to me to indicate an identity and a membership in the more inclusive, but no more clearly defined, Indian civilization.

Although the East Indian group I studied in Guyana recognized the necessity to have the Brahmin involved in certain ritual performances, and identified other persons as "Sudra"[4] and therefore, appropriate to perform certain drumming tasks in the Kali Mai puja (religious healing ceremony), this fact cannot be said to be a recognition of the four-level varna model of caste hierarchy (Srinivas 1957). "Superiority" is apparently a complex function of achieved status, affluence, prestige, and reputation for being a "religious" person who fulfills obligations as the community defines them. If we think of

---

[4]My informants would sometimes use the word "Sudra" and sometimes "Untouchable" and sometimes "Pariah" to refer to the drummers. Also, when the Brahmin was not available, other individuals of doubtful varna, but who identified themselves as religious persons, would perform religious ceremonies.

caste in terms of specific characteristics, such as prohibitions on eating and social interaction, ascribed occupation, caste endogamy, limited mobility, and fear of ritual pollution (Desai and Damle 1957), then caste cannot be said to exist in Guyana. Also, in contrast to India, where even today caste plays a significant and fissiparous role at the ballot box (Bose 1961: 152), in Guyana it contributes to massive "bloc" voting. "Apanjat," the unofficial slogan of the Indian domi- nated PPP (People's Progressive Party) at the 1961 general election, meant a vote for your own diffuse *kind,* not for your own particular jati (caste). This appeal was to Indian cultural identity, based on religion not on caste as in India.[5]

It is central to the concept of sanskritization, developed by Srinivas (1956) to explain caste mobility, that any time a non- Brahminical caste or tribe enlarges its vocabulary to include Sanskrit terms, it becomes sanskritized. Srinivas' assumption here is that ac- ceptance of the symbol (karma, dharma, papa, punya, maya, moksha, or other) is equivalent to the acceptance of the symbol's discursive, Vedic, theological content. It is debatable, even for India, whether these terms in current usage are Sanskritic, theological ideas, based on Sruti (revealed Vedic texts), the primacy of caste, and the Brahmin as hierarchical varna benchmarks, or more simply part of the process of persons acquiring the verbal symbols for higher inter- personal status. The implication, of course, is that Hindu theological content and caste framework are ubiquitous and inhere in reified fashion in the symbol itself.[6] When the sanskritization process in rela- tion to usage of Sanskrit symbols is applied to an overseas Indian com- munity (and there is no reason why it should not be), then the assumptions underlying sanskritization become even more doubtful. I often heard among Indians in Guyana, who could speak no Indian

---

[5]It remains to be seen what direction will be taken by the other Indian parties that have been formed under the encouragement of proportional representation to fight the national elections in Guyana. As of this writing, a month before the general elections on December 7, 1964, there were, be- sides the PPP, at least three other "Indian" parties, not including the Guiana United Muslim Party. Conceivably, these new parties must find some other appeal than Indian "apanjat" identity in order to compete with each other and the PPP. This need may lead to sectional, class, and occupational appeals.

[6]Although I am here stressing the symbol aspect of sanskritization, it also includes customs and beliefs.

language and were comfortable only in English, such terms as "sana-tan dharma," "karma," "darshan," and "maya."

They remind me of the way thoroughly acculturated and as-similated Jews in America use in their speech such typical Hebrew and Yiddish expressions as "kosher," "bar-mitzvah," "shiksa," and "goyim." To claim that the use of such words is indicative of a process of "Talmudization" or "Judaization" would be ridiculous. What it does indicate, however, is the use of certain shared symbols with affective charge which serve to emphasize a common Jewish identity. With respect to this identity, it is irrelevant whether the speakers in any way *practise* Judaism: orthodox, conservative, re-form, ritually correct, of Sephardic, or Germanic, or Portuguese origin. Accordingly, I raise the question whether it is possible to have an Indian (Hindu) identity outside the dominant and traditional framework of caste—religious behavior.

I attended numerous Bhagwats in Guyana. These are meetings for the purpose of community Hindu religious instruction and may last over one to several days depending upon the amount of money the sponsor has and is prepared to spend. At these meetings a Brahmin usually reads from some of the sacred texts in Sanskrit or Hindi, then translates to his audience and dilates interpretively. At one such Bhagwat of about 500 men, women, and children there was much use of Sanskritic terms by the speakers and pandits in the course of the English exegesis. Of even more importance, perhaps, to the creation of a Hindu identity was the honored place accorded the regional chairman of the Sanatan Dharma Maha Sabha, a Hindu religious organization. He was invited to address the meeting and in his ad-dress said:

> A view has been expressed by some very learned people that Hinduism is fast dying out in this country.[7] If these people express such views they could not be very learned indeed. We in British Guiana, we the Hindus, in British Guiana, have suffered tremendous handicaps. Our forefathers came to this country as indentured laborers. We brought

---

[7]In later talks with me, this extremely well-informed and intelligent Hindu leader, educated in England and America, told me that he was re-ferring to the anthropologist R. T. Smith, who worked in the area and who expressed such a view in his book *British Guiana* (1962).

with us our rich culture. I will briefly mention some of the handicaps. Not too long ago, if you were a Hindu, certain jobs were not open to you. Something else. You have to change your religion before you could get the top jobs in this country. Hinduism at that time was meant for the laboring class. When our boys and girls go abroad for professional training they leave from British Guiana very simple Hindu homes. When their parents send them off, they do a jandhi (religious ceremony). When they pass their exam abroad and they write their parents, every time they (parents) do a jandhi. But, when they come back they start with their collar and tie jobs, they feel that this is not a religion they must associate with. Fortunately for us, this idea is gradually going. I will say thanks to the present government that we have been able to get Hinduism on the same footing as all other religions. No longer are special jobs meant for people who have special religious background. We now have equal rights as anybody else. We have come a far way but we still have a much further way to go.

Our Dharma is being threatened by a number of different things. As you know, our organizational machinery functions in a very limited way, because of several drawbacks. Many religious organizations come into this country. One I know gets about $200,000 every year, and they purchase valuable equipment, loudspeakers, microphones, and what not, and they go about encouraging our people to clap hands, and saying things which are very, very strange to us. How we have been able to survive this is still a big question. They have been plugging at us all the time, as they see such a large gathering here this evening it only goes to show how much faith we have in our Dharma.

I must tell you that nothing is achieved by just sitting back and doing nothing about it. We of the Maha Sabha, we are trying to get our Hindu brothers and sisters organized. We feel that if we work together as one body, as one voice, we would have a bigger say. We will be able to stand up and profess when bad things are perpetrated on us. As you know, not too long ago, a Culture Council was established in this country. Not a single Hindu was on the original committee, although there were 27 people. Because the Maha Sabha was organized we made representation and we pointed out to the people concerned that the Hindus have brought a certain amount of culture in this country. We are not against anybody, we are saying that if we are going to form a Guianese culture, then we are going to make a contribution too. Because of representations we now have four other members on this Culture Council. I can go ahead and cite you dozens and dozens of instances, where because we were not organized, because we function as separate entities, lots and lots of advantage have been taken of us.

I don't want to continue much longer, ladies and gentlemen, but I ask all of you to listen carefully to what this learned pandit tells you. Anything we do now must be done with a purpose. Put power into practice. As the speaker before me said, in the past jandhis were very rare. Now the pandits don't even have time, there are so many. This is a good thing. It shows that there is with us religious reawakening. We can practice our Dharma without any fear or without any favor.

The jandhi (sometimes spelled *jhandi*) would seem to be a fairly reliable index of consciousness of Hindu cultural kind, if not ego identity. A jandhi, in Guyana means "a flag."[8] According to my informants, this is generalized to mean a religious service, usually presided over by a Brahmin pandit, at a devotee's home, in which the jandhi or flag is consecrated and then planted in the yard. As one travels along the coast of Guyana, the easiest way to identify Indian homes from the others is by the red, yellow, and white flags outside.[9] According to one Brahmin informant, the poet Tulsi Das provides the justification and authority for the jandhi is some poems celebrating Hanuman, the monkey god who is the Hindu ideal of loyalty and devotion. Apparently quoting Tulsi Das,[10] my informant recited:

Hand, one with spear, one with flag. If you want to destroy yourself, you use the spear. If you want to be victorious, you use the flag. The flag should not stick on the ground, but be stuck on a bargat (?) tree which should be of sandalwood, not of bamboo.

His explanation for the jandhi in Guyana is that since there were no temples in which to worship, the people requested the Brahmins to put the sacred flags in their homes, which they could

---

[8]According to I. P. Singh (1961: 193), in the Sikh village he studied in the Punjab, "jand" means tree (*Prosopis spicigera*). It is the abode of Valmiki, the holy man who reputedly wrote the epic *Ramayana* in Sanskrit.

[9]During the racially violent summer of 1964, in British Guiana, the Maha Sabha protested to the British Governor, Sir Richard Luyt, against the treatment British troops were giving to Hindus who had red jandhi flags in their yards. The Maha Sabha said that British soldiers would enter and search such homes under the impression that a red flag indicated communist sympathies and concealed weapons.

[10]Tulsi Das translated Valmiki's *Ramayana* into Hindi. Popularly, the epic is known as Tulsi-*Ramayana* and not Valmiki-*Ramayana* (Ghurye 1953: 67).

then treat as places of worship. The red Hanuman flag is the most popular, but there are also frequent jandhis to the potent sun (white) and to the healing powers of Durga (yellow flag). The average cost to the householder for a Hanuman Jandhi is about five dollars, which includes the Brahmin's fee. A Durga Jandhi is the most expensive. All of the pandits I interviewed said they were performing more jandhis now than in previous years. One man, 57 years old, said that in 1963 he performed 750 Hanuman Jandhi, 700 Surujnarayan Jandhi, and 300 Durga Jandhi. All of these ceremonies were done within a radius of twenty miles.

Whatever the origin of the jandhis, the Bhagwats in Guyana seem to be the equivalent of the Indian harikatha. Srinivas makes the point that the harikatha is another Sanskritic vehicle. However, as in Guyana, the harikatha, or Bhagwat can be a vehicle for many things. At one harikatha I attended in India, it was addressed, not by a Brahmin pandit, but by a casteless sadhu on the harikatha "lecture circuit" in the Punjab. This particular sadhu delivered an indictment of materialism in general and of America in particular. He said:

> When America attacked Korea . . . the Chinese, who were styled by the Americans as apes, made an army out of nothing and threw back the armed might of the Americans. You should also remember that apes defeated Ravana . . .

This homily was thrown in while telling the *Ramayana* story. In this case, since the audience knew the epic well, it was only necessary to cite parts of it in order to score points. The use of the word "ape" recalls Hanuman, the monkey worshiped in India as Ram's greatest devotee, and serves to stir up race feeling.

As Opler has remarked (1955: 153):

> The manner in which the villages will absorb and respond to these new ideas which sweep in from the West and East or which are being generated in India today is perhaps even more important than the manner in which it copes with Sanskritic rites.

This statement applies also to overseas Indian communities. However, although there does not seem to be any doubt, despite the winds of change, that Hindus in India retain Hindu identity, the question is raised as to whether the overseas Indians retain it. Basic

Hindu identity is presumed gone and what remains of Hindu identity is put into the category of "survivals," or trait persistence. In his review of the East Indian family overseas, Davids (1964: 395) puts it this way:

> We might say that an alien resident group's necessity to maintain its self-identification and pride of heritage in a hostile, thoughtless world has kept the superficial appearance of Hindu living in action beyond the continued existence of its necessary sub-structure.

However, this view of cultural survivals, or cultural persistence, does not necessarily come to grips with its significance. The importance is not in the degree to which there is conformity to the "original" structure, as in the case of marriage practices, caste observances, or ritual performances, but whether the new cultural mosaic results in personalities which are more similar to those of the original culture than they are to the "new" personality in the second country. In the case of Guyana, it is presumed that the process of "creolization" is the new, dominant cultural pattern shaping the emerging, or emerged, Guyanese personality. This presumption is doubtful. Apart from the 11 per cent or so of the population which is considered to be "mixed" and so "creolized," Guyana's population still consists of almost 50 per cent Indians, of whom the majority are Hindu. It seems to me that anthropological students of Guyana have been more concerned with the descriptive *form* of Hindu survivals rather than their socio-psychological function. Thus it is possible to discuss Kali Puja in Guyana and say that the form includes possession and trembling similar to that found in part of south India. The function, however, might be described as continuing to perpetuate the dependency relationship between the child and mother found in India and apparently persisting in Guyana.

Besides sanskritization, another concept—the Great Tradition—has been developed to try to explain the synthesizing, integrating processes at work in Hinduism in India, which presumably result in Hindu identity not only for the tribe, or lower caste, but for the individual as well. This theory was primarily developed by Robert Redfield (1955) and Milton Singer (1955, 1958). It is more optimistic, perhaps because liable to even more ambiguity, about the enduring vitality of Hinduism even if caste withers away. The Great Tradition in India is linked to Sanskritic tradition in India, within a qualified Brahminical, specialist, and caste scaffolding. Generally, it is identified with a sacred culture. The Little Tradition is represented in the local forms of Hindu practice. The dialectic consists of the transformation of the Little Tradition into the Great Tradition, primarily through sanskritization, and its carriers, Brahmin literary specialists.

I believe there is just as much logic in assuming that every overseas Indian community represents the "Little Tradition" as there is in Srinivas identifying the remote tribal Coorgs (1952) as in the "Little Tradition." The remarks of Robert Redfield are particularly relevant here. In discussing the intellectual problems involved in "thinking about a civilization," and particularly Indian civilization, he says (1957: 2-3):

> The problems of delimiting a civilization in time and in space involve not only special knowledge about people and institutions at many times and in many places but also the choices the mind makes as to the kind of thing that civilization is. . . . As I think of the civilization as persisting for hundreds or thousands of years I am choosing the characteristics that make it that same thing, in spite of changes, throughout that time. I find its limits according to the conception I have of its substance. If I am content with a conception that identifies Indian civilization with geographic limits, say, the Indian peninsula, then Indian civilization is whatever goes on within those limits, and nothing else. If I identify civilization with political unity, the Roman civilization changed its borders in time and in space as Roman rule changed, and perhaps Indian civilization did not come about until the Guptas or until British rule. But if I choose to think of civilization as a characterizable way of life, wherever and whenever it is found and whether or not present in a single political order, then the problems of civilization take different turns: I must decide as to the substantial qualities that make that civilization the one thing that it is.

In a society such as Guyana, where almost 50 per cent of the population is now of East Indian origin and of predominantly Hindu persuasion, it seems appropriate to use the term "civilization" rather than "ethnic group" or "subculture" to attempt to understand it. The problem is to identify what is meant by the Great Tradition, or the terms used as synonyms for it—"cultural consciousness," "mental outlook," "ethos."

If we turn our attention from caste as structure, to caste as a reflection of a particular religiously based psychological constellation, or Great Tradition,[11] some peculiarities of Indian behavior in Guyana seem to be clarified. Thus Jayawardena (1963) points to the "striking frequency" of disputes over prestige that take place on Guyanese plantations.[12] One term that describes these offenses and disputes that ensue is "eye-pass." Some significant characteristics of these disputes are that they apparently do *not* take place between persons of well-defined different status, but "occur between persons of comparable prestige" (1963: 88) and they are argued before the public. An important motivation is the redressment of a real or imagined insult or humiliation which lowers a person's "dignity and prestige by repudiating what is justly his due." Some other terms for this kind of ubiquitous dispute, which to my mind stress hierarchical and status quo characteristics, are (1963: 72):

> . . . *take advantage 'pon, become biggety, play big, play bad, play manager, play white man, play mannish, play power-man* . . .

In all disputes, the effort is to restore the relationship to its status quo, which bears the name of "mati" (1963: 80). Jayawardena conceives mati not only as a condition where the status quo prevails but also as representing a concept of egalitarianism. However, he points out that although the term is flexible ". . . it implies persons of equal social status and power. A labourer never refers to a manager as his mati . . ." (1963: 49). Nevertheless, when in his summary Jayawardena talks about eye-pass disputes as helping "to maintain the egalitarian social norms . . ." (1963: 142), I believe he distorts (because of an egalitarian bias?) what he has earlier established—that disputes do not take place between persons of lower and higher prestige. Here is no across-the-board egalitarianism, and mati is not democracy.

The remarks of a Guyanese informant relative to caste, locally referred to as "nation," bear on this concept of mati. My informant said that a "low-nation man can't request a high-nation man to do anything." Referring to himself as the high-nation man, my informant

---

[11]An analysis could be made of caste in terms of Kardiner's "secondary institutions" in relationship to basic personality. See Kardiner (1945).

[12]His analysis uses the parameters of social system and the "positive functions of conflict" (1963: vii).

said he would assist "only if me please to help them." Neither would
he eat at a "low-nation" house. "They would laugh me if me eat
them."

It seems to me comparison can be made here between mati and
the maintenance of caste status quo. Caste, like mati, theoretically
suggests an egalitarian oneness (Hsu 1963: 188; Prabhu 1958: 331).
However, the concern with status, or prestige, which is essential to
eye-pass and mati, is also basic to Hindu social organization (Hsu
1963: 181). An important difference between conflict (eye-pass) and
mati (status quo) and conflict (caste fission) in India, seems to be
the greater potentiality which exists for mobility in the Guyanese
situation. Nevertheless, Hsu's comment on fission in caste seems to
apply also to the eye-pass-mati situation (1963:184) :

> [It] is fed by the fear of loss of caste, conformity, and the desire to
> rank higher on the same caste ladder.

In his discussion of the psychological basis of caste in India, Hsu
touches upon several features which contribute to another way of
looking at the eye-pass-mati conflict situation in Guyana. He says
(1963:189) :

> The individual can never be satisfied with the status quo. He will try
> to change the name of his caste; he will develop new subcastes; he will
> find justification in obscure myths, folk-tales, and sacred scriptures for
> raising the status of his caste . . . These are unending processes in Hindu
> society.

Hierarchy is basic to the psychological underpinning of caste
(Hsu 1963: 181) and also is central to the "egalitarian" plantation
worker in his concern for mati and prestige. Actually, I am suggesting an equation here between the minutiae with which caste is pre-
occupied and with eye-pass offenses which constitute the minutiae
which dominate mati. As Hsu puts it (1963: 181; my italics) :

> Ritual purity or food taboos are two of the most ubiquitous but arbi-
> trary signs limiting, demarcating, and defining specific boundaries of
> sociability, belonging and status. *As soon as one sign for ritual purity
> or food taboo is eliminated another will take its place unless there is
> basic change in the idea or hierarchy and attitude toward it.*

I believe the essential characteristics of eye-pass and mati, like
caste as described by Hsu (1963: 180), for India:

> . . . are not merely that its members entrench themselves behind its

walls but also that they constantly seek to break out of one set of walls into another for which they claim superiority.

On the same page, Hsu (1963: 180) further makes the point that status, or hierarchy, is:

> . . . the most basic ingredient in the Hindu way of life in its actuality. Its link with the supernatural-centered ideal is not only that the universally demanded status in India is ritual status but also that Atma is the apex of all statuses toward which all must increasingly strive . . . In this atmosphere dissatisfaction with the status quo is a foregone conclusion.

If we turn now from this discussion of caste, eye-pass, and mati to specific personality characteristics for the Hindu as described by Hsu, there again seems to be remarkable similarity with the Guyanese Hindu.[13] The significance of this similarity of personality is to be found in the equally striking similarity between the politics of "racism" in Guyana and the politics of "communalism" in India as the milieu for the development of a Hindu identity. This similarity is discussed later.

For Hsu, the key to an understanding of Hindu personality in India is in the "supernatural-centered orientation of life . . ." (1963: 4). On the basis of brief field work in Guyana, I believe this orientation applies to the Hindu there as well. This orientation, says Hsu, leads the Hindu ". . . to seek solutions to his life's problems by leaving himself in the hands of gods or persons who, compared with him, enjoy higher statuses or possess greater powers" (1963: 7). This attitude encourages attitudes of dependency and submission to authority (1963: 175). There is also a "lack of close human relations" (1963: 175). Furthermore, the "dominant mother-son relationship is conducive to diffused unilateral dependence" (1963: 243). It means that the individual need feel no resentment against being a recipient,

---

[13]Using a similar framework of Hindu religious postulates for an analysis of Hindu personality, Taylor (1948: 12) emerges with a strikingly similar profile. He is not mentioned in Hsu's bibliography, and his work seems generally to be overlooked. Some of his conclusions: "Hindu basic personality is characterized by a sense of conformity in place of personal initiative, responsibility is exercised without personal authority . . . security is associated with the sense of dependence and self-respect with a sense of helplessness."

nor need he feel obligated to reciprocate what he has received. This "diffused outlook" will inevitably be correlated with a strong feeling of mutual uncertainty and even distrust among men (1963: 176). This dependency and diffuseness is reflected in the Hindu attitude to the gods (1963: 54):

> The worshipper-dependent can expect much more from the gods than he gives to the gods. With a high degree of feeling for mutability of all things, the worshipper-dependent is [prone to] extreme passivity, fasting, abstention, and other forms of austerity, regardless of the reasonableness of the desired object or solution as measured by human capabilities.

The prayers I heard to Hindu gods in eleven Kali temples scattered from Georgetown to villages on the upper Corentyne, and in numerous Hindu ceremonies, reflect this dependency and diffuseness. Here are two prayers to two of the major deities worshiped. They are similar to prayers to Hanuman, Ganesha, and Krishna.

(1) *Prayer to the Sun, "Soojnarine"*:[14] Oh Lard, you is the creator in dis worle, you have powers, you have heat, you show us light in the worle. Bless everybadi, bless the worle to give up lots of fruits and everybadi must be happy. Now, who have sick, Oh Soojnarine, you have power to give sick, you have power to take sick and by de heat in you in our body, well dat is de way we got to beg you. We don know how to pray to you, we don know how to talk to you, so I am begging you, Soojnarine, help. Whatever sick we have, help, and I wan you to bless dis place. Anybadi who bow to you and give you his heart, please take away all their worries and bless them, dat is de prayer.

(2) *Prayer to Kali:* Oh, Mudder, I am begging you, I don know how to pray to you, I don know how to talk to you, I do na have power to come afron o you, but I'm de devoter to you. I am de pujari (temple caretaker) and I am begging you dat we want to do you wuk at dis time and I want everything shud be in order. You give and you take, and you can give me sense to gat anyting. Anyting we want to do for you, must lead me. Dat is my begging for you. Now we pray to you. We don know that if you will listen my praya. I don know which time that you will listen to my praya, and den you will be able to bless me

---

[14]This is Surya in the Hindu pantheon. The spelling is that used by my Guyanese assistant who was asked to reproduce the prayers phonetically.

and everybadi who come to you to tek away all dose sick, all dose worry. You give and you must have ta take from what I am going to beg you.

It is significant that Rorschach interpretations[15] of protocols I administered to six informants bear a striking similarity to Hsu's interpretations of Hindu projective test material (Hsu 1963: 263-311) as well as to his analysis of Hindu personality presented above, which was independent of the test material. Hsu's psychological material on Hindus in India and my material on some Hindus in Guyana also show a remarkable identity with the conclusions drawn by Kardiner and Ovesey (1951) in their study of the American Negro. There is no need here to be drawn into the argument concerning the differences and similarities between caste as it exists in the United States and India. It is necessary only to point out that as the concept is used by writers on the subject of Negro-white interaction, it refers to the way status differences are maintained while containing hostile acting out (Dollard 1949). I am concerned with its effect upon personality, even though "it" may not be clear. If "Hindu" is substituted for "Negro" in the conclusions of Kardiner and Ovesey (1951: 337-338), the similarities to Hsu's characterizations of Hindu personality emerge. Thus:

> . . . the major features of the [Hindu] personality . . . include the fear of relatedness, suspicion, mistrust, the enormous problem of the control of aggression, the denial mechanism, the tendency to dissipate the tension of a provocative situation by reducing it to something simpler, or to something entirely different. All of these maneuvers are in the interest of not meeting reality head on.

I will quote from only one of the Rorschach interpretations of my informants. However, the major themes run through all the others.

> Like the others, he too is prone to avoid expressing emotions or feelings. However, there are indications within his record that he can,

---

[15]The interpretations were made by Dr. Reuben Silver, Chief Psychologist, Department of Psychiatry, Albany Medical College. Although Dr. Silver knew I had been studying the Kali Mai worshippers in Guyana, he knew little more than that about the culture and had no previous knowledge about Hindus or Hinduism, or Guyana.

indeed, engage in an affectional relationship, though he usually prefers
not to. His effort and energies are extended in a fashion to make it
appear as if he were exceedingly interested in the welfare of people.
If he is, he isolates this interest so that he can do things for people
without actually feeling emotion or without expressing emotion. It is
interesting to note that in his protocol he sees his role as being a rather
passive individual . . : Actually he sees his role as being a rather
precarious one. Indeed he sees himself as potentially being able to be
destroyed and thrown from a position which he would like to attain,
namely to be in a passive-dependent relation with a mother figure. His
hostility takes a much different twist than did the others. Here, I don't
really believe that he expresses great amounts of hostility. Basically he
sees himself as being the object of other people's aggression but somehow he does not seem to be overly concerned about the aggressing
people. He has occasions when his perceptions become somewhat
distorted. This is especially true in the case of stimuli which evoke
dependency, sexual responsiveness or sensuality, and situations which
deal with familial interactions. I see that he has a disturbed relationship
with mother figures in the sense that he fears them, that he cannot
interact smoothly, that he almost stands in awe of them. It is important
to note too that when occasions arise to make him feel threatened and
uncomfortable, he will if possible, resort to the unimportant minutiae of
his environment and retreat to the security of his own fantasy. The
picture that is displayed here would make one wonder about his
ability to function adequately. Were this record occurring in a person
from our culture, I would seriously wonder about the level of this
man's integration.

R. T. Smith's analysis of the social structure in Guyana (1962)
does not deal with the area of personality. His position in regard to
the two major groups, Indian and Negro, is that of the liberal advo-
cate of the "melting pot" theory—or its Caribbean equivalent, creolization. Thus, referring to Indian religious organizations such as
the Sanatan Dharma Maha Sabha, he says (1962: 110-111; my
italics) :

Apart from the performance of traditional Indian rituals which have
tended to lose most of their original significance, the major emphasis
is upon the making of elaborate speeches in which social shortcomings
are condemned and the moral "upliftment" of all Indians is urged.
In the management of the religious societies great emphasis is placed
upon the conduct of meetings, the election of officers, the keeping of

minutes and the making of speeches in which a proper command of English is demonstrated. . . . The position is, then, that the Indian's emphasis upon the value and worth-whileness of "our Indian culture" is really a mode of expression of his desire to be treated on terms of equality within a Guianese universe. *It is most emphatically not an expression of separatist tendencies.*

This was written in 1961. In 1963 and 1964, when I spent brief periods of time in field work in Guyana, the Sanatan Dharma Maha Sabha was anything but a conventional moral "upliftment" organization. With branches in almost every Indian community, it had become not only the cultural and religious voice of the Hindu personality, but an extremely active rehabilitation and relief agency for displaced Indians following racial riots in the prolonged strike against the sugar industry.

Smith's political liberalism leads him even further away from at least some village realities when he says: "Far from being unfriendly or inhospitable, Indians are extremely pleased when members of other races show an interest in their cultural heritage and religious beliefs" (1962: 141). That is surely so on the face of things. Yet, in three villages I visited on the Corentyne, I was assured by local Hindu religious leaders that there were no Christians in their village, and that if any Christians should come, whether foreign missionary or baptized Indian, they would be stoned out of the village. Their tolerance of the Christian missions with buildings on the main road was in direct proportion to their estimate of their ineffectiveness.

Because of Smith's belief that in Guyana ". . . the whole society shares a common cultural equipment which can serve as the basis for unity, as the foundation for creativity and future growth . . ." (Smith 1962: 198), he looks with favor upon Indian religious missionaries coming there. He believes some "have done good work in helping the local Indians to break down some of the defensive attitudes and to interest other races in Indian traditions" (1962: 141).

In 1963 I met one of these Indian sadhu (holy men) missionaries in Guyana. I had known him in India as a founding member of the semigovernment organization of sadhus, the Bharat Sadhu Samaj. This man is well known for his belief that sadhus should not only teach but rule as well; indeed, that only sadhus are sufficiently disinterested in self to be the proper rulers of people. In Guyana he was hosted by several prominent Indian civil-service officials and his meetings were attended by cabinet-level officials of the government. Members of the several regional Sanatan Dharma Maha Sabha organizations told me that the original cultural purposes of the organization were quite compatible with political aims. Depending upon the political sympathies of those to whom I spoke, I was assured the government was either supporting or subverting the Maha Sabha. In a private interview with the sadhu, who is called a "missionary" by his supporters, he told me that he believes a Hindu consciousness and organization could be effectively built up on a noncaste base; indeed, that it would be "stupid" to attempt to urge caste obligations or consciousness in Guyana, "because the people here have none of their old traditions." He saw this as being quite compatible with the aims of "dharma," or the "path of duty."

The basis for this compatibility is in the "fit" that the concept of dharma has with the Hindu personality. In the practice of dharma there is no provision for the autonomous individual. Dharma is a system of ritual, functional, obligatory and moral relations between the individual, the group, the cosmos. Dharma is also the one Sanskritic word that is perhaps best known, and used by Hindus.

In the growth and development of the Maha Sabha in Guyana, we can see the growth and development of a Hindu cultural identity which does not basically depend upon respect for the Brahmin or caste and ritual observance. This is a cultural identity where rites are secondary to ideology (dharma).

An editorial comment in *Sandesh,* the monthly newsletter of the Maha Sabha youth section, which bears the masthead motto "Nothing Can Save You Except Dharma," clearly makes the point:

> Any attempt to suppress and undermine our Hindu Culture would be as wasteful as it would be wicked. It would be wasteful because it would be an attempt to deprive Guyana of Hindu Culture which is part of Guyana Culture. It would be wicked because it would reject the legitimate right of Hindus to assert their separate identity. Preserving our identity is our moral and bounding duty; and since this may very well be questioned, let me say that the eagerness of Hindus to retain their culture is neither strange nor unnatural. The Irish, after years of subjection have gone some way towards reviving their language and culture. The Welsh, while sharing a common political allegiance

with the English, still proudly proclaim their Welshness. In Canada, the French vigorously struggle for the same rights. Why then should any attempt be made for the Hindus in Guyana to be deprived of their heritage?

The loss of our individuality will surely mean the loss of that inner inspiration which urges us to noble heights. Subservience to a foreign culture curbs the growth of our personalities, hinders the full development of our thoughts and encourages servility. It would be the last step on the road to extinction. Would it be fair to ask us to abandon a heritage which has inspired and supported innumerable generations for thousands of years? To ask us to abdicate our culture in favour of another is to ask us to commit an act of self-obliteration and to live permanently in a state of ridiculous imitation. *So Protect your Dharma and your Dharma will protect you.*[16]

As keeper of the rites, the Brahmin will continue to play a role of diminishing influence in relation to the increasing importance of religious organization. As a self-conscious representative of religious organization, he will play a more important role. Indeed, it is only as he identifies with organization, ideology, and Hindu identity that he will achieve respect and power. This may partly explain the interest shown by Brahmin pandits in Guyana in conversion. Thus, of the 16 pandits I interviewed in 1964 in Guyana, 6 indicated that they had been involved in converting Christians to Hinduism. This is quite different from the view that respect for the Brahmin is the natural accompaniment of caste obligations. Hindu purity no longer depends upon a taxonomy of mutual exclusion, and ritual precision, diet, and occupational ranking. The internal hierarchy has become dichotomous—all Hindus who do not intermarry with Negroes and other races are supporters of the dharma. Purity no longer depends upon an upward mobility in imitation of the Brahmin. Ethnic scrupulosity is sufficient for the new polarized varnadharma.

This kind of analysis pushed further leads me to conclude that what Guyana has been recently going through is not, as newspapers

---

[16]This appeared in Vol. 1, No. 2, June, 1964, some six months before national elections under a system of proportional representation which gave a plurality to the Hindu-identified People's Progressive Party, but power to a coalition between the Negro dominated People's National Congress and the United Force, dominated by wealthy Portuguese, Colored Indian, and foreign interests.

and Western political pandits would have it, a racial clash, but is instead a classic case of communalism. To my knowledge, this term communalism and all it implies has not yet been used in reference to Guyana. I believe this may be partly due to the influence and insistence of West Indian journalists and novelists such as V. S. Naipaul, who sees East Indian cultural continuity as a myth and describes it as a pathetic joke, and to other "realists" who see the conflict either in terms of competition for riches and political power, or Colonial office manipulation, or the behind-the-scenes manipulation by foreign investors.

Yet, if I have succeeded in making some sort of case for the existence of a Hindu identity and personality in Guyana, then there are very real parallels to be drawn between the Hindu-African conflict, and psychological "acting out," and the Hindu-Muslim split in pre-Independence India, which finally led to violence and partition.[17]

Dumont (1964: 47) defines communalism as the "affirmation of the religious community as a political group." He makes some important distinctions between communalism and nationalism (1964: 48):

> Communalism, on the one hand, differs from nationalism in the place that religion sems to play in it, while on the other, the religious element that enters into its composition seems to be but the shadow of religion, i.e., religion taken not as the essence and guide of life in all spheres, but only as a sign of the distinction of one human, at least virtually political, group against others.

Cosmopolitan liberals in Guyana could not understand how Indians and Africans, who lived with each other "like brothers" could kill each other. When all kinds of political Machiavellian explanations failed to satisfy, the idea of an archaic racism founded in primitive rage, lust and fear universal to mankind, was put forward. But, as Dumont (1964: 56) says, referring to partition in India:

> . . . people who lived together for centuries do not really constitute a society if their values have not fused. . . . coexistence was empirically accepted without being legitimized, and was therefore, together with the cultural symbiosis, at the mercy of a change of power.

---

[17]Talk of partition has been persistent in Guyana both before and after the elections in 1964.

This is equally true of Guyana.

It seems clear that the four major causes of division between Hindus and Muslims sketched by Dumont for India, and resulting in the excesses of communalism, can equally be applied to the situation in Guyana.[18] These four factors, and their analogs for Guyana, are:

1. "General social fusion" did not occur between the Hindus and Muslims during the long period of Muslim domination. For Guyana, the "creolization process" would be the equivalent of social fusion. Regardless of the reasons, it seems that creolization has not been a dominant process in Guyana.

2. Before the Western and Christian challenge, the Hindus and Muslims in India reaffirmed their religious and cultural identity by recalling past glories and engaging in a revivalistic religious renaissance which drew the two groups even further apart. This pattern also has been manifest for Guyana, only this time the encounter is between Indian Hindu and African Christian.

3. The middle-class Muslim fear that an independent India would see a "Hindu Raj" exactly parallels the fear of the African group in Guyana. As Dumont says, "the difficult transition to a democratic ideology was left entirely in the hands of the middle classes, where rivalry developed between members of the two communities ..." (1964: 53).

4. Division and communalism were given further impetus in India by the institution of separate electorates urged by the minority Muslims, in which Muslims alone would be able to vote for Muslim members in the government. The equivalent for Guyana was the imposition of proportional representation, also designed to protect against the real or imagined fear of a "Hindu Raj."

The melting pot or creolization approach to Guyana would like to establish a dialectic between Indian and African social structure with a synthesis into a third or Guyanese culture. It seems to me that the Indian in Guyana is presently engaged in his own identity dialectic

---

[18]Dumont acknowledges that his analysis is based upon the work of Beni Prasad, an Indian professor of political science, who wrote *India's Hindu-Muslim Questions*, London, 1945.

in the interplay between the Little (Guyanese) Tradition and the Great Tradition of Hinduism. The result is likely to be a renaissance neo-Hinduism coming into ever exacerbating conflict with a Christian and Western-supported African government in Guyana.

REFERENCES

BHARATI, AGEHANANDA
1964   "Possession and divination among Lohana Hindus in East Africa."
        Paper delivered at the 63d annual meeting, American Anthropological Association, Detroit.

BOSE, N. K.
1961   "Some aspect of caste in Banga." pp. 135-156 in *Sociology, social research and social problems,* R. N. Saksena, ed. New York: Asia Publishing House.

BROWN, W. NORMAN
1961   "The content of cultural continuity in Asia." *Journal of Asian Studies* XX:4:427-434.

CHICAGO, UNIVERSITY OF (COLLEGE)
1957   *Introduction to the civilization of India; changing dimensions of Indian society and culture.* Chicago: Syllabus Division, University of Chicago Press.

DAVIDS, L.
1964   "The East Indian family overseas." *Social and Economic Studies* 13:3:383-396.

DESAI, I., and Y. B. DAMLE
1957   "A note on the change in caste." pp. 277-287 in University of Chicago 1957.

DOLLARD, J.
1949   *Caste and class in a southern town.* New York: Harper and Bros. [1st ed. 1937, 3d ed. 1957]

DUMONT, L.
1964   "Nationalism and communalism." *Contributions to Indian sociology* VII:30-70.

FURLEY, W. W.
1965   "Protestant missionaries in the West Indies: Pioneers of a non-racial society." *Race* VI:3:232-243.

GHURYE, G. S.
1953   *Indian Sadhus.* Bombay: Popular Book Depot.

HOROWITZ, M. M.
1963 "The worship of South Indian deities in Martinique." *Ethnology* II:3:339-345.

HSU, FRANCIS L. K.
1963 *Clan, caste and club.* Princeton: D. Van Nostrand Co.

JAYAWARDENA, CHANDRA
1963 *Conflict and solidarity in a Guianese plantation.* London: University of London Monographs in Social Anthropology No. 25.

KARDINER, ABRAHAM
1945 *The psychological frontiers of society.* New York: Columbia University Press.

KARDINER, ABRAHAM, and LIONEL OVESEY
1951 *The mark of oppression.* New York: W. W. Norton and Co.

KLASS, MORTON
1961 *East Indians in Trinidad.* New York: Columbia University Press.

MARRIOTT, MCKIM, ed.
1955 *Village India.* Menasha: American Anthropological Association Memoir No. 83.

OPLER, M. E.
1955 "Review of [Marriott] *Village India.*" *Far Eastern Quarterly* 15: 146-153.

PRABHU, P. H.
1958 *Hindu social organization.* Bombay: Popular Book Depot.

REDFIELD, R.
1955 "The social organization of tradition." *Far Eastern Quarterly* 15: 13-21.

1957 "Thinking about a civilization." pp. 1-10 in University of Chicago 1957.

SINGER, M.
1955 "The social organization of Indian civilization." *Diogenes* 45:84-119.

1958 "The great tradition in a metropolitan center: Madras." *Journal of American Folklore* LXXI:347-388.

1961 "The cultural pattern of Indian civilization: A preliminary report of a methodological field study." *Far Eastern Quarterly* 15:23-36.

SINGH, I. P.
1961 "Religion in Daleke: A Sikh Village." pp. 191-219 in *Aspects of religion in Indian society*, L. P. Vidyarthi, ed. Meerut: Kedar Nath Ram Nath.

SMITH, RAYMOND T.
1962   *British Guiana.* New York, Toronto, London: Oxford University Press.

SRINIVAS, M. N.
1952   *Religion and society among the Coorgs of South India.* London: Oxford University Press.

1956   "A note on Sanskritization and Westernization." *Far Eastern Quarterly* XV:4:481-496.

1957   "Varna and cast." pp. 270-276 in University of Chicago 1957.

TAYLOR, W. S.
1948   "Basic personality in orthodox Hindu culture patterns." *Journal of Abnormal and Social Psychology* 43:3-12.

TRINIDAD

The Failure of Caste in Trinidad[1]

BARTON M. SCHWARTZ

Today, the East Indians in Trinidad constitute more than 40 per cent of the island's total population. Initially, East Indians were brought to Trinidad as indentured laborers to work on the West Indian sugar estates. The abolition of slavery by Great Britain in 1834 and the subsequent refusal of Negroes to continue as plantation laborers created critical economic problems for the West Indian planter class of the early nineteenth century. Continued success of the sugar estates depended ultimately upon finding a new and steady source of cheap but relatively efficient labor. Following unsuccessful attempts to import Portuguese, Maltese, and Chinese workers, the planters turned to India.

[1]This paper is based upon material collected during a field investigation of East Indians in Trinidad in 1961 and 1965. The research was made possible through grants from the George C. Barker Memorial Fund; Center for the Study of Comparative Folklore and Mythology, University of California, Los Angeles; the Graduate Research Center, University of California, Los Angeles; and the American Council of Learned Societies. I wish to thank each for their support.

India's vast population, lack of steady year-round occupations, decline of handicrafts resulting from the industrial revolution in England, excessive and fluctuating land taxes at the end of the eighteenth century, the occurrence of frequent famines, and the lack of easily accessible economic alternatives open to the majority of the peasant population are cited as major factors for the successful response to the demand for plantation labor from abroad (Kondapi 1952: 2 ff). Methods of recruitment of laborers in India and per capita financial rewards paid to the recruiters of labor were, at least, catalytic agents contributing to the general success of the program (Kondapi 1952: 8 ff).

The indenture system, sanctioned by the government of India, provided the means for recruitment of Indian labor to be transported to the West Indian sugar estates. The diagnostic features of this system are succinctly summarized by Kondapi (1951: 8):

> The chief features . . . were five years of stereotyped State regulated labour, denial of the right to change the employer or employment, recruitment of labour units and not families, gross disproportion of men to women emigrants, payment of emigration charges for recruitment by the employer and the denial of increased wages in spite of increased prices and profits. The employer was under a legal obligation to provide fixed wages, free housing, medical attendances and other amenities.

At the end of this five-year period, the East Indian indentured laborer had three alternatives: (1) to reindenture himself, (2) to return to India, or (3) to become an independent farmer or laborer in the West Indies. Return to India entailed the possibility of being subjected to gross retribution for breach of caste restrictions, whereas continued residence in the West Indies offered the possibility of improved social and economic conditions. Some of those who remained in Trinidad received land in lieu of their return passage or were given the opportunity to purchase small tracts. In addition, they were able to continue as free plantation laborers.

The indenture system continued for a long enough period of time and a sufficient number of indentured laborers decided upon the third alternative to establish the core population of a transplanted East Indian society. High birth rates completed the transformation of the population into a strong competitive minority. Recent estimates indicate that the East Indians will assume majority proportions in the very near future. Says Braithwaite (1953: 15) :

> The most important of the differences in fertility rates and the one most visible is the differential rate between the East Indians and Negroes. The East Indian group which for so long enjoyed minority status . . . threatens within the next couple of decades to become the largest single group in the country and to constitute in fact a majority of the population.

During the initial stages of East Indian settlement in Trinidad the perpetuation of caste names and certain elements of caste behavior provided a method of adaptation. Indentured laborers brought to Trinidad were recruited as individuals and not in groups. Such persons had to relate to one another, and, therefore, had to structure their relations in familiar terms. One aspect of traditional culture that contained the capacity to achieve this need was caste. A person could be categorized on the basis of his traditional caste affiliation, and patterns of expected behavior could have been derived from such social recognition. However, the circumstances of the indentured migration simultaneously allowed, even stimulated, changes in ascribed caste status. Since he was removed from traditional restrictions of social mobility in India and was less well known in the new environment, it was relatively easy for an indentured East Indian to assume a caste status higher than his original one. Few people were able to challenge pretensions of this kind. Even more important, those who were able to support such pretensions in Trinidad, with compatible economic and/or political success were able to achieve their claims. While pretensions of this kind may have been the object of some skepticism on the estates, the East Indian who left the estate to become an independent farmer or to engage in the urban life of Trinidad found few, if any, who would be able to seriously threaten his pretensions.

Closely related to this caste passing is the fact that high-caste East Indians composed a minority of the indentured laborers. In fact, near the end of the nineteenth century the emigration agent was asked not to recruit high-caste laborers (Comins 1893: 80). The low incidence of high-caste laborers lends some validity to the frequent claim by many contemporary East Indians in Trinidad that there are no "true" Brahmins on the island. The lack of large numbers of high-caste persons, together with the inability to transplant the rigors of the caste system, invited individuals to assume a higher caste position; the positive advantages of high-caste status must have still been fresh in the minds of the indentured, the restrictions to mobility traditionally exerted from the "top" were considerably weakened, and the upper levels of the status hierarchy, by virtue of their relative lack of numbers in Trinidad, could absorb new members.

Though many people obviously viewed the assumption of a higher caste name as a method for success, others apparently were content to retain the caste ascribed by their birth. The possibility of social embarrassment always existed for those who attempted to claim a higher status, and many of the indentured had no basis or support for such mobility. In the final analysis, challenges against the legitimacy of an individual's caste affiliation had little continued significance. They did, however, carry the potential of defaming an individual's character, especially during the earlier indenture period.

On the other hand, the rejection of high-caste Indians by the sugar estates as desirable workers provided sufficient reason for those members of the lower castes to adhere to their ascribed caste position. Persons belonging to low castes were sometimes, but not always, promoted to positions of drivers (overseers). Such promotion even caused conflict on the estates during the indenture period when members of high-caste groups refused to work under drivers of low caste (Comins 1893). In this sense, low-caste status had the potential, at least temporarily, of greater success in the context of the estates. A similar situation remained once the East Indian left the estate as an indentured laborer. If the independent farmer required cash, he worked for the estate as a free laborer. Choice of such individuals may very well have involved the general criterion of caste affiliation, insofar as it was related to more effective labor.

Consequently, from one point of view, the existence of caste names in Trinidad constitutes what appears to be the final phases of an earlier adaptive mechanism, a mechanism employed by East Indians to order relations in accordance with traditional and well-known aspects of culture, a mechanism to achieve mobility, and a mechanism to achieve success in the new environment.

Increased mobility relative to caste status in Trinidad was, how-ever, an important factor which compromised continued endogamous marital practices. Even during the early part of the indenture period complete caste endogamy was impossible, and as Comins points out, "Members of the Chattri, Rajput and Thakur class frequently get married to or form connections with women of a lower class" (1893: 79). The fact that many East Indians were claiming a higher caste status prevented them from maintaining endogamous relations based on traditional caste ascription. Hence endogamous practices in such cases were based upon an individual's *new* caste status rather than his original one. Where status mobility was not involved, endogamy based on original caste ascription was probably more closely approximated.

Still another factor was important in relation to caste endogamy during the indenture period in Trinidad: the small ratio of inden-tured females to males. Precise numbers are not readily available for all years of the indenture period. However, the following examples will clarify the relative proportions of males to females. In 1877-1878, Richards reports that only 6,044 females were among the emigrants from Calcutta (Richards in Klass 1961: 18). For Trinidad in 1907, Banks reports 2,010 indentured laborers entered Trinidad. Of this number, 558 were female (1907: 22). Niehoff (1960), deriving data from Kondapi (1951) and the Emigration Reports of 1905, 1907, 1908, shows the ratio of men to women among the indentured labor-ers range between four to one and three to one. The suggested dis-parity between the sexes illustrated by these examples appears to be accurate and representative. For an even earlier period (1851-1870), Erickson, giving "a composite of the yearly totals issued by the land and emigration commissioners," reports that indentured East Indians transported to Trinidad numbered 23,903 men and 8,434 women; a ratio of almost three to one (1934: 146). This extreme disparity between numbers of male and female emigrants was an important factor which restricted endogamy based upon original caste affilia-tion. In addition, the fact that high-caste males married low-caste females, thus reducing the number of "proper" eligible partners, made the adherence to traditional endogamous practices more difficult for males of the lower castes.

In spite of the practical problems which severely limited adher-ence to caste endogamy along traditional lines, the conception of caste endogamy was probably firmly embedded in the minds of the indentured emigrants, and was applied as a means of limiting membership in newly constituted quasicaste groups of Trinidad. Where status mobility was achieved individuals no longer identified themselves with their caste affiliation in India. The new status became the effective status. Although this may have presented some problems during the early indenture period, after one or two generations the new status became an accepted fact. Consequently, while caste endogamy may have been the ideal form of marriage in Trinidad, increasingly such practices appear to have been based upon the new rather than the original caste status. Gradually, however, other criteria became more important in determining suitable marriage partners. Criteria such as economic status, religious affiliation, ethnic group, success in Trinidad society, and the like became important considerations which were able to override caste affiliation (new or old). Caste endogamy, then, constituted the preferred rather than the prescribed form of marriage at this time.

It is difficult to enumerate those characteristics of caste which were introduced into Trinidad by the emigrants. Pollution practices were probably not very rigid, what with the nature of the emigration centers and accommodations allowed while traveling to Trinidad. Segregation which approximated caste prescriptions in any form was near impossible during these times. A similar situation prevailed on the estates. In each case, accommodations were crowded without any serious attempt made to segregate individuals of high or low caste, food was obtained from common stocks, and constant physical contact was inevitable. Constant pollution of this nature would require, ideally, almost constant purification, a relatively difficult matter, especially during the time spent at the emigration centers and on board ship. In light of these enforced breaches of caste restrictions, it is logical to infer that a great many of the insulative and isolative aspects of caste decreased in importance.

Traditional aspects of caste carried to Trinidad were severely modified. Whatever the elements of caste introduced into Trinidad, they were derived from traditional caste as modified, interpreted, and remembered by the indentured laborers—a relatively inaccurate replica of caste in India. It remains for us to analyze those aspects of caste which remain in Trinidad today as reflected by the village studied.

Boodram,[2] the village studied, is best described as a dispersed community which incorporates three main territorial divisions within its boundaries. These territorial subunits were more distinct in the past and are being obscured at a very rapid rate. Previously, heavily wooded areas separated these units, but today, households increasingly disrupt this former segregation. The fact that new households are being constructed in this manner does not reflect an influx of new population elements, but results directly from the increased importance of the nuclear family household in Boodram.

The actual population of Boodram is approximately 850 persons distributed in the proportions shown in Table I. Of this total figure (850), only 24 are Creole. These individuals are not significantly affected by the general patterns of behavior common to Boodram, and are, therefore, not considered in the study except for purposes of contrast in relation to specific data. The Creole population is residentially segregated from the East Indian population and maintains kin and friendship ties with other villages. Therefore, the total East Indian population of Boodram is 826. Out of the 826 East Indians, 19 are Muslim, while the remaining 807 are Hindus or recently converted Hindus who still retain nominal affiliation with the Hindu sects of Boodram. The population is grouped into 136 households scattered throughout the village.[3]

TABLE I. POPULATION OF BOODRAM

	Male	Female	Totals
Adults	169	164	333
Children	261	256	517
Totals	430	420	850

[2]Boodram is a pseudonym given to the village in which the investigation was carried out. The designation "Hindu" is used throughout the paper as a loose classificatory term.

[3]Previously, I had reported 137 households (Schwartz 1964a). Upon reexamining my data, I find this to be incorrect; 136 households is the correct figure.

Declining Patterns of Endogamy

One may not agree that endogamy is the basis of caste, but it cannot be disputed that endogamy is extremely important for maintaining and perpetuating caste. The assumption is made that while endogamy is not the basis of a caste system, it is one of the necessary factors for the existence and perpetuation of caste.

Consideration of the various levels of organization among East Indians in Trinidad, as reflected in Boodram, will clarify the marital patterns that exist. First, East Indians comprise a distinct ethnic group in opposition to other similar groups on the island—Creole, Chinese, Armenian, and the like. East Indians are endogamous within their own group. The overwhelming tendency is for East Indians to marry other East Indians.[4] This statement is validated by the fact that only a fraction of the East Indians in Trinidad have become significantly creolized in spite of conscious efforts on the parts of other ethnic groups to achieve admixture.[5] In one case in Boodram where a female East Indian had married a Creole male and several offspring resulted, the children all married East Indians. For Boodram, ethnic group marriages are 99 per cent endogamous and only 1 per cent exogamous.

The second level of group analysis involves the major dichotomy within the East Indian population: Hindus and Muslims. Although this dichotomy is essentially religious, nationalistic overtones do exist. Both groups are endogamous. Scattered incidents of exogamous marriages can be found in most of Trinidad, but these are, by far, the exception rather than the rule. The fact that a higher incidence of exogamy occurs among the Muslims of Boodram is a function of the small numbers of this group in the village. Exogamous marriages of this type are highly unique and certainly are not representative of the general Muslim population of Trinidad.

Closely related to the above is an analysis of marital patterns by

---

[4]Forces at work in Trinidad are moving in the direction of cultural and racial integration. It may not be too long before this tendency is significantly altered.

[5]Exact measurements of "creolization" are difficult. Crowley (1960), however, presents a convincing argument for a greater degree of creolization among East Indians than is usually reported.

religious affiliation, based on 91 marriages recorded in Boodram (Table II). Two major sects of Hinduism are represented in Boodram: Sanatan Dharma Maha Sabha and Siva Narayani. Both sects are island-wide organizations, but the Sanatan Dharma Maha Sabha is reported to be more extensive, more influential, more orthodox, and more traditional than the Siva Narayani (Klass 1961: 145 ff.; Niehoff 1960: 113 ff.). Individuals who claim membership in the Sanatan Dharma Maha Sabha are known as Sanatanists; members of the Siva Narayani are commonly referred to as Seunerinis. Other religious categories used in the table are self-explanatory. Clearly, religious endogamy prevails. In Table II, of the 91 marriages, 69 are endogamous within religious groups, while only 22 are exogamous. Therefore, on the basis of this sample, 76 per cent of the marriages

TABLE II. MARRIAGE BY RELIGION IN BOODRAM

Group (Female)	Group (Male)	No. of Marriages
Sanatanist	Sanatanist	45
Sanatanist	Seunerini	2
Seunerini	Sanatanist	3
Sanatanist	Muslim	1
Muslim	Sanatanist	3
Sanatanist	Presbyterian	2
Presbyterian	Sanatanist	1
Catholic	Sanatanist	2
Seunerini	Seunerini	17
Presbyterian	Seunerini	5
Presbyterian	Muslim	1
Catholic	Seunerini	1
Muslim	Muslim	2
Catholic	Muslim	1
Catholic	Catholic	5
Total Number of Marriages		91

are endogamous according to religious-group affiliation, and 24 per cent are exogamous. These proportions are increased even more if all Hindu sects are grouped together. Then endogamous marriages comprise 81 per cent of the total number of marriages and exogamous unions only 19 per cent. Such a categorization is, however, a distortion of the cultural situation and would be similar to grouping all Christians of different sects together as a single socio-religious category.

At another level of organization are the caste groups. Assuming for the present that caste groups do exist, at least nominally, among East Indians in Trinidad, they may be listed for Boodram as the following:

Ahir	Kshatriya	Maraj (Brahmin)
Bhat	Kurmi	Musahar
Chamar	Mahli	Nau
Dusad	Mala	Teli

There is an additional group which has been categorized as a caste in other parts of Trinidad (Klass 1961) : the Jangli group. I am not convinced that the people known as Janglis in Boodram meet the requirements even of a nominal caste, though it is beyond the scope of this paper to detail the religious and economic factors which lead me to this view. Most Janglis are adherents of the Siva Narayani sect, engaging in certain ritual practices which are viewed with some skepticism by other Hindus. Until recently they were territorially segregated from the rest of the population in Boodram. In addition, most of these individuals follow a pattern of life which is closely associated with subsistence activities, a pattern that was even more prevalent in the past. Some of their characteristics may give them the appearance of a caste, but in order to validate such a categorization further explanation must be given. Since the Jangli group is recognized as distinct from the remainder of the East Indian population in Boodram, however, it will be treated as a caste group for the purpose of analyzing marriages by caste.

The pattern of marriages among the caste groups listed above is shown in Table III.[6] Of the total marriages by caste 45 per cent are endogamous and 55 per cent are exogamous. Although these percentages clearly indicate that caste endogamy is not the prominent marital pattern, the proportion of endogamous marriages is somewhat distorted by the Jangli. Their high incidence of endogamy is explained by their former territorial segregation, Siva Narayani religious affilia-

---

[6]The discrepancy between 91 marriages for religion and 92 for caste is based on one case where religious affiliation could not be sufficiently validated and was, therefore, excluded. The inclusion of this case in either category does not alter the relative proportions in any significant manner.

tion, and the fact that they were viewed as "wild" people by other East Indians in Boodram. All other groups among the East Indian population show a higher incidence of exogamy than endogamy.

It was not until a relatively few years ago that the Jangli people began to interact significantly with other members of Boodram. They resided in a heavily wooded area of the village where no roads existed and seldom appeared except to purchase goods which they could not produce themselves. Because it was difficult for other villagers to make contact with Janglis, interaction was minimal. In addition to the rough terrain which made contact difficult, interaction was further discouraged by the fear among outsiders of entering the Jangli section of the village and by the reports that Janglis had the practice of hiding from anyone who entered their area. Hence they became known as

TABLE III. MARRIAGE BY CASTE IN BOODRAM

Caste Group	Total No. of Marriages	Endogamous Marriages		Exogamous Marriages	
		No.	%	No.	%
Ahir	20	1	5	19	95
Bhat	3	0	0	3	100
Brahmin	13	3	23	10	77
Chamar	33	7	21	26	79
Dusad	5	2	40	3	60
Jangli	29	20	69	9	31
Kshatriya	5	2	40	3	60
Kurmi	6	1	17	5	83
Mahli	1	0	0	1	100
Mala	5	0	0	5	100
Musahar	2	0	0	2	100
Nau	3	0	0	3	100
Teli	7	0	0	7	100
Muslim	6	2	33	4	67
Creole	5	3	60	2	40
	143	41	45	102	55

Note: In computing over-all percentages, the numbers for exogamous marriages are not to be counted as equivalent to the endogamous numbers. Thus, a marriage between two Ahirs is counted as one endogamous union; but a marriage between an Ahir and a Brahmin is recorded twice, once under each caste category. The sum of exogamous marriages in the table, therefore, should be halved to make it comparable to the sum of endogamous marriages.

"wild" people. About 1950, the roads of the area were improved to the quality of traces (narrow roads). Following completion of these traces, interaction between the Janglis and other East Indians of Boodram increased at a rapid rate. Recently, exogamous marriages have begun to take place.

There is one additional aspect of group analysis which can be considered in relation to caste: marriage patterns within the varna classification. Although classification of nominal caste groups into varnas does not exist formally in Boodram, we may use traditional categorization for purposes of determining the extent of varna endogamy. The Brahmin varna includes only Brahmins, sometimes called Maraj in Trinidad. Kshatriyas, sometimes referred to as Chattri, and Bhats are the only groups included in the Kshatriya varna. The Vaishya varna is made up of Ahirs, Kurmis, Malas, and Naus. Finally, the Sudra varna includes Chamars, Dusads, Mahlis, Musahars (actually a tribal designation), and Telis. Although Klass (1961) assigns the Jangli to the Sudra varna, I have no data which would validate such a classification. Therefore, they have been excluded from this analysis of varna marital patterns. In a similar manner, Muslim and Creole marriages have been excluded. If all the varnas in Table IV are grouped together, 53 per cent of the total considered are endogamous, and 47 per cent are exogamous.[7]

In light of the data presented, the pattern of exogamy is beyond doubt. However, the Sudra varna indicates a relatively heavy concentration of endogamy which requires explanation. Several interpretations of this phenomenon may be given. First, the hypothesis could be presented that there exists a conscious attempt on the part of the East Indians in Trinidad to practice varna endogamy. I have no data to support such a contention, and I believe that this explanation incorporates an unwarranted bias reflecting the traditional values and practices of Indian culture.

---

[7]The critical reader will note a difference in the number of cases for the summary charts on caste (Table III) and varna (Table IV). This discrepancy is due to the fact that marriages of caste members involve some groups not found among the varnas. In order to arrive at Table IV from the count in Table III, the Jangli (29), Muslim (6), and Creole (5) must be subtracted from the 143 total given in Table III to arrive at the total of 103 marriages in Table IV.

TABLE IV. MARRIAGE BY VARNA IN BOODRAM

Varna	Total No. of Marriages	Endogamous Marriages		Exogamous Marriages	
		No.	%	No.	%
Brahmin	13	3	23	10	77
Kshatriya	8	2	25	6	75
Vaishya	34	8	24	26	76
Sudra	48	24	50	24	50
	103	37	53	66	47

Second, an alternative hypothesis might suggest that endogamy is consciously practiced by East Indians in Trinidad between the twice-born groups on the one hand and the low castes, on the other. Once again, I was unable to collect data which would validate such a conscious practice by the people of Boodram. However, this interpretation appears more plausible than the first but still retains the fallacy of superimposing the traditional values of Indian culture upon East Indians involved in a significantly different society.

The final alternative which explains the relatively heavy incidence of endogamy among Sudra groups resorts to the social and economic factors which prevail among East Indians in Trinidad. All of the families justifiably included in the Sudra varna are also the ones most closely associated with the basic subsistence pursuits. Consequently, they tend to occupy a lower position in the economic hierarchy. Since economic status is an important factor in the selection of a marriage partner, it is logical that the heaviest concentration of endogamous marriages would occur among those groups engaged in subsistence activities rather than between subsistence workers and those more intimately connected with the wider cash economy. Further, families adapted to subsistence labor are least able to take advantage of the economic alternatives offered by the wider economy. These families have a tradition of unskilled labor perpetuated during the indenture period on the estates. The practice of selecting marriage partners from groups with a similar life pattern holds true not only for the Sudra groups but also for the other caste groups who are more closely linked to the cash economy. Further evidence for this interpretation obtains from the fact that most of the exogamous marriages of the Jangli group are with individuals who are also subsistence workers.

Only in recent years has this pattern been disrupted. The increase of economic opportunities resulting from increased industrialization, in addition to the constant pressure placed upon the Sudra groups, has forced their greater involvement in the cash economy and has decreased their reliance upon subsistence activities. Hence the frequency of exogamous marriages has increased among these groups. The hypothesis may be presented that the greater the involvement in the wider cash economy, the less the reliance upon subsistence activities, and the higher the frequency of exogamous marriages among the different economic groups among rural East Indians in Trinidad. This postulate will apply only until such time as more refined and distinct socioeconomic categories establish themselves. Then there may be a marked decrease in socioeconomic "class" exogamy, at least on a temporary basis. Such a hypothesis must, however, be tested in a variety of rural situations.

If caste among East Indians in Trinidad is perpetuated on the basis of endogamous patterns of marriage, Boodram is an exception. Not only do endogamous patterns fail to exist, but marital trends appear to be quite the opposite. As revealed by our data, endogamous marriages take place in only 45 per cent of the cases with regard to caste and in 53 per cent of the cases with regard to varna. In contrast, ethnic-group endogamy occurs in 99 per cent of the marriages reported, and religious-group endogamy is found in 76 per cent of the marriages.

Economic Counteractions against Caste Organization

The economy of Boodram is based primarily upon rice, coconut, and cocoa cultivation, and wage labor. Rice is the major subsistence crop, while cocoa and coconuts are cash crops which provide the currency necessary for active participation in the wider economy. Wage labor is highly desired by most villagers either as a temporary or permanent involvement, but the opportunities are relatively limited. Consequently, the majority of Boodram's inhabitants are in competition for those opportunities that do arise. These three major categories of economic activity are highly suggestive of the transitional nature of rural East Indian society in Trinidad. When the total economic complex is analyzed, the increasing movement away from subsistence activities toward greater involvement and participation in a cash economy becomes clear. There is little doubt that the rural East Indian is being drawn more and more into the broader Trinidad economy. The number of stable economic units which transcend the family is minimal. In fact, the transitional nature of the economic situation is a stimulus to the complete breakdown of permanent cooperative economic groups as well as stable economic relations that one may expect to be associated with subsistence activities.

Cooperative economic groups and activities are present in Boodram, but they occur in relation to the production of subsistence crops only. The integrative function of such groups has limited and specific significance only. Their occurrence does not precipitate unification of other permanent groups, nor does it lend support to existing socioeconomic groups in any important way. Rice cultivation provides the best example of such cooperative economic activity. Cooperative labor is necessary for three major operations in the production of rice: planting, harvesting, and threshing. Work groups are formed at the beginning of each rice season by nuclear families engaged in this subsistence activity. Such economic groups are formed by mutual consent, and labor is exchanged on a reciprocal basis. All members of the group will work on a single family's rice land until the task is completed, at which time they will commence the same operation on the next family's land, and so on, until the operation is completed for all families who are members of the group. This system is known as guayap.[8]

The prescribed sexual division of labor for rice cultivation in Boodram emphasizes the fact that the nuclear family is the minimal unit that may aspire to membership in these cooperative economic groups. Planting and harvesting of the rice are female activities, while threshing the rice is a task performed by male labor only. Hence, in order to discharge the obligations of membership, all adult mem-

---

[8]The term *guayap* is described as the reciprocal exchange of labor or mutual aid. It is seldom used by the majority of the villagers. Further, there is no local Hindi meaning for this term, and it is doubtful that *guayap* is a Hindi word at all. More likely it is a local term describing this situation. Klass (1961) reports the term *hur* for similar economic activities in Amity.

bers (and many times children) of the nuclear family must provide labor. An individual who is not a member of a nuclear family rarely, if ever, participates in the guayap system.[9] In reality, then, there exist two cooperative groups based upon the sexual division of labor: the woman's group and the man's group. Each has the same general obligation, the mutual exchange of labor, but each is involved in a different task performed at a different time. Both groups are unified by the economic reality that both the man's and the woman's labor is necessary for a successful crop.

Although kinship is a necessary factor determining the minimal unit of membership in the guayap system, it has no further importance. Beyond the nuclear family, kinship is not a factor which has positive relevance to group formation. Cooperative economic groups may consist of two or more members who are related, but this composition results from factors other than kinship. The major determinants of group formation are: (1) common economic interests and goals (rice cultivation), (2) the ability to supply both male and female labor, and (3) continuous positive relations (nonconflict relations) between those families who are group members. Consequently, these cooperative groups are usually composed of neighboring households or of those families who are intimate friends. There is no evidence that caste affiliation is a factor taken into consideration. I have witnessed groups composed of individuals who were nominal members of various castes working together as a cooperative unit. This practice extends to a common sharing of food and water prepared by each member family. In order to save time when the rice is being threshed, the female members of the participating families will bring food and water, separately at times but more frequently in specified sequence, to the fields where they are then shared by the male members. Common sharing is especially evident in regard to drinking water, which is

---

[9]Reference is made to those few individuals who live by themselves. An individual without a nuclear family in the village would not be able to engage in rice production without incurring an additional cash liability for labor. The fact that he cannot offer female labor to a cooperative unit eliminates him as a potential member. The only alternative left to him is employment of wage labor. Even if he were successful in hiring individuals to perform the necessary tasks, the cash expense would approximate the cost of purchasing the rice necessary for his consumption. Therefore, it is not likely that such an individual will be found engaging in rice cultivation.

usually brought to the fields in a five-gallon container that serves as a common water supply for all men in the group.

Two major points are relevant here. First, commensal concepts of pollution are not observed, and second, pollution derived from physical contact is not recognized. This becomes evident when the composition of the guayap groups is revealed. Four guayap groups with which I was especially familiar had the composition shown in Table V.

Although the caste composition is not known for all guayap groups in the village, it is clear that there is no correlation between cooperative economic activities and caste affiliation. If any significant relationship between caste and guayap groups did exist, further membership restrictions would be imposed to insure a more consistent extension of caste principles. These are not found in fact. In addition, it is obvious that the composition of guayap groups is not based upon similarity of caste membership, nor are isolative or insulative procedures imposed in this context as a means for maintaining group individuality.

These cooperative economic units do not maintain a stable membership over time. Realignment with the same group by a member family in succeeding years is not viewed as obligatory, nor is it expected. Guayap groups are formed at the beginning of each rice season and terminated at the end. Factors which oppose continuous group membership are far more frequent and effective than those which operate to keep the same member families together as a unit over a period of years. Although conflicts and disputes are probably the most frequent causes for the nonpermanent nature of guayap units, other factors are also relevant. These include the acquisition of permanent wage labor by a member which decreases his ability to

TABLE V. GUAYAP GROUP COMPOSITION BY CASTE

Group 1	Group 2	Group 3	Group 4
Brahmin	Brahmin	Kshatriya	Ahir
Kshatriya	Mala	Ahir	Kurmi
Ahir	Ahir	Jangli	Jangli
Dusad	Dusad		Chamar
Chamar			
Teli			

provide the time and labor expected of him as a group member, dissatisfaction on the part of a member with the work performance of other members, or movement from the village.

Cooperative economic groups formed to answer the labor requirements involved in the cultivation of rice are characterized by: (1) being temporary rather than permanent, (2) involving the mutual exchange of labor only (as opposed to services or goods), (3) requiring the nuclear family as the minimal unit member, (4) not being based on extended-kinship ties, (5) requiring continuous positive relations between all members, (6) being subject to frequent disruptive forces, and (7) not being affected by caste in any way.

Participation in the wider cash economy of the island is achieved by various types of economic activities. For Boodram, these are coconut and cocoa production and wage labor. Each of these economic categories is characterized by the fact that individuals enter into them primarily as a means for acquiring cash in order to meet the necessary costs of living. Coconut and cocoa production are individual enterprises and have no relation to group affiliation. That a person enters into such economic activities is an individual decision—one which is partly influenced by the degree of availability of necessary resources—but there exist no restrictions, incentives, or obligations derived from any social group, and certainly none derived from caste.

Wage labor takes several forms in Boodram, ranging from that of the temporary local laborer who periodically accepts work from a cash-crop producer to that of the permanent town employee. These multiple forms of wage labor can be grouped into five distinct categories: (1) local temporary wage labor; (2) local permanent wage labor; (3) estate work; (4) temporary wage labor outside the village; and (5) permanent town work. While these categories do not approach the nature of corporate groups, the categories are more than an analytical device since the villagers recognize them as real economic categories characterized by a particular position in the local status hierarchy. Two major criteria distinguish each economic group from the others: (1) place of employment and (2) permanence of work.

Conversely, there are no criteria which relate these categories of wage labor to caste. Wage labor is an individual matter rather than one for the group. There exist no prescriptions or proscriptions defining or limiting the specific occupational endeavors in which an individual may participate. Even minimal economic boundaries are absent, and occupational inheritance is entirely inapplicable. Caste affiliation, as such, does not determine, influence, or correlate with any specific type of wage labor, and in this sense all types of wage labor are based upon open competition. Further, there is no concerted group action to restrict an individual from participating because he is labeled as a Chamar or a Brahmin or a member of any other caste. That a lack of correlation exists between economic activities and caste on the basis of occupational membership is shown by the representation of caste labels for the economic categories listed in Table VI.

The fact that only Kshatriyas comprise the category of large business proprietors may be due to the small numbers involved. Alternatively, the fact that these individuals are large business proprietors may be the reason they claim Kshatriya status. Muslims have been included in the categories shown in Table VI to show their representation in the various economic activities of Boodram.

That caste has no relation with economic activities in Boodram

TABLE VI. CASTE REPRESENTATION BY ECONOMIC CATEGORY

Economic Category	Castes Represented
Large Business Proprietors	Kshatriya
Permanent Town Workers	Brahmin, Kshatriya, Ahir, Chamar, Dusad, Muslim
Local Craftsmen and Entrepreneurs	Bhat, Ahir, Nau, Chamar
Shopkeepers and Market Vendors	Brahmin, Kshatriya, Ahir, Chamar
Complete Cash-Crop Producers	Brahmin, Kshatriya, Ahir, Kurmi, Mala, Muslim
Estate Workers	Ahir, Dusad, Chamar, Teli, Musahar
Permanent Local Laborers	Chamar, Dusad, Teli
Subsistence Farmers	Brahmin, Kshatriya, Bhat, Ahir, Mala, Kurmi, Nau, Chamar, Dusad, Teli

is explained by five major factors (in addition to other more minor ones). (1) There is no economic interdependence in the village of a permanent or consistent nature. (2) Occupational specialization is minimal. (3) Those economic groups that do exist are temporary in organization and have no essence of corporativeness. (4) Numerous economic alternatives are potentially and actually available to the villager. Finally (5), the existence of a wider cash economy as a major force impinging upon the life of the rural villagers, in addition to exerting pressures for conformance to the cash economy, is a force counteractive to subsistence patterns of life as well as to the economic interdependence and integration associated with such activity. Under these circumstances, economic activities, groups, and systems which lend positive support to the over-all organization of caste have been largely removed and have not been replaced by alternatives that might achieve similar results. Economic reinforcement of caste organization and principles as found in India (jajmani, malnad, and other similar systems) is not present in Trinidad.

Considerable research in India has established the importance of economic integration of social units within the caste system. More, such research has indicated successfully that the introduction of new economic factors into the system may provoke two major forms of response. On the one hand, increased mobility may result. Caste groups, on the basis of their ability to acquire new economic wealth and power, have been able to raise their position rather significantly within the caste system (Bailey 1957 ; Srinivas 1956). Here, the economic factors responsible for the disruption occur within the system, and the system, though disrupted in terms of the original hierarchy, is reestablished along the same principles. That is to say, the system itself is not immediately altered in any significant manner ; there is only a rearrangement of groups within the hierarchy. Once such groups approximate achievement of the new status, they tend to reinforce the traditional aspects of the system in order to validate and secure their newly acquired status in the hierarchy. The other response to the introduction of new economic factors into the caste system results in significant structural modification and/or gradual destruction of the over-all system. It removes from caste the aspect of economic integration. Introduction of new economic factors that would tend to remove or decrease the significance of traditional relationships associated with and conducive to the perpetuation of the jajmani system (or similar systems) would, conceivably, tend to weaken caste. Also, the availability of multiple economic alternatives to a large segment of the population would, similarly, result in a form of economic competition which is not conducive to the perpetuation of caste as a form of organization of social units.

Recognition of these responses suggests a clear explanation in regard to economic integration according to caste principles in Trinidad. There is nothing to suggest the establishment in Trinidad of a hierarchy of social groups which have functional or structural resemblance to those of India. More, the data show no significant and consistent economic integration of social units of this type ; the principles of economic organization in Trinidad are contrary to this form of reciprocal integration and dependency. Further, the short time during which the East Indians have been in Trinidad mitigates against establishing a tradition of social rigidity which could incorporate economic forces into the general framework of the system without leading to modification of the social structure. Consequently, the interpretation of economic factors as related to caste in terms of this alternative is not satisfactory.

The economic situation is more reasonably interpreted as a response similar to the second found in India, but in modified form. The economic climate which is extant in Trinidad and which incorporates significant competitive forces is not conducive to the transplantation of caste as an organizational system, nor is it possible to incorporate those economic factors which are necessary to caste. In fact, the economic forces and trends in Trinidad are counteractive to and mutually exclusive of precise economic integration of the type required by caste.

Ineffective Panchayat Organization

There are five major agencies of social control in Boodram. Each is characterized by a different degree of use and success. Two of these are associated with the islandwide socioreligious organization, the Sanatan Dharma Maha Sabha, and claim partial similarity to the traditional organs of social control in India, the panchayats. Both local Maha Sabha groups claim to be recognized as representative of the larger organization in Boodram. Because of this split, and the consequent division of the village population, neither is very successful in the area of social control. Yet both state the existence of panchayat organizations within their respective groups. More, they express a commitment in terms of "duty" to solve problems and conflicts that occur among East Indians in Boodram, but neither group has been utilized by the villagers to any high degree. Not one dispute occurred that was heard and settled by the panchayats of the local Maha Sabha groups while I was in the village. Equally important, only vague recollections of previous panchayat action existed—no specific instance could be recalled or related.

The third organ of social control in Boodram is the village council. This group is deemed the local representative of the Trinidad government and is, theoretically, directly responsible to the council of the county in which Boodram is located. Membership in the village council is open to all who are willing to participate and pay nominal dues. The majority of the villagers display little open interest in this organization, and the most active participants appear to be the younger males of the village. The leaders of the village council related that they had the power to arbitrate disputes, but have never done so. Further, they have no records of nor do they recall ever having settled a dispute formally. The stated purpose of their "power" is to keep minor disputes out of court. However, the people of Boodram do not make use of the village council in this capacity. Not one person could give me any concrete indication of such a situation.

The fourth method of social control in Boodram focuses upon the village pandit. For the most part, attempts by this religious specialist to maintain control within the village are limited to the settlement of disputes between two or more individuals or families. These controversies seldom, if ever, involve serious crimes. Translated into the language of our legal code, conflict situations in which the pandit is involved would come under the category of civil action or minor torts.[10]

There are several obstructions which prohibit the success of the

---

[10]It is not intended to superimpose our legal nomenclature upon activities which occurred in village Trinidad. Rather, this statement is given as a point of familiarization.

pandit in such procedures. A pandit requested to act in an extralegal capacity usually recognizes that: (1) his recommendations are not always accepted; (2) his decisions may not be treated as final; and (3) his suggestions are not always viewed as the best alternatives possible. In spite of these restrictions for success, the pandit's participation in matters of this type is continued and constitutes a significant contribution to the maintenance of social control among East Indians in Boodram. His major purpose is to keep situations of this kind out of the courts.[11]

The final alternative in the area of social control, and the one most frequently and successfully used, involves the police and the local courts. Most of the individuals in Boodram will use these constituted governmental agencies more readily than they will those alternatives which resemble traditional Indian methods of social control. This occurs in spite of the fact that use of the courts involves financial expense. However, the courts render decisions which can be enforced, whereas the panchayat organizations lack the power for extended and continuous enforcement. The fact that most disputes, covering a wide range of cases, are referred to these agencies by the villagers illustrates the intimate association the villagers have with the island-wide sociopolitical mechanisms. There is no territorial restriction involved, no group reprisal, and the individual does have the ability to seek the intervention of higher legal and political authority. More, the upper political echelons are in direct association with local communities. All of these factors constitute a force contradictory to the perpetuation of traditional methods of control found in "traditional" village India.

Four main generalizations can be derived from the presence of alternative methods of social control in Boodram, together with the extant system of social democracy. (1) Traditional methods of social control are not successful due to their incapacity for significantly enforcing any decisions they may make. (2) Local representatives of political agencies of the island's government constitute the main source for the satisfaction of disputes or conflict situations. (3) Local East Indian groups have little significance in the area of social control

---

[11]See Schwartz 1965a for a somewhat more detailed report of the extralegal activities of the pandit in Boodram.

and have no relation to voting practices, but particular individuals within the community (pandits) provide an important alternative of control. (4) The individual, as opposed to the group, is incorporated into the larger political system through his power of elective representation. This is encouraged not only by the government, but also by the opposition party (the Democratic Labor Party—DLP) and the Sanatan Dharma Maha Sabha as supporters of the DLP.

A situation of this nature is highly incompatible with the existence or perpetuation of caste organization. Social control compatible with a viable caste system is manifest in the panchayat (council of five) organization. Panchayats assume two major forms in the traditional system of India: the caste panchayat and the village panchayat. Both of these agencies of social control reinforce the over-all system of caste. Caste panchayats maintain conformance to culturally prescribed rules of behavior for their members and their members only. On the other hand, village panchayats are frequently multicaste and enforce conformity to culturally accepted behavior relative to the interrelations among castes of the village. In this way, the village panchayat maintains and perpetuates a rather delicate balance of intercaste behavior and maintains the unity necessary to support common multicaste tradition. These two aspects of social control result in the direct support of the vertical and horizontal aspects of caste organization.

None of these characteristics can be found in Boodram. There, panchayat organizations are ineffective essentially by reason of the fact that they are not able to enforce any decisions they may make. Consequently, they are no longer an acceptable agency for social control in the village. In addition, the situation in Boodram is such that there are no prescriptions based upon corporate groups, on corporate group membership, or on corporate group action. That is to say, traditional norms have been disrupted to the point where normative behavior is not known by all members of the village in relation to all others. Consequently, sanctions are unstable.

Emphasis in Boodram is upon the individual rather than upon the local group. The placement of such emphasis appears to be the logical result of several related factors. First, there is an obvious lack of village corporativeness, either by contraposition or by interdependence, which, in turn, restricts the effective operation of group mechanisms of social control at this level. Indeed, social units which are necessary prerequisites for the existence and operation of such agencies of social control are absent. Second, corporate groups at the sub-village level are generally not present. Where group factions exist, the resulting units are integrated with referents beyond the village rather than within the village. More, such social units have no effective basis for integrative action within the village. Third, the village is a geographical unit more than a unified administrative one. Finally, readily available and acceptable alternative behavorial norms, which result from the force of other cultural elements found in the plural society, are increasingly prominent. Individuals may participate acceptably in the broader society on a different normative basis.

The fact that behavorial alternatives exist severely weakens enforcement of traditional prescriptive behavorial patterns. Equally important to the presence of factors which contradict caste is the reality of a social democracy which denies to caste the restricted political environment it is dependent upon for complete and uninterrupted expression. When all aspects of the sociopolitical complex are viewed in their totality, it is understandable why these dimensions of caste have not been perpetuated in rural Trinidad.

Conclusions

The major conclusion to be drawn from the data presented for Boodram is that caste does not exist. In addition to the lack of adequate economic and political factors basic to caste organization, seven specific social and cultural elements indicate the nonexistence of caste among East Indians in Trinidad. (1) Groups which operate as definite and permanent corporate units (socially, politically, or economically) do not exist in Boodram. (2) Concomitant with the first element, there is no interdependence among groups within the village. The basis for economic, social, or political interdependence is lacking in Boodram. (3) Groups larger than the nuclear family are not seen as occupying a status position in a definite hierarchy. Rather, individual nuclear families are the status units. This is evidenced by the rapid breakup of the extended family, differential status achieved by nuclear family units of the same extended family, and the competitive economic situation (Schwartz 1965b). (4) The perpetuation of traditional aspects of East Indian culture is not sufficient or crucial enough to enable the insulation and isolation of caste groups if they did exist. Pollution concepts, for example, are rare in Boodram. Where they do exist, they exist on an individual basis. It is obvious that selective perpetuation of traditional East Indian culture exists in Trinidad. Not only do large, island-wide East Indian socioreligious organizations dedicated to this activity adhere to a selective process, but individuals, owing to the fluid economic and political environment, are able to discriminate also (Schwartz 1963). Differential religiosity[12] and the ineffectiveness of traditional agencies of social control (panchayats) in Boodram are clear examples of such selective perpetuation of cultural elements. (5) Endogamous marriage is not of sufficient frequency to allow the existence of caste, much less its perpetuation. (6) The rural village is not a corporate unit composed of interdependent or contraposed groups. (7) Finally, there is no significant or intimate contact maintained with India that provides an effective stimulus to the perpetuation of caste in Trinidad. Even if intimate contact were maintained with India, the breakdown of caste in that country today would weaken India's capacity to reinforce or stimulate caste among East Indians in Trinidad.

If caste does not exist among East Indians in Trinidad, why then does one find the perpetuation of caste names (Chamar, Teli, Ahir, and the like)? More, why is it that the majority of East Indians in Boodram can be associated with a particular caste name? Before answering these questions, three points must be reiterated. (1) It must be recognized that caste names are not an important factor determining status or interaction in Boodram. (2) Caste names are infrequently used in normal conversation among or about individuals in the village. (3) Finally, caste names are used more by members of the older generations than those individuals of the younger generations.

---

[12]Religiosity is used here to mean the differential degree of adherence to a specific body of religious beliefs and practices. The concept of religiosity and its application are presented in a somewhat more precise form in an unpublished manuscript (Schwartz 1964b). The information given in this manuscript was presented originally in slightly different context before the Southwestern Anthropological Association meetings, April, 1963, at Riverside, California. It is the author's intention to publish this manuscript in the near future.

Hence the presence of caste names, while it does not indicate the existence of caste, does point to an earlier period where caste names constituted an adaptive mechanism. That is to say, the attempted but unsuccessful transplantation of caste into Trinidad as an adaptive mechanism was sufficient to allow the perpetuation of caste names and certain elements of caste behavior. However, without the rigid structure of the caste system present, such elements of behavior were perpetuated in modified form. The rapid and erratic changes in caste status by East Indians during the indenture period attest to this. Caste endogamy at this time was preferred, but not prescribed in behavorial terms. Gradually, other more pertinent criteria determining suitable marriage partners achieved enough importance to supersede traditional caste affiliation as a primary consideration. Criteria such as economic status, religious affiliation, ethnic-group membership, and style of life in the new environment became more basic considerations. After all, partners to a marriage, especially in recent years, had no behavioral commitments to caste if they had any caste affiliation at all. Rather, they retained the traditional caste affiliation of their grandparents. Caste affiliation considered in the selection of mates was that of the individual's elder relatives whose caste he had perpetuated in name only. Hence, while some may still consider caste endogamy as preferred, its incidence is decreasing and its importance as a criterion of marital suitability has declined with reference to other factors. In fact, caste endogamy more closely approximates an ideal form of marriage rather than a preferred form, an ideal form for a limited number of people.

There remains that minority group of East Indians who are responsible for the conscious perpetuation of caste names and the association of caste names with specific individuals in Boodram. Reference is made to those individuals who are especially concerned with the perpetuation of traditional Indian culture. The pandit, of course, is the major proponent of such action. In fact, the pandits in Boodram are probably the only persons able to assign a caste to every individual in the village. When I asked many of the lay villagers to tell me the caste of their neighbors or someone on the other side of the village, the answer usually was "I don't know," or "I don't worry with things like that." The same answer came from those who had revealed intimate information to me in other areas. This is not to say that individuals in Boodram know only their own caste names, rather, they have little concern with knowing the caste names of all individuals of the village—such knowledge is not essential for their behavior. It is more important for them to know where an individual is employed, whether or not he has engaged in rice production this year, or to what conflict situations he has become a party. Things of this nature are widely known throughout the village.

Many times the knowledge of a person's caste name is derived from his parent's or his grandparent's caste name. Several individuals in Boodram, when asked what caste they were, replied that they must be of the same caste as that of their parents, but that they really did not know and have little concern with things of this kind. Frequently, individuals will leave the determination of caste to the pandit when the time arrives for marriage negotiations for their children. Therefore, while caste may be considered at the time of marriage, it is not crucial. Caste endogamy in Boodram is not expected.

In addition to marriage, concepts traditionally associated with caste are manifest in one other form of behavior in Boodram today: conflict situations. Infrequently individuals will attempt to embarrass a person publicly by making reference to his supposed caste name. However, such intended degradation is always placed in the context of the individual's elder relative's caste or in relation to the situation in India. Remarks such as, "Your grandfather came from the lowest nation in the world," or "If you were in India, you would belong to the lowest nation in the world," are typical in contexts of this sort. I have never heard, nor do I have any reports of such a statement as, "*You* are of the lowest nation in the world." Reference is not made to the present, but to the past or to traditional culture in India. Embarrassing or derogatory statements of this kind have no real consequence, but they do serve as a minor method for the perpetuation of caste names.

To summarize briefly, it is evident that ideas of caste survive in Boodram in relation to marriage, to conflict situations, and to genealogical status. However, caste itself does not exist.

At least one other major aspect must be considered in this respect. Gough (1960) and others have pointed out that caste organizations in India have assumed functions so remote from their traditional ones that they are no longer castes. A similar situation must be considered for Trinidad. Has caste in Trinidad assumed some other form—one derived from traditional caste organization?

If one considers only the possible aspects of caste introduced into Trinidad by indentured laborers, the situation into which they were brought (estates), and the nature of contemporary village groups and patterns of interaction, it is evident that corporate groups along caste lines are nonexistent. Further, there is no conclusive indication that such corporate groups ever existed among East Indians in Trinidad. Corporate characteristics are synonymous with a relatively high degree of group unity (at least on a temporary and repetitive basis). Ultimately, this would be based upon elements of common caste tradition. Where corporate groups are found in Boodram, caste elements, caste behavior, and caste traditions have no relevance to the unification of the group.

In conclusion, then, the major factors which account for the failure of caste as an organizational system among East Indians in Trinidad are subsumed by three broad categories: historical factors associated with the indenture period, the broader economic and political structure of Trinidad, and the forces extant in a plural society. The ideas and concepts introduced by the indentured East Indians were not sufficient to transplant caste into Trinidad as a viable system which was able to withstand the pressures encountered.

The fact that Trinidad is a plural society exposes traditional aspects of East Indian culture to extreme and multiple forces directed toward assimilation and amalgamation. Though ethnic-group isolation exists in many respects, the multiple ethnic groups existing in the plural society of Trinidad are moving in the direction of establishing shared cultural characteristics which cut across ethnic lines. Hence, one finds the acceptance by East Indians, of cultural elements associated with Creoles, and the converse. A similar situation exists in varying degrees for all ethnic groups in Trinidad. Caste, however, is not one of the acceptable aspects of traditional East Indian culture that could conceivably be shared by other ethnic groups. Conversely, there are no significant external mechanisms for the reinforcement of caste, such as support from India.

When all of these factors are viewed as a totality in relation to the perpetuation of East Indian caste in Trinidad, it is little wonder that caste has failed as an organizational system. Positive reinforcement of traditional caste is minimal, whereas negative forces directed toward the nonperpetuation of caste as a system of organization are overwhelming.

REFERENCES

BAILEY, F. G.
1957   *Caste and the economic frontier.* Manchester: Manchester University Press.

BANKS, C.
1907   *Report on emigration from the Port of Calcutta to British and foreign colonies.* Calcutta: Bengal Secretariat Press.

BRAITHWAITE, LLOYD
1953   "Social stratification in Trinidad." *Social and Economic Studies* 2:2, 3:5-175.

COMINS, D. W. D.
1893   *Note on emigration from India to Trinidad.* Calcutta: Bengal Secretariat Press.

CROWLEY, DANIEL J.
1960   "Cultural assimilation in a multiracial society." pp. 850-854 in *Social and cultural pluralism in the Caribbean,* V. Rubin, ed. Annals of the New York Academy of Sciences, 83 (Art. 5).

ERICKSON, EDGAR L.
1934   "The introduction of East Indian Coolies into the British West Indies." *The Journal of Modern History* VI:2:127-146.

GOUGH, E. KATHLEEN
1960   "Caste in a Tanjore village." pp. 11-60 in *Aspects of caste in South India, Ceylon, and North-West Pakistan,* E. R. Leach, ed. Cambridge: Cambridge University Press.

KLASS, MORTON
1961   *East Indians in Trinidad.* NewYork: Columbia University Press.

KONDAPI, C.
1951   *Indians overseas 1838-1949.* Madras: Oxford University Press.

NIEHOFF, ARTHUR, and JUANITA NIEHOFF
1960   *East Indians in the West Indies.* Milwaukee: Milwaukee Public Museum Publications in Anthropology, No. 6.

SCHWARTZ, BARTON M.
1963   *The dissolution of caste in Trinidad.* Ph.D. dissertation. Ann Arbor: University Microfilms.

1964a   "Caste and endogamy in Trinidad." *Southwestern Journal of Anthropology* 20:1:58-66.

1964b "Religiosity and the perpetuation of Hinduism." Unpublished manuscript.

1965a "Extra-legal activities of the village pandit in Trinidad." *Anthropological Quarterly* 38:62-71.

1965b "Patterns of East Indian family organization in Trinidad." *Caribbean Studies* 5:1:23-36.

SRINIVAS, M. N.
1952 *Religion and society among the Coorgs of South India.* London: Oxford University Press.

1956 "A note on sanskritization and westernization." *Far Eastern Quarterly* 15:4:481-496.

1957 "Caste in modern India." *The Journal of Asian Studies* 16:4:529-548.

TRINIDAD

The Function of Caste among the Indians of the Oropuche Lagoon, Trinidad

The island of Trinidad has 827,958 people, 43.31 per cent (358,-588) of which are of African ancestry, 36.47 per cent (301,947) East Indian, 16.27 per cent (134,748) mixed or colored, and 3.93 per cent (32,675) of other ethnic background (Trinidad Population Census, 1960, Vol. II, Part A, Table 5, pp. 1-2). The Creoles (the name used on the island for people of African ancestry) were brought as slaves to work on the sugar plantations while the Indians were brought at a later date as indentured laborers for the same plantations.

Physically, most of the island is covered by gently rolling hills. There are two other types of terrain, however. In the north there is a range of heavily forested low mountains and at three places along the coasts there are low-lying, marshy areas. Two of these swampy areas have been largely drained and are now used for cultivation. It is principally the Indians who have settled them. The two largest concentrations of rural Indians on the island are those at the Caroni Swamp on the northwest coast just south of Port-of-Spain and those in the Oropuche Lagoon in the south.

The "community" discussed in this report is the Oropuche Lagoon. The main towns from which the data were gathered are Debé and Penal. Both are known as "Indian" towns and both do have a majority of East Indians in their population. Debé at the time of the study had an Indian population over 95 per cent while Penal had an estimated 75-80 per cent population of Indians. There are smaller towns in the Oropuche area which are also predominantly Indian. In fact, the entire area is mainly Indian. To the east, south, and west the Creole population constitutes the majority. The whole area is regarded as conservative, that is, as a region where Indian culture has survived with less alteration than in the more urbanized regions or regions where the Indians are a minority group.

The reason for selecting the lagoon area for study rather than a particular town or village is that these are not viable social entities as they are in India and the non-Western world in general. In fact, the towns and villages of the Oropuche area are administrative units in the Western sense but possess practically none of the characteristics which cause the Indian village to be considered a viable unit in itself. There are no panchayats or any other kind of village rule, land has little meaning other than purely economic, there are no village godlings or rituals, and people stay where they do almost entirely for economic reasons. Furthermore, the towns and villages of the area lack almost completely the isolation of a village in India. Transportation is highly developed and travel is comparatively cheap. There are buses and jitneys, and many people have cars of their own. The Indians of the area, like the residents of other parts of the island, travel frequently, not only from town to town and from village to village but also to and from the urban centers of San Fernando and Port-of-Spain. The Oropuche Lagoon, then, is a social unit of significance only because it contains a concentration of rural Indians. It differs from other regions of Trinidad only because there are many more Indians and many more Indian institutions in it than in regions of the same size elsewhere.

The occupational pursuits of the Indians in this area are primarily agricultural. The main crops they cultivate are sugar cane, cacao, and rice, the first two as cash crops and the last for their own consumption. The economic position of the Indians varies from that of wage laborers on the large sugar estates to independent cacao farmers who own several hundred acres. Indians also engage in store-keeping and other businesses, and a good proportion work as clerks, teachers, and in other white-collar jobs. Finally, a considerable number work in the oil fields nearby, but principally in office jobs or handling motor vehicles. All in all, there is a considerable diversity of jobs among Indians and this diversity seems to be increasing.

The religious affiliation of the Indians in the area reflect the island-wide proportions, in which 65 per cent are Hindus, 17 per cent Muslims, and 19 per cent Christians (Kirpalani 1945: 61). Almost all Christian Indians are converts since coming to the island. These Christian Indians are comparatively well educated and in positions of importance in the community.

Probably the two most important social institutions brought from India, particularly by the Hindus, have been the extended family and the caste system. However, the extended family is found in many other parts of the world, while the caste system seems to be very particularly Indian. Although there are institutions like caste elsewhere, the pervasiveness with which it affects individual behavior in India make Indian society different from almost all other societies in the world. Probably the most significant characteristics of these hereditary socioreligious groups that we call castes are marital exclusiveness (caste endogamy), ritual cleanness, economic position (the lower castes in general being the poorest), and hereditary caste occupation. Moreover, these caste groups are arranged in hierarchical order, the Brahmins being in the highest position and the unclean castes, now referred to in India as harijans or "scheduled castes" being in the least-favored position. However, even in India these characteristics have been changing rapidly during the last few decades.

One can assume that this system was brought in some form to Trinidad by the immigrants, though the immigration system must have weakened it. In the first place most of the recruits were obtained from widely separated areas of northern India. The caste alignments would differ in these different areas even when the name of the caste was the same. Moreover, most people would not have known one another, so there was no practical way of keeping a person from up-grading his caste position. The face-to-face continuity of village relationships was lost. Rather than a series of functioning castes being transported to Trinidad, there were groups of people who brought along the caste idea and realigned themselves when they settled into their new environment.

There are scattered statements of social commentators indicating that caste ideas were still functioning among Indians in the early days. However, these are almost exclusively in regard to Brahmins. Whether the individuals were truly Brahmins it is impossible to know, though one suspects that many such persons had assigned themselves to the Brahmin caste for the privileges they thought this status would give them. Collens (1886: 190) mentioned that Brahmins tried to hold themselves apart and stated:

> The sceptre of the maharaja Brahmin dwindles to the insignificance of a hoe handle but poor as he is he will look down on his caste inferiors.

Morton also states that Brahmins were not supposed to work but were to be provided for by the offerings of their disciples. He describes one Brahmin who picked out his eyes so he would not have to work (1916: 69). Morton must have been unaware of the fact that most Brahmins were engaged in secular work in India at this period, most often as farmers. The Brahmins that came to his attention must have been priests, either real or assumed. This fact would not be too surprising since Morton was a Protestant missionary intent on converting the Indians. Brahmin pandits or priests probably created some opposition to his efforts. Evidently Brahmin priests did receive some recognition in the early days. Gamble, another missionary, reported (1866: 46):

> There are some of the Brahmin caste among them [Indians] and it is revolting to see the way a woman, for instance, will drop down, touch the foot of this holy Brahmin, and then kiss the hand that has been in contact with the priest's foot.

Whatever the ideas regarding caste behavior were that the immigrants brought, they were assaulted from many sides in the new environment. There was practically no sympathy by non-Hindus toward the institution of caste, even in those few instances where there might have been a minimum of understanding as to what it was. Ritual cleanness could be observed only within the Hindu community, which was a minority group. Marital exclusiveness could be observed, but again only among Hindus. But outcasting, the most effective punishment for violation of ritual observances and marriage with outsiders, was very difficult to impose. The Hindu who violated traditional observances could simply move to another community if his fellows tried to apply too much pressure. And one quite important factor in weakening the structure was that the economic and occupational foundation for caste was eliminated almost completely in Trinidad. Traditional caste occupations found no place in the commercial farming economy of Trinidad. All men started out on an equal basis as plantation laborers. Whereas in India the agricultural landholders tend to be of the higher castes while the agricultural laborers tend to be of the lower castes (or at least possess only small parcels of land), in Trinidad all were landless to start.

It might sound from the above that nothing has survived of caste as an institution. This impression is not quite true. Evidently, the system of caste is too integral a part of Hindu culture for the idea to be completely eliminated in two or three generations, despite difficult circumstances. In the Oropuche area most people still do know something about both the system and individual placement in it. There is a hierarchy generally accepted by most Hindus. The following are the main castes of the area in the order of their prestige, the highest at the beginning and the lowest at the end: Brahmin, Gosain, Chattri, Kayasth, Bania, Kurmi, Ahir, Koiri, Barhai, Kahar, Chamar, Dom, Dhobi.

The list is no absolute hierarchy, but rather a vague general consensus of ranking. Caste ideas are not so explicit that unanimity about position can occur. The classification reflects the situation in north India quite well. In Uttar Pradesh, the center of the Hindi-speaking area, Brahmins or Chattris (sometimes called Thakurs or Kshatriyas) are generally conceded to be the castes of highest prestige ; in most villages the wealthiest landholders are from one or the other. The one exception occurs in western Uttar Pradesh, where many villages are dominated by Jats (Lewis 1958: 87-88 ; Marriott 1955: 174). The Gosains, though less numerous than the Brahmins, are religious leaders of great respect. Hutton mentions them as being important religious leaders in the Assam Valley (1951: 98) while Ibbetson states that Siva temples were always built by Banias and served by Gosain priests (1883: 146-147). In my own research in central Uttar Pradesh I heard little about Gosains. Either they were not active in the area in which I was working or else their position had declined in India in the interval since the immigrants came to Trinidad. However, Lewis does mention that in a village near Delhi which he studied a Gosain had displaced a Brahmin priest in the local Siva temple (1958: 229).

The castes of the Oropuche region which fall between the Chattris and the Chamars would be classified in north India as ritually clean though below the level of the top three and usually not important landholders. The three lower castes are those which in India are classified as ritually unclean, the "untouchables" or "scheduled castes" in modern political parlance.

There are some Indians in the Oropuche region that have come from parts of India other than the north central region, Hindustan. But they are very few and the numerical superiority of the north Indians seems to have been great enough that their language and cultural patterns have become the norm. Today, practically all Indians in Trinidad who speak any Indian language speak Hindi. Only once did we (my wife or I) hear any other Indian language spoken. In all large public gatherings and in all rituals where an Indian language was used, it was Hindi. The data concerning emigration indicate the same provenance of these immigrants. The main port of debarkation was Calcutta, and from the emigration reports of the early twentieth century, as well as from the *Indian Centenary Review,* the proportion of emigrants from Hindustan was 80-90 per cent (Kirpalani and colleagues, 1945: 35). In the Report of Emigration of 1908, when 2,446 Indians came, 2,351 or 96 per cent were from the three north central provinces, the United Provinces, Oudh, and Bihar.

In the Oropuche region, what distinctions there are in the Hindu community are focused mainly on the high and low castes. There is still some deference shown to Brahmins and there is a feeling among Hindus that Brahmins are somewhat special. This feeling is probably due to their services as priests. The majority of Brahmins do not perform any ritual services but this situation is no different from that in

India. Brahmins are still thought of by devout Hindus as potential priests. At prayer meetings (puja) in the Oropuche region, Brahmins are usually served first. There are still a few occasions when a Brahmin's feet will be touched by the faithful in honorific greetings. Also, some informants reported that devout Hindus would sometimes bequeath land or animals to Brahmin priests in their wills. The term *panditji* (*ji* being an honorific suffix) is still used in conversations to refer to a Brahmin, whether or not he is a priest. I knew a local Brahmin who operated a service station and another who practised law, both of whom were referred to by this honorific title.

Brahmins have taken up all sorts of occupations, as have Chattris and members of the other "twice-born" castes. Even those few Brahmins who do serve as priests usually engage in some other kind of occupation. The majority in the Oropuche region have a certain amount of land which they tend when they are not serving at rituals. Others can be found in various occupations, from the highest to the lowest. I knew of one who worked as a taxi driver during the day and at night attended the different religious functions as a priest. There are even Brahmin proprietors of rum shops, though I do not believe these are part-time priests. Because the Brahmins are supposed to be devout men they are criticized much more than other "clean" caste members when they violate traditional practices.

The upper castes have retained a vestige of the "twice-born" ritual. They observe the ceremony of the investiture of the sacred thread, jeneo, but unlike their ancestors in India they do not continue to wear it through the rest of their life. They wear it for a few days after the ceremony, during certain ritual occasions in their lifetime, and again sometimes in old age when they can concern themselves with the needs of the spirit without the problems attendant to mingling with non-Hindus in the workaday world. According to belief in the Oropuche region, the only requirement for wearing the thread is that the wearer be ritually clean at the time, abstaining from alcohol, meat, and "unclean" things. They do not believe this kind of abstinence is possible for long; consequently they wear the thread for short periods only, when the ritual laws can be observed.

Least of all is heard about the castes in the middle ranks of the hierarchy, presumably because there is nothing to be gained prestige-wise by accentuating their caste position nor is there a stigma of uncleanness attached to their status. The members of the low castes still carry some of the stigma of their traditional position. A Hindu who wishes to insult another will frequently call his antagonist a "Chamar" (the leatherworking caste). An incident which took place in Debé illustrates how this term will be used. A group of Indians had gathered to hear a man explain how a certain spirit had appeared on several occasions. During his explanation another Indian in the group interrupted him periodically to clarify or elaborate certain portions of the story. Finally the speaker stopped in exasperation and addressed the kibitzer:

> Man, you're a jackass and from the lowest nation on earth, the Chamars, and if you don't keep quiet I'm not going to tell any more of this story.

I do not know if the man was a Chamar or not but the term was obviously used as an insult.

The only residence clusterings by caste that were found were those of low castes. This isolation is probably largely due to their habit of raising pigs and eating pork. Outside the town of Debé there is a hamlet known as Dom Village, said to be inhabited exclusively by Doms. Also one end of Penal has a heavy concentration of low-caste Hindus, most of whom raise pigs. Another custom which still persists among the low castes which probably helps perpetuate the image of their uncleanness is animal sacrifice. These rituals usually involve pigs, though goat sacrifice was reported as taking place less frequently. Such sacrifices are typically performed to malevolent village godlings (deota) or to the Hindu goddess Kali. There is annual sacrifice in Debé performed by the low-caste community, in which a collection is taken up by the women for the animal.

Food taboos dictated by caste membership, particularly those concerned with pork and beef, still remain among the Hindus of the area. As noted above, pork is not considered a proper food for any other than the lowest castes. This outlook parallels the situation in India. A new problem occurs among the Oropuche Hindus, however, as a result of intercaste marriage. Women of "clean" castes sometimes marry low-caste men. In such a case the wife will cook pork for her husband but will not eat it herself.

The one other food which Hindus of the area avoid eating is

beef. Cows are not treated as sacred as they are in India, but it is readily noted that many Indians in the area keep milk cows. Bullocks are more rare since they are hardly needed for draft purposes in Trinidad's comparatively mechanized economy. There are still a few water buffalo for the swampy areas of the lagoon, but motorized vehicles are rapidly replacing them also. The cow serves almost entirely as a source of food, which to the Hindus consists entirely of dairy products. We learned of no instance when cows were butchered by Hindus. In the Penal market, where Indian vendors predominated over Negroes in a ratio of four to one, there were eight Negro butchers and only four Indian ones. Two of the Indians were Muslims who did sell beef, and one was a low-caste Hindu who sold pork. We did not find out the caste affiliation of the fourth Indian. There was no bias against selling fish; out of a total of twenty fish vendors, fourteen were Indians. The proportion of Indians selling goods other than meat was much higher.

The repugnance toward the idea of eating beef is deeply rooted in the Hindu personality, even in those who have adopted new religious beliefs. The reaction remains well after the theological justification for it has been taken away. The Christian Indians we knew in the Oropuche area, whose parents had been converted from Hinduism, still found it practically impossible to consider eating beef. My wife and I witnessed an incident which demonstrates the strength of this attitude where the participants were a relatively well-educated and Westernized Christian couple. Both were teachers in a Christian mission school. We stopped with them at a roti shop. Roti, which is served all over the island, is unleavened Indian bread which is folded together to contain a curry sauce. The most popular curries are those which contain fish, shrimp, goat meat, or potatoes. However, some shops, which are usually operated by Muslims or greatly Westernized Indians, advertise beef roti. It was dark when we stopped at this particular shop so we were not able to identify it easily. I ordered chicken roti for my wife and myself while the Indian husband ordered two roti of potatoes. The Indian wife shortly discovered a piece of meat in hers. She became disturbed and was sure it was beef. Her husband chided her and continued to eat his even though it contained small bits of meat also. He became irritated too, however, and went back to the stand to demand replacements without meat. The boy at the stand then admitted putting a little meat in them—just for flavor. He did replace one for the husband, however, without meat. The wife would have no more though and threw hers away.

We knew individual Indian Christians who would not cook beef at home, even when some family members would eat it. Only rarely would they cook pork. In some cases when grown children ate pork or canned beef from Argentina, the parents would not allow them to cook it on the same stoves they used. Whenever beef is eaten it is usually this canned meat, which is relatively cheap and does not need to be cooked on the day it is bought, a necessity for fresh meat in a hot place where refrigerators are not usually a part of the household furniture. Also, canned meat comes from outside the country and in its processed form only remotely suggests the cow from which it is derived.

Chicken and eggs are considered only slightly less polluting than pork to middle- and upper-caste Hindus in India (Hutton 1951: 77). However, the attitude toward fowl in the Oropuche area of Trinidad has changed perhaps more than toward any other meat. Almost all families keep a flock of scrawny chickens and there is little objection toward eating either the birds or their eggs. The same is true of fish. In India the attitude toward eating fish seems to be closely related to their abundance—that is, in areas where fish are scarce they are not looked upon as a desirable food while in localities where they are abundant, even the higher castes eat them freely (Hutton 1951: 77). Bengalis, who live in an area where there are plenty of fish, are known throughout India as fish eaters, regardless of their caste position. It is probable that the abundance of fish in Trinidad has helped bring about this almost complete acceptance. Fish is both cheap and readily available in comparison to meat. Not only is a great variety of fish to be had in the week-end markets, but also there are fish peddlers on bicycle who travel the lagoon roads during the week. No meat can be purchased from such traveling merchants.

Probably the most popular meat among Hindus in the Oropuche area, even as in India, is goat flesh. If a Hindu will eat any kind of meat, he will accept goat. Goats are relatively plentiful in the area, since they require relatively little care or space in an economy where meat production is only a subsidiary activity. The relative market prices for the different meats seem to reflect these preferences. At the time the study was made, goat meat sold for about $1 per pound, chicken for 90c, pork for 75c, and beef for 65c. The demand for goat flesh being the greatest, it was the most expensive, while the demand for beef being least, it was the cheapest. The cost of fish was much less than for any of the animal meats, ranging from 10c to 40c per pound. Hindus who subsist entirely on a vegetarian diet are rare. Some pandits, all saddhus (religious ascetics), and a few very devout Hindus do not eat meat, but these constitute only a minute proportion of the total Hindu population.

Evidence of touch pollution among Oropuche Hindus is almost entirely lacking. The only vestiges we noticed were at some ceremonial functions. At Hindu weddings or prayer meetings, though Muslim and low-caste friends were invited, there was some effort made to keep them from touching the food while it was being prepared. The presumable reason was that though the middle- and upper-caste Hindu did not object to the "unclean" ones eating the food, they wanted their own food handled only by fellow "clean" Hindus. We knew one Muslim woman who was widely accepted among Indians and was much in demand to help with the cooking at such rituals, but orthodox families would not allow her to come inside the cooking shed at their affairs. When she did assist in the preparation of food it was done outside, and consisted primarily in peeling vegetables. Her main job was to help serve the cooked food.

One other custom which may have some connection with touch pollution is the manner of serving at weddings and prayer meetings. The cooked food is placed on the leaf of a plant similar to the banana, though stronger. Each guest gets one, which is discarded when he is finished eating. Thus the guests touch no vessels. This custom does not provide strong evidence of beliefs in touch pollution, however, as these leaf dishes serve almost the same function as paper plates in the United States.

There is practically no relationship between caste membership and occupation in the Oropuche region except for pandits and a scattering of individuals who follow some traditional work which produces marketable goods or services in the Trinidad economy. Barhai (carpenters) are still to be found in house construction and a few make traditional Indian drums. There are a few Kahar who make traditional pottery vessels, particularly the lamps for the festival of

Divali, and also new types of vessels which can be sold in the Trinidad markets. There are also some basket makers who follow their traditional caste occupation. Some Chamar women still serve as traditional midwives. In general, though, the economy of the area, as with the rest of the island, is so geared to imported goods that the craft worker has great difficulty in showing even a small profit. There are many other jobs available that are much more remunerative.

One of the strongest bulwarks of the caste system in India is intracaste marriage. Even in India's urban environments marriages between individuals of different caste are very rare. In the Oropuche area of Trinidad the situation is quite different. It is perhaps in this area of caste behavior that the contrast between Hindu customs in India and those in Trinidad is so striking. Marriages between castes in the Oropuche area are quite common, with probably just as many intercaste marriages as intracaste ones, despite the fact that Hindu parents still have a strong voice in selecting spouses for their children. In fact, the institution of the Hindu family seems to have survived much better than that of caste. The Indians seem to view marriage as the focal point in the affairs of the family and have retained much Indian tradition in it. The majority of marriages are arranged by the parents or responsible elders. There is very little social discourse between young unmarried people. Indian girls do not go on dates or to dances and a girl is suspect if she is seen talking to a young man alone.

The normal procedure is for the parents to locate a mate. Then the boy is brought to the girl's house, where she can see him and speak to him briefly. The young people's wishes are then weighed and if they agree the parents go ahead with the marriage arrangements. If the young people do not agree, the parents may apply considerable pressure, though it is rare to ignore the young people's wishes entirely. Between the time of the agreement and the marriage ceremony the boy will be allowed to visit the girl at her parents' home several times. We knew women though who had never seen their husbands before their marriage, or who had seen them so briefly that they were not sure who they were. A variation takes place when the boy sees a girl whom he likes in a public place and who then asks his parents to arrange a marriage with her. If she seems suitable, the parents will often do so.

The Hindu system of courtship and marriage is thus still quite

Indian and marital choice is still primarily in the hands of the elders. Furthermore, it contrasts greatly with the Creole union, which is characterized to a high degree by concubinage, and with what is called the nonlegal union, which has been described (Matthews 1953: 2) as a relationship of two marriageable people:

> Living under one roof . . . without any formal religious, civil, or social ceremony.

The Hindu union is practically always validated by a ceremony, either traditional or conforming to modern Trinidad laws. Though the Hindu rite was not considered legal until 1946, the Indians had continued to perform the traditional ceremony since they arrived on the island, which made the union legal in their eyes (Francis 1950: 56, 69). These unregistered marriages came to be known as "under the bamboo," because the ceremony was conducted in a temporary bamboo structure. The marriage ritual still is probably the most important socioreligious event that Hindus observe. Usually there is a series of events from Friday night until Sunday evening, for which a considerable amount is spent on food and drinks. Also, in the Oropuche region dowries continue to be an integral part of the arrangements, ranging from a few dollars up to $500, and including material goods of considerable value among the well-to-do families.

Despite the fact that marriage among Hindus has retained many of the traditional aspects, intercaste unions are common. Parents prefer to get mates of the same caste for their children but this consideration does not seem as important as others such as financial position and degree of education. The families do try to avoid the extreme in their selections; that is, high-caste parents try to see to it that their children, particularly girls, do not get low-caste mates. There is precedent for this preference in the Indian custom of hypergamy (Hutton 1951: 53-54). However, in the Oropuche region even marriages between widely separated castes are accepted, though frequently these are not arranged in the orthodox manner. We knew of one marriage between a Brahmin boy and a Chamar girl, which had been arranged by the father after the couple had lived together for six months. The father then called in a pandit for a brief ceremony and had the union registered. However, the father remained so angry that his son finally moved out of the house with his Chamar wife.

People of different castes have been intermarrying so long by now that parents frequently have difficulty in deciding to which caste their children belong. In general, the Hindus of this area take the attitude that a child belongs to the caste of the father, which seems to indicate Western influence on their ideas. In India such a problem does not occur because the mother and father are almost invariably of the same caste. In Trinidad the matter of caste status is of so little importance in comparison with other status markers, though, that some Hindus have forgotten what caste they belong to. One would suspect that these are usually people of low caste to whom it is convenient to forget their position in the hierarchy, but the significant fact is that a Hindu can be accepted within the community without any caste affiliation and still be considered a Hindu.

The primary kind of punishment meted out to caste offenders, outcasting, has practically disappeared. It was reported that efforts to ostracize a caste fellow were still occasionally made for two offenses only: for incest and for a married man running off with an unmarried girl. The methods of punishment were refusal to go to social or ritual functions at the offender's house or to eat with him. However, it was readily admitted that these measures were difficult to apply since the man would simply leave the community. Though people could remember caste councils held for the purpose of outcasting someone, they could not remember any for a long time.

To sum up, caste is functionally a matter of little concern in this Hindu community. To explain why, one needs to realize that these people are descendants of uprooted Hindus who, though they carried the idea of caste with them to their new homeland, undoubtedly changed their specific affiliation in numerous instances. A Trinidad Indian could never be sure that another's stated caste affiliation was his actual one. Secondly, two of the major props of caste behavior were very difficult to maintain in an environment where the Hindus were a minority people and where the majority had a quite different cultural background. Both caste occupations and rules of ritual cleanness dictated by caste membership were very difficult to maintain in this unsympathetic environment. And finally, the most potent means of enforcing conformity to caste rules in India was almost lost—that of outcasting, or social ostracism. The aberrant Hindu could move into the Creole community if his caste fellows tried to apply pressure.

The Hindu family system survived much better than did the caste system, presumably because the family is a smaller unit and the means of control are more easily applied, even when the culture is under pressure.

REFERENCES

CENTRAL STATISTICAL OFFICE
1960 Population Census 1960. Vol. II, Part A, Table 5, pp. 1-2. Port-of-Spain: Government Printing Office.

COLLENS, J. H.
1886 *Guide to Trinidad*. Port-of-Spain: Trinidad.

FRANCIS, ELIOT
1950 *Laws of Trinidad and Tobago*. London: C. T. Roworth.

GAMBLE, REV. W. H.
1866 *Trinidad: Historical and descriptive*. London: Yates and Alexander.

HUTTON, J. H.
1951 *Caste in India*. 2d ed. London: Oxford University Press. [1st ed., 1946; 3rd ed., 1961; 4th ed., 1963]

IBBETSON, DENZIL C.
1883 *Report on the revision of the settlement of the Panipat Tahsil and Karnal Parganah of the Karnal District, 1862-1880*. Allahabad: Pioneer Press.

KIRPALANI, MURLI J., MITRA G. SINANAN, S. M. RAMESHWAR, and L. F. SEUKERAN, EDS.
1945 *Indian centenary review, one hundred years of progress*. Port-of-Spain: Guardian Commercial Printery.

LEWIS, OSCAR
1958 *Village life in Northern India*. Urbana: University of Illinois Press.

MARRIOTT, MCKIM
1955 "Little communities in an indigenous civilization." pp. 171-222. in *Village India*, McKim Marriott, ed. Menasha: American Anthropological Association Memoir No. 83.

MATTHEWS, DOM BASIL
1953 *Crisis in the West Indian family*. Port-of-Spain: Government Printing Works.

MORTON, SARAH E., ed.
1916 *John Morton of Trinidad*. Toronto: Westminster Co.

TRINIDAD

Caste among Hindus in a Town in Trinidad: San Fernando

COLIN CLARKE

The town of San Fernando is located on the west coast of Trinidad and faces Venezuela across the Gulf of Paria. In 1960 San Fernando had a population of 39,000 and was the second largest town in the island. During the nineteenth century the town was confined to the steep western slope of Naparima Hill, but the more recent suburbs extend inland across rolling country. San Fernando has been surrounded by cane fields for more than a hundred and fifty years, and most of the land on the periphery of the town is still cultivated by a large sugar company. However, a considerable amount of cane land has been built upon, and the residential area of the town extends northward as far as the Texaco oil refinery at Pointe-à-Pierre. The borough of San Fernando claims to be "the industrial capital of Trinidad," but its industrial character depends more on the adjacent oil and sugar companies than upon the smaller industries which are located in the town. A large proportion of the 7,000 men who work at the Texaco oil refinery live in San Fernando, and the town may

165

safely be described as one of the most prosperous in the British West
Indies.

East Indians were imported into Trinidad between 1845 and
1917 for employment as indentured laborers on the sugar estates.
Although East Indians have been living in San Fernando for more
than a hundred years, they still comprise less than a quarter of the
town's population. The Negro ethos of the newly independent state
of Trinidad and Tobago is resented by almost all East Indians, and
no less so by those living in San Fernando. However, the East Indian
community itself is highly segmented, and comprises three main religious groups—Hindus, Muslims, and Presbyterian Christians. Hindus
comprise less than 8 per cent and Muslims less than 6 per cent of the
population of San Fernando. Presbyterians form the largest East
Indian group and account for nearly 10 per cent of the town's inhabitants (Table I).

TABLE I. THE PROPORTION OF HINDUS, MUSLIMS, AND PRESBYTERIANS IN THE
POPULATIONS OF SAN FERNANDO AND TRINIDAD

	San Fernando		Trinidad	
	No.	%	No.	%
Hindu	3,047	7.6	190,403	23.0
Muslim	2,318	5.8	49,736	6.0
Presbyterian	3,848	9.6	32,409	3.9
Other Christian East Indian	1,083	2.7	29,399	3.5
Total East Indian Population	10,296	25.8	301,947	36.5
Remainder of Population	29,534	74.2	526,010	63.5
Total Population	39,830	100.0	827,957	100.0

Source: 1960 Census.

The Presbyterian Church was established by Canadian missionaries during the second half of the nineteenth century with the object
of converting the Muslims and the "idolatrous" Hindus. The activities of this denomination in south Trinidad were directed from San
Fernando. The significance of the Presbyterian Church for the Hindus
lay in the fact that it offered not only an alternative religion and

philosophy of life, but that it first of all provided primary schools, and later, in the twentieth century, secondary schools, a teachers' training college, and a theological college. By equipping students for white-collar posts in the colony, the church provided East Indians with an alternative to the cane fields and an opportunity to escape from the poverty with which a "coolie" was associated. Many Hindus, and a smaller number of Muslims, took advantage of the facilities of the church in this way, and all those who wanted to become school-teachers in the Canadian Mission Indian Schools, as they were then called, were prevailed upon to become Christian.

The proportions of East Indians and of Hindus and Presbyterians in San Fernando differ significantly from their representation on the island as a whole (Table I). East Indians comprise only 25.8 per cent of the population of San Fernando compared with 36.5 per cent of the population of Trinidad. Proportionately, Presbyterians are more than twice as numerous locally as they are nationally, and Hindus are three times as numerous nationally as they are locally. While Hindus (and East Indians generally) are still largely rural in location, Presbyterian East Indians have shown a tendency to live in towns. The demographic situation in San Fernando is therefore atypical of conditions obtaining throughout the island. The prosperous industrial economy of the town, the religious and educational influence of the Presbyterian Church, the small size of the Hindu community and its contact with Negroes, at least on the economic plane, have created a situation which may have hastened change in the social institutions of the "town Hindus." In the light of these factors it is proposed to examine the institution of caste as it is practised by the 3,000 Hindus who live in San Fernando.

Breakdown of the Caste System

Hutton has described a caste system as ". . . one whereby a society is divided up into a number of self-contained and completely segregated units (castes), the mutual relations between which are ritually determined in a graded scale" (1961: 50). If this definition is accepted as a yardstick, it is clear that the caste system, as such, has broken down among Hindus in San Fernando. There is no caste organization, no caste council, and no set of rules to regulate inter-caste relationships and obligations at either a personal or group level. Children are not initiated into caste, and castes do not discipline their members for breaking caste rules; indeed, there are no rules. Caste is a problem for the individual or for the family; excluding considera-tion of religious and political institutions, caste does not affect any larger organized group. Occupational segregation and specialization have disappeared, and there is no congruence between the occupa-tions of the Hindus of San Fernando and the traditional pursuit of their castes in nineteenth-century India. An important exception to this, however, is the exclusiveness of the orthodox priesthood, mem-bership of which is still confined to Brahmins.

The dissociation of occupation from caste has led to the break-down of the jajmani system, which bound certain castes in patron-client relationships. The term *jajman* (patron) is known to very few Hindus in San Fernando, and almost all of those who recognized it thought that it referred to the relationship between guru and chela. One informant, however, said that his dead father, a Brahmin pandit (priest), had been a jajman who retained the services of a Nau (bar-ber). The Nau had helped him in religious rituals, and had also cut the hair and trimmed the finger and toe nails of the members of the pandit's family. This pandit had been born in India and had lived there until he was a young man. He thought that nail trimming and hair cutting were polluting, and otherwise would not have employed the services of the Nau. The sons, however, did not retain the Nau after their father died.

The dissolution of the link between occupation and caste illus-trates the extent to which the concepts of purity and pollution have lost their meaning, especially in secular contexts. Even at wedding ceremonies the Nau's tasks are performed by other individuals, and one Muslim woman from San Fernando frequently plays the part of the Nau's wife in Hindu marriages. Untouchability has disappeared, and, with one or two exceptions, commensality has become the norm. The dilution of the concept of pollution has broken one of the pillars of the caste system and has reduced the hierarchical distance be-tween most, if not all, castes. Only Brahmins who have taken the janeo (sacred thread) are particularly aware of pollution, and priests who have become temporarily polluted during their toilet preparations loop their sacred thread over one ear. The conditions under which individual Indians were recruited, shipped across the polluting "black waters," indentured, and put to work as laborers on sugar estates in Trinidad, must have made it impossible for the East Indians to attempt to reconstitute the caste system had they actively sought to do so.

In San Fernando few rituals are performed by one caste and not by another. The number of Chamars and Madrassis is too small for them to have maintained the Kali Mai ritual and the fire-pass, both of which were formerly held in the sugar area around San Fernando. The castes have no myths, heroes, or heritage of their own. In fact there has been a "generalization" of Indian culture which has effaced the cultural variations which were associated with caste in India. (See Crooke 1896.) Passage of time, the small size of the membership of some of the castes, isolation from India, and the work of the Brahmin-led Sanatan Dharam Maha Sabha, the orthodox Hindu religious organization in Trinidad, have been responsible. The movement in San Fernando towards a common, Brahmin-controlled Hindu religion has reached the stage where 114 out of the 131 Hindus who answered a questionnaire survey in San Fernando and who knew the religious sect to which they belonged said that they were Sanatanists. Of the remaining 17 respondents, 5 were members of the Arya Samaj, 6 were Seunerinis, 5 were Kabir Panthis, and one, a man born in the Punjab, was a Punjabi Guru Nanic. The priesthood of the three major nonconformist sects, the Arya Samaj, Siva Narayani (Seunerini), and Kabir Panth, is open to non-Brahmins, but there are no non-Sanatanist priests living in the town, and caste priests have disappeared. Before he died, three years ago, a priest of the Arya Samaj lived in San Fernando, but he was a Brahmin. All the public religious rituals which were performed during the period of the writer's field work in San Fernando were presided over by Sanatanists. All five weddings witnessed in San Fernando were conducted by Brahmin pandits, and all of them followed the ritual prescribed by the Pandits' Council of Trinidad and Tobago, an organization closely associated with the Sanatan Dharam Maha Sabha. There was no variation in the marriage ritual from one caste to another, although the weddings between Brahmin children involved a greater show of wealth and a larger cavalcade of pandits than was usual at lower-caste weddings.

A few Brahmins claim to know their gotra, but gotra exogamy is not practiced, and no distinction can be made between the twice-born varnas and the Sudras in this respect. The life-cycle rites of all Hindus are virtually identical, irrespective of caste, but there are two important exceptions. It is commonly agreed, as in India, that only the three "twice-born" varnas—the Brahmin, the Kshatriya, and the Vaishya—may take the janeo. Furthermore, the castes of the two lower varnas, the Vaishya and the Sudra, have been less dutiful than the Brahmins and Kshatriyas in observing Hindu customs and rituals. The sacred thread is taken by only a few Brahmins, and the only Vaishya to take the janeo in the area in recent times was a Baniya. All adult Hindus who die from natural causes should, ideally, be cremated, but the practice is only now being revived, and it is rare for members of varnas lower than the Brahmin and Kshatriya to be cremated rather than buried.

No neighborhoods or streets in San Fernando are confined to any one caste or group of socially equal castes because of caste as such. While it is true that Hindus have tended to congregate on the fringe of the town (Figure 1), it cannot be said that there is even a Hindu quarter. In fact, the Hindu community is widely scattered throughout the town; only in Kakatwey, the shanty town, do Hindus comprise more than 32 per cent of the population, and here the common denominator is not so much race or religion or caste as poverty. But there are two important areas, one in the north of the town and the other in the south, where Hindus comprise between 18 per cent and 31 per cent of the population. Both areas are located in new suburbs, and both are served by a mandir (temple). The area in the south surrounding the Todd Street mandir has a large number of Brahmin inhabitants. Other castes are not excluded from the area, which is one of the best residential districts in town, provided they can afford to rent or purchase property there. The map (Figure 1) suggests that the scatter of the Hindu population is unfavorable to both caste and Hindu group organization, unless they are achieved through the only Hindu institution in town, the mandir. No one can remember a

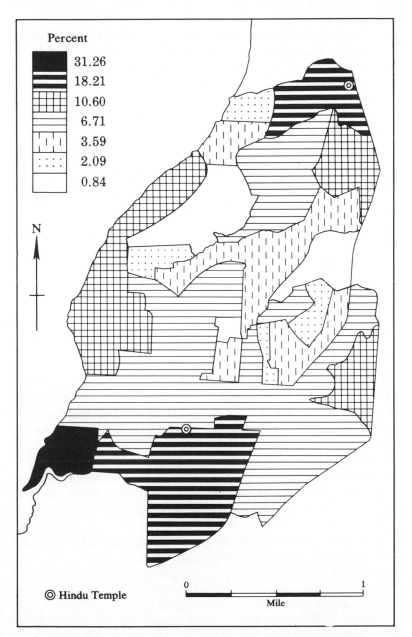

Percent

31.26
18.21
10.60
6.71
3.59
2.09
0.84

N

◎ Hindu Temple

0   1
Mile

FIGURE 1. SAN FERNANDO: 1960 CENSUS DISTRIBUTION OF HINDUS.

panchayat (council) being called to regulate the affairs of the Hindus living in San Fernando. But the fact that more than one-third of the Brahmins live within a quarter-mile radius of the mandir is not fortuitous, since caste is an important consideration in the context of religion and ritual.

The caste system has broken down, but caste is important in the Hindu religion and in the Hindu family, where it affects the choice of marriage partner. Persistence in one institution is frequently linked with persistence in other institutions in this way. It is proposed to examine what remains of caste, to list the caste of Hindus who live in San Fernando, to compare caste and varna with class, to examine the extent to which these residual castes have remained "segregated" or endogamous, and to consider the importance of caste in the priest-hood, religion, and secular affairs.

Castes in San Fernando

The writer surveyed a systematic, random sample of adult East Indians in San Fernando in 1964 as part of a project the main purpose of which was to examine the relations between the East Indian and Negro communities.[1] Every sixth East Indian name recorded on the list of electors for San Fernando in 1961 was selected, and the ensuing survey covered just over 500 respondents, 149 of whom were Hindus. Each respondent was asked to state his or her caste, the caste of his wife or her husband, and the caste of the parents of both the respondent and the spouse. Table II gives as complete a picture of the caste composition of the Hindu community of San Fernando as it has been possible to prepare. The caste of the respondent and the respondent's spouse, where it was given, has been listed, and the traditional occupation of each caste in nineteenth-century India recorded.

Only 20 out of the 149 Hindu respondents did not know their caste. The caste of 223 adults, 123 men and 100 women, has been re-corded in Table II; and among these 26 castes are represented. The

---

[1] The field work was carried out by the writer and his wife between January and September 1964. The field work was financed by a grant from the Research Institute for the Study of Man, New York.

TABLE II. THE CASTE OF A SAMPLE OF MALE AND FEMALE HINDUS IN
SAN FERNANDO (RESPONDENT AND SPOUSE)

Caste and Varna	Traditional Occupation of Castes	Male	Female	Total
BRAHMIN				
Gosain		3	1	4
Maharaj	Priests	32	22	54
Subtotal		35	23	58
KSHATRIYA				
Chattri	Warriors and rulers	22	22	44
Subtotal		22	22	44
VAISHYA				
Ahir	Graziers	20	13	33
Baniya	Traders	3	3	6
Barhai	Carpenters	0	2	2
Gadariya	Shepherds, Goatherds, and Blanket Weavers	1	1	2
Jaiswal	Traders	1	0	1
Kahar	Cultivators, Fishermen, and Carriers of Palanquins	3	1	4
Kewat	Fishermen, Boatmen, and Cultivators	1	0	1
Koiri	Cultivators	4	3	7
Kori	Weavers	0	1	1
Kurmi	Market Gardeners	10	8	18
Lunia	Cultivators and Makers of Earthworks	3	1	4
Madrassi	Name given to people from South India *(see text)*	2	0	2
Mali	Gardeners	0	1	1
Mallah	Fishing and Boating	1	0	1
Nau	Barbers	1	2	3
Patitar	*(see text)*	1	0	1
Sonar	Goldsmiths	0	1	1
Teli	Oil Pressers, Traders, and Cultivators	2	0	2
Vesh	*(see text)*	1	1	2
Subtotal		54	38	92
SUDRA				
Dusad	Plowmen and Village Menials	6	5	11
Seunerine	*(see text)*	1	0	1
Chamar	Tanners and Leather Workers	5	11	16
Subtotal		12	16	28
Dass	*(see text)*	0	1	1
Total		123	100	223

26 castes have been placed into four main groups which correspond to the varna system of India. The fifth group, Untouchables, who are outcastes in India, does not exist in Trinidad. Varna is rarely mentioned explicitly when caste is discussed by Hindus; but they think in terms of high, medium, and low castes, and varna adequately expresses this rank order. The four varnas are ranked hierarchically; the highest is the Brahmin, followed by the Kshatriya, Vaishya, and Sudra.

The Brahmin or priestly varna in San Fernando comprises two castes, Gosain and Maharaj. The Gosain caste is very small, but it is agreed among the Brahmins that it is the highest jat (caste) or "nation." The name Maharaj or "great ruler" has been adopted as a surname by many Brahmins. They claim membership in the Maharaj caste but most do not know their original caste or subcaste. However, the names of some Brahmin castes, notably the Dube, whose members were able to recite two Vedas, and the Misir, have been retained as family names. There is only one caste in the Kshatriya varna, the varna of rulers and warriors, and it is called Chattri; no subcastes are known. The third varna is the Vaishya, comprising 19 castes. In India the members of most of these castes were involved in trading, agriculture, fishing, and rural crafts. In north India, the Kewat caste was sometimes listed as a subcaste of the Mallah; the Jaiswal was associated with the Baniya; and the Mali, Koiri, and Kurmi were closely aligned. It has been reported that castes are ranked within the Vaishya varna in at least one rural area in Trinidad (Klass 1961: 60). The breakdown of caste feeling between castes of this varna in San Fernando has been such that ranking is not significant, if present, and these castes have simply been listed alphabetically. Three castes—the Dusad, Seunerine, and Chamar—comprise the Sudra varna. In India the Dusad caste were plowmen, watchmen, and village menials; the Chamar were tanners, leather workers, and day laborers; and the Chamarin (female members of the Chamar caste) were midwives. Because they worked with skins of dead animals, and especially of cows, the Chamar were ostracized and despised throughout North India.

The ideas behind varna have been kept alive by the traditions of the people and revived by Hindu religious texts such as the *Bhagavadgita*, the Gita Press paperback translation of which is owned by many

Hindus. In Chapter 18 of the *Bhagavadgita,* the varnas are ranked in the sequence given in Table II. In India it has been suggested that varna is associated with race or skin color, the high castes being light and the low castes dark. This tradition is still maintained in San Fernando, and one saying warns Hindus against people whose color and caste do not coincide in this way: "Beware of the black Brahmin and the fair Chamar." In Trinidad, the preeminence of the Brahmins is accepted because of their traditionally high ritual status; the rank of the other castes is measured by their approximation to the Brahminical ideal. Varna has remained fixed, but the membership of the varnas, especially of the Vaishya and Sudra, has become mutable. Klass reports that Sudras who renounce pork eating can become Vaishya (1961: 59). But social mobility is not achieved by castes as a whole, as in India, but by individuals. In San Fernando a Maharaj who eats pork is a "pork Maharaj," and because of this pollution can be considered lower even than Chamar. However, because class is more important than caste in the multiracial community of San Fernando, very little encouragement is given to members of the low castes to upgrade themselves by adopting orthodox Hindu behavior, although one example of this process, which Srinivas (1952) has termed "sanskritization," will be described later.

Some of the names of the castes given by Hindu respondents in San Fernando are not recognizable as Indian caste names: these are Madrassi, Patitar, Vesh, Dass, and Seunerine.

The term *Madrassi* is an umbrella title applied to the descendents of indentured laborers who were shipped from South India through the port of Madras. The customs and rituals of this group were different from those of the majority of the indentured Indians who came from the North-West Provinces and Oudh. Some Madrassis claim that they are divided into two groups—the Moon-Sammies, who are Brahmins, and the Mootoos, who are Sudra. Neither of the two Madrassis who were interviewed mentioned this division. The distinction must have been unknown to, or disregarded by, other East Indians, who used to consider all Madrassis lower than Chamar. One Madrassi informant said that his mother-in-law, who was a Christian like himself, rejected him, albeit temporarily, with the charge that "Madrassi and Nigger is de same ting." However, the Madrassi caste in San

Fernando is sufficiently inconspicuous for it not to rank locally as Sudra.

The word *Vesh* is the Trinidad Hindi for *Vaishya*. Vesh has been listed as a caste, although it is clearly meant to represent varna and not caste.

The word *Patitar* is a misspelling of the word *Patidar*. Only one family of Patidar was interviewed, and they had come from Gujarat in India, where the caste is well known. They are recent immigrants and own a jewelry business. The Patidar respondent has been classified as Vaishya, although the caste really stands outside the Trinidad varna system. Over a dozen "Indian" families originating mostly from the Bombay area now live in San Fernando. They own dry-goods and jewelry businesses in and around the town, and, with some of the Muslims, have engrossed the business of goldsmithing, which traditionally was the preserve of the Sonar caste. The Bombays keep ritually and socially aloof from the descendants of the indentured Indians, and many bring brides from India for their young men.

It has not been possible to discover what the name *Dass* means, and the only member of that caste, a woman, has not been included in the varna system.

There is no caste called Seunerine, although there is a religious sect (Siva Narayani) of that name. The sect draws the greater part of its support from the Sudras, and the Seunerine has therefore been placed in the Sudra varna.

The striking features of the caste list (Table II) are the numerical preponderance of the three twice-born varnas over the Sudras, and the fact that not only do the Brahmins and Kshatriyas together outnumber the Vaishyas, but that the Brahmins also outnumber the Kshatriyas. The numerical size of the various varnas in San Fernando is quite the reverse of the proportions that obtained among the original immigrants (Comins 1892: 37), and the reverse of the proportions that have recently been recorded for the Trinidad village of "Amity" (Klass 1961: 61). Klass found that over half the males in "Amity" were Sudra, and that well over half the Sudras were Chamar. In San Fernando, also, over half the Sudras were Chamar, but only 12.5 per cent of the Hindus are Sudra.

The overrepresentation of the high castes in San Fernando may be accounted for by the differential social, economic, and geographic mobility of representatives of the various castes. During the early decades of the twentieth century, the Brahmin priests were among the wealthiest and most powerful members of the Hindu community. It is probable that the higher castes were particularly self-confident and ambitious, and therefore more likely to look for the opportunities for material advancement which were available only in schools and occupations in the town. It is also possible that many low-caste members of the Hindu community, who were born or came to live in San Fernando, were converted to Christianity. The Presbyterians rewarded achievement and not caste, although achievement may not have been dissociated from caste. To a large extent the Presbyterian Church provided a way not only out of the cane fields but also out of what remained of caste.

In addition to the urbanization of the higher castes and conversion of the lower ones, falsification of caste may also have occurred. It is suspected that some lower-caste Indians claimed the status of Brahmins when they came to Trinidad. However, the penalty of ridicule and even of beating was reserved by the community for those who were discovered, and this must have discouraged most Hindus from falsifying their caste.[2] But some probably tried and succeeded. If the breakdown of the caste system facilitated falsification of caste, the movement of Hindus into the town of San Fernando must have facilitated it similarly, if in lesser degree. During the last generation two men, one the son of a Kshatriya father and the other "a half-way Muslim," have claimed and been accorded Brahmin status. The man of Kshatriya origin is politically one of the most powerful East Indians in San Fernando. His wealth, and the high caste of his father, have made him readily acceptable to all Brahmins. Furthermore, his claim was to the secular rank of Brahmin and not to the ritual office of priest. Nowadays, the caste of almost all the Brahmins in San Fernando is undisputed, and several of the Brahmins have ancestors who were pandits in the area.

---

[2]The caste of East Indians from Grenada is treated with suspicion; their background is obscure, and a remarkably large number of them claim to be Brahmin or Kshatriya.

Caste and Class

The ascriptive ranking of the most significant castes in San Fernando is as follows:

Varna	Caste
Brahmin	Gosain
	Maharaj
Kshatriya	Chattri
Vaishya	Baniya
	Ahir
	Kurmi
	Koiri
Sudra	Chamar

For many Hindus caste presents no great problem. In their working life in town, race and class are infinitely more important to them than caste. Many Hindus say that caste does not matter and some deny that it exists. It is significant that caste is one of the few basic elements of Indian culture that the Hindus do not claim to have preserved. Since the Vaishya are the largest varna in San Fernando, and since they are not particularly caste conscious, it is not surprising that the opinion which prevails is the one that caste no longer matters. However, the opinions of some individuals differ widely from this view, as the following quotations from respondents and informants show.

[*An Ahir, male, aged 28*] The caste system is not the best thing, but I'm in it and what can I do? Quicker trust a Maharaj than a Chamar. The Chamar think and act low.

[*A Madrassi, male, aged 43, a laborer*] There was an old woman who used to offer me food on a leaf because I was a low nation. She was a Kurmi.

[*A Chamar, male, aged 47, a fitter in a refining plant*] The only hope for Hindus who are not Maharaj is to become Christians, when their status of life will become changed in the eyes of these Brahmins.

[*An Indian-born Brahmin, a school teacher*] Caste is silently felt, especially in the upper bracket. . . . No one is diffident about caste in Trinidad, but many are arrogant. . . . The high castes are arrogant.

The Brahmins and Kshatriyas are proud of their caste, and the names Gosaine and Maharaj appear frequently as the surnames of Brahmins. The fact that a considerable number of Brahmins have adopted the title Maharaj during the last twenty years suggests that Brahminism has increased and not decreased in importance in San Fernando. Some Brahmins are admired by the lower castes, especially if they are the sons of respected pandits or elders, and their advice on personal problems may be sought and taken. The Kshatriyas carry the surname or suffix "Singh," and this is their panache. The Vaishyas are relatively indifferent to caste, largely because it does not place them in a critical position socially. However, Chamars are still looked down upon by the higher castes and are sneered at when their behavior is considered offensive. The word *Chamar* is used as a blasphemy; certainly it is one of the worst names that a Hindu can be called. Two important facts are therefore clear: (1) Caste rankings focus on the low status of the Chamar and the high status of the Maharaj. (2) Caste may become crucial for Hindus who aspire to leadership within the community.

When comparing caste with class, it must be remembered that the comparison is not between caste which is static and class which is mutable. The comparison is between two variables which are partly interrelated. Caste, varna, and class have been compared in Table III. Only those castes have been listed whose representatives were employed or were seeking employment. The members of each caste have been divided into three social categories.[3] Social group I, the upper class, comprises owners of large properties and businesses, executives, and professional people who earn an annual income of more than 7,500 Trinidad and Tobago dollars.[4] Social group II, the middle class, is made up of white-collar workers, proprietors of small shops and properties, teachers, and skilled and semiskilled workers. The income range of persons included in this group is between $1,500

---

[3]The data referring to occupation and income were collected in the writer's survey.

[4]One Trinidad and Tobago dollar is worth approximately four shillings sterling, in United States money 59 cents. All figures relating to incomes are in Trinidad and Tobago dollars.

TABLE III. CASTE AND CLASS IN SAN FERNANDO

| Caste and | Social Groups | | | | |
Varna	Group I	Group II	Group III	Not Placed	Total
BRAHMIN					
Gosain	0	2	1	—	3
Maharaj	6	16	11	—	33
Subtotal	6	18	12	0	36
KSHATRIYA					
Chattri	4	10	8	—	22
Subtotal	4	10	8	0	22
VAISHYA					
Ahir	2	8	11	—	21
Baniya	0	1	2	—	3
Gadariya	1	0	0	—	1
Jaiswal	0	1	0	—	1
Kahar	0	1	2	—	3
Kewat	0	0	1	—	1
Koiri	0	1	3	—	4
Kurmi	0	1	9	—	10
Loniya	0	0	3	—	3
Madrassi	0	0	2	—	2
Mallah	0	0	1	—	1
Nau	0	0	1	—	1
Patitar	0	1	0	—	1
Teli	0	2	0	—	2
Vesh	0	1	0	—	1
Subtotal	3	17	35	0	55
SUDRA					
Dusad	0	0	6	—	6
Seunerine	0	0	1	—	1
Chamar	0	1	4	—	5
Subtotal	0	1	11	0	12
Don't know	0	8	12	—	20
Won't answer	0	0	1	—	1
Not placed	—	—	—	3	3
Subtotal	0	8	13	3	24
Total	13	54	79	3	149

and $7,500 per annum. Social group III represents the lower class, and comprises vendors and unskilled laborers, all of whom receive less than $1,500 per annum.

Out of the 149 persons whose caste, occupation, and income have been analyzed, 9 per cent belonged to social group I, 36 per cent to social group II, and 53 per cent to social group III ; 2 per cent were not categorized according to social groups. The Maharaj caste accounted for almost half the membership of group I, and Brahmins and Kshatriyas together made up 10 of the 13 members of the group. The only other members of group I were two Ahirs and one Gadariya. No other Vaishya and no Sudra belonged to group I. Thirty-six per cent of the total sample belonged to group II. Of the 46 members of this group, 28 were Brahmin or Kshatriya. Ahirs accounted for 8 of the 17 Vaishyas who were members of group II. Only one Sudra, a Chamar, ranked as high as group II. Group III is the largest and the lowest social group among the Hindus in San Fernando. Brahmins and Kshatriyas together formed 25 per cent of this group, Vaishyas 44 per cent, and Sudras 14 per cent ; 17 per cent could not be grouped according to caste and varna. It is significant, however, that 11 out of the 12 Sudras in the sample fell into group III. There is a strong tendency, therefore, for the Brahmins and Kshatriyas to be associated with groups I and II, for the Vaishyas to be associated with group III and to a lesser extent with group II, and for the Sudras to be linked with group III.

Although the link between caste and secular occupations has been severed, caste has become closely associated with socioeconomic class. The varna stratification of the Hindu community has been partly harmonized with the class structure of the total society by becoming subordinate to it. There is a strong correlation between high class and high caste, and between low caste and low class, while the Vaishyas are a median group in both caste and class structures. But although caste is an attribute of social status, caste applies only to the Hindu community, and a certain amount of disharmony exists between the two systems of stratification and the two sets of social values with which they are associated. The high social status of Brahmins belonging to group I is grudgingly recognized by members of the Negro community, but they do not appreciate that Brahmins are the elite of the caste system. Disharmony is most marked when Vaishyas and Sudras are members of group I and Brahmins and Kshatriyas are members of group III. One-third of the Brahmins and Kshatriyas in the sample were classified as lower class, and their low social status is readily acknowledged in the Negro community. However, although their status is low, these Brahmins usually receive favorable treatment by their class superiors in the Hindu community and are respected at religious ceremonies. The status and roles ascribed to low-class Brahmins or high-class non-Brahmins clearly depend upon the racial or religious group with which they associate, and if it is the Hindu group, then on the secular or religious nature of the context.

Within the Hindu community caste is a social attribute in its own right. Consequently, caste can be set in the social balance against class when an individual's social status is being defined. Occupation and wealth determine a Hindu's social status in secular affairs, and caste either adds to it or detracts from it. It is therefore possible, though rare, to find high-class Chamars who are important members of the community. Examples drawn from the composition of friend-ship lists illustrate the relationship between caste and class in determining social patterns among the Hindus.

Friendships are developed bilaterally through both caste and class structures, although class is usually more important. The Vaishyas who were recorded as members of group I (Table III) are accepted as friends and business associates by the high-class Brahmins in San Fernando. Similarly, a middle-class Brahmin and a middle-class Vaishya are close friends, while the same Vaishya is friendly with another Vaishya who is recorded in group I. Ties of friendship and occasionally of family link Brahmins of different but adjacent social classes. However, these relationships are most firm when the caste and class statuses of the individuals concerned are similar. In religious settings, caste is the most important factor. This point is particularly significant because the Hindu community is a religious group and religious services and events account for a large part of the social activities of its members. However, persons of low caste can, and frequently do, avoid caste by not attending public services and functions.

Class modifies caste in secular settings, while caste modifies class particularly, but not exclusively, in religious contexts. Only in the latter does "sanskritization" of behavior become more important than the acquisition of wealth as a method of achieving social mobility. This difference indicates the extent to which Hindus have accepted some of the socioeconomic values of Trinidad society. Nevertheless, the polarization of the high caste and class status of the Brahmins and the low caste and class status of the Chamars has reinforced the social importance of caste and varna. In San Fernando it is argued that the Brahmins have proved their superiority in the competitive field of business, while the Chamars have reached their own level. The wealth of the Brahmins has confirmed their long-established dominance, and failure to possess Brahminical status detracts from the rank of even high-class Hindus. Evidence of the importance of varna is provided by the attempts of some rich Hindus to claim Brahminical status by falsifying their caste.

Endogamy and Exogamy

Most authors who have written about caste in India are agreed that subcaste endogamy is one of the strongest characteristics of the system. In San Fernando, only 3 respondents, two Ahirs and one Chamar, mentioned their subcaste. The Ahirs belonged to the Goalban subcaste; the Chamar was a Jaisvara. All three claimed that their subcaste was the highest in their respective castes. This kind of claim suggests that there is an element of caste feeling and a desire to appear to be of a higher caste among some members of the Sudra and Vaishya varnas. However, the failure of over 98 per cent of the respondents to mention subcaste shows the extent to which caste has been "generalized." If caste endogamy exists in San Fernando, it can do so only at the caste level and not at the subcaste level.

Most East Indians marry endogamously, as do most Hindus. A high proportion of Hindu marriages are still, to a greater or lesser extent, arranged by parents, though usually with the children's consent. The caste into which 96 men and 96 women married[5] has been

<hr />

[5]There are four types of marital unions among Hindus in Trinidad: customary, legal, customary and legal, and common-law. Certain important factors which distinguish one form of marital union from the others should be made clear. *Customary* marriages, while generally recognized and accepted by the Hindu community, are not legally valid unless accompanied by registration. Conversely, when Hindus are married at a registry office, their unions are unaccompanied by religious rites and receive no customary sanction from the Hindu community, but are *legally* binding. *Customary and legal* marriages are recognized by the larger society and by the Hindu community, but only pandits who have been licensed as marriage officers can perform customary

set out in Table IV. Out of these 96 couples, exactly half married endogamously and half exogamously, and this fact helps to explain the imbalance of the sex ratio in the castes recorded in Table II. The frequency and caste range of exogamy differs very greatly among castes and among men and women of the same caste. The experience of the men is examined in detail.

Of the 24 Maharaj men, 15 married Maharaj women, 4 married Chattris, and 5 married Vaishyas. Of the 3 Gosain men, 2 married

TABLE IV. CASTE AND MARRIAGE IN SAN FERNANDO

Caste of Hindu Women	Caste of Hindu Men																		
	Gosaine	Maharaj	Chattri	Ahir	Baniya	Gadariya	Kahar	Kewat	Koiri	Kurmi	Lunia	Madrassi	Mallah	Nau	Teli	Vesh	Dusad	Chamar	Totals
Gosaine	1																		1
Maharaj	2	15										1			1				19
Chattri		4	12	2			2			1	1								22
Ahir		1	5				1			2	1	1			1				12
Baniya				1	1					1									3
Barhai						1				1									2
Gadariya		1																	1
Kahar		1																	1
Koiri									2										2
Kori														1					1
Kurmi		1	1	1	1			1	1	3									9
Lunia																	1		1
Mali										1									1
Nau		1							1										2
Sonar			1																1
Vesh															1				1
Dusad			2														3		5
Chamar			1	1	1								1				2	5	11
? Dass			1																1
Totals	3	24	15	13	3	1	3	1	4	9	2	2	1	1	3	0	6	5	96

weddings which are also lawful. Although the *common-law* union is widespread in the West Indies, it is a misnomer for it receives no legal sanction whatsoever. While common-law unions are distinguished from customary marriages by the Hindu community, the two are categorically similar in legal terms. Of the 96 unions examined in this paper, 43 per cent are both customary and legal, 21 per cent are customary, 17 per cent are legal, and 19 per cent are common law. All are treated as marital unions.

out of caste, but to Maharaj women in both instances. Of the 15 Chattri men, 12 married endogamously and 3 exogamously, 2 to Vaishyas and 1 to a Chamar. Caste exogamy is particularly high among the castes of the Vaishya varna, 31 men out of the 43 having married out of caste. Eight of the 13 Ahir men, 6 of the 9 Kurmis, and 2 of the 3 Baniyas married exogamously, as did all the men of the Gadariya, Kahar, Kewat, Mallah, Lunia, Teli, Nau, and Madrassi castes. Although village and town exogamy are usually practised in Trinidad, the small size of the last 8 castes and the absence of strong caste feeling among the castes of the Vaishya varna probably accounts for this high rate of exogamy. While 3 of the 6 Dusads married endogamously, the highest record for caste endogamy was found among the Chamar men. Not one of the 5 had taken a non-Chamar spouse. The nearest approach to orthodox caste endogamy occurred in the Maharaj, Chattri, and Chamar castes. The polarization of caste is again remarkable. No Maharaj has taken a Chamar bride, and no Chamar has received a non-Chamar bride.

It has already been demonstrated that varna closely approximates class in San Fernando, and that it provides a valuable frame for analyzing caste status. In fact, the ranking of castes in the varna system is more important for most Hindus than caste as such. This is clearly shown by the fact that while 47 of the 96 Hindu unions that have been analyzed are caste endogamous, 70 are varna endogamous and only 26 varna exogamous (Table V). Of the 27 Brahmin men, 9 married out of varna ; 4 married Kshatriyas and 5 married Vaishyas. Not a single Brahmin married a Sudra woman. Of the 15 Kshatriyas, 12 married endogamously and only 3 exogamously, 2 to Vaishyas and 1 to a Sudra. No Kshatriya man married a Brahmin woman. The most interesting aspect of varna endogamy in San Fernando occurs among the Vaishyas. Although caste exogamy is high among the Vaishyas, varna exogamy is not. Only 13 of the 43 Vaishyas married out of varna, 6 to Kshatriyas, 2 to Brahmins, and 5 to Sudras, and this exogamy again illustrates the median position of the varna. Out of the 11 Sudra males, 10 married endogamously and only 1 exogamously, to a Vaishya. Of the Brahmins, 33 per cent married out of varna, as did 20 per cent of the Kshatriyas, 30 per cent of the Vaishyas, and 9 per cent of the Sudras. The fact that varna exogamy occurs more than twice as frequently between adjacent varnas (18 examples) as between nonadjacent varnas (8 examples) provides independent confirmation of the hierarchical ordering of the varnas.

Using the four varnas as a yardstick, it is possible to measure the relative frequency of hypergamy and hypogamy among the Hindus in San Fernando. Out of the 26 cases of exogamy there are 17 of hypergamy and 9 of hypogamy (Table V). There are almost twice as many cases of women as of men marrying into varnas higher than their own. Furthermore, the caste range of hypergamous unions is greater than for hypogamous ones. No Kshatriya man married into the Brahmin varna, but 4 Kshatriya women did. Two Vaishya men married Brahmins, but 5 women did. No Sudra man married a Kshatriya, but 1 woman did. One Sudra married a Vaishya, but 5 women did. The only varna which did not accept a Sudra woman in a marital union was a Brahmin. With the exception that 6 Vaishya men and only 2 Vaishya women married into the Kshatriya varna, women of lower varnas have been able to enter unions with higher-varna mates far more frequently and more easily than have men. There are two cases of hypergamy within both the Brahmin and Sudra varnas to confirm this point.

TABLE V. THE PATTERN OF VARNA ENDOGAMY AND EXOGAMY IN SAN FERNANDO

Varna of Males	Varna of Females				Total
	Brahmin	Kshatriya	Vaishya	Sudra	
Brahmin	18	4	5	0	27
Kshatriya	0	12	2	1	15
Vaishya	2	6	30	5	43
Sudra	0	0	1	10	11
Total	20	22	38	16	96

The frequency of hypergamy, 17 cases out of 96 unions, is not particularly high. But the reason why it plays such a large part in varna exogamy can be explained by the fact that Hindu children, at least in San Fernando, inherit caste patrilineally.[6] There was no example in the sample of a person adopting his or her mother's caste.

---

[6]The Niehoffs report that children inherit the caste of the parent with the higher caste. See the Juanita Niehoffs' report (1960: 98).

This fact does not, of course, rule out the possibility that some Hindus may attempt to adopt their mother's caste if it is higher than that of their father and is particularly prestigious. Because of caste pride and a feeling of superiority, Brahmin fathers are reluctant to "down-caste" their daughter's children, and lower their own standing, by arranging hypogamous marriages, especially with Sudra boys. The higher castes are much less likely to object to unions with lower-caste girls, especially if they are light-skinned, beautiful, wealthy, or have had a secondary-school education. However, the possession of outstanding qualities and the membership of a high social class also modifies the attitude of Brahmins towards boys of lower castes. In the south of Trinidad a pandit recently married his daughter to a Chattri boy whom he favored because the boy was well-placed financially and had a fair skin. Nevertheless, the caste into which a wife was born can very easily be concealed by a husband's high-caste surname, and this undoubtedly facilitates hypergamy among the Brahmins and Kshatriyas.

In an attempt to obtain further information about the attitude of Hindus toward caste endogamy and exogamy, the 149 respondents in the survey were asked to agree or disagree with the statement, "People of different nations (castes) should not marry each other." The replies have been scaled against each caste and are given in Table VI. Out of the 128 respondents whose caste was known, only 34, or 27 per cent, were in agreement with the principle of caste endogamy. Of these 34, 28 were representatives of only 5 castes, the Maharaj, Chattri, Ahir, Baniya, and Kurmi. Only one Sudra, a Dusad, agreed with the statement. It is impossible to say whether this represents a breakdown of caste feeling or whether it is simply lip service to egalitarian principles. Only 41 of the 94 respondents who disagreed with the statement had married out of caste themselves, but the discrepancy between theory and practice may be due partly to the fact that marriages are still arranged and tend to reflect the parents' rather than the child's views about caste. One important point is that 16 of the 34 respondents who agreed with the statement and favored caste endogamy had, in fact, married exogamously. It is possible that exogamy is used as an explanation, or an excuse, for an unsatisfactory marriage. The fact that 40 per cent of the Brahmins, 25 per cent of the Kshatriyas, and 23 per cent of the Vaishyas stated that they favored caste endogamy undoubtedly provides a basis for the practice

TABLE VI. RESPONSES TO THE STATEMENT "PEOPLE OF DIFFERENT NATIONS
(CASTES) SHOULD NOT MARRY EACH OTHER," TAKEN FROM THE
SAMPLE SURVEY IN SAN FERNANDO

Caste of Respondent	Agree	Disagree
Gosain	0	2
Maharaj	14	21
Chattri	6	18
Ahir	4	20
Baniya	2	1
Gadariya	0	1
Jaiswal	1	0
Kahar	1	1
Kewat	0	1
Koiri	1	3
Kurmi	2	6
Lunia	1	2
Madrassi	0	1
Mallah	0	1
Nau	0	1
Patitar	0	1
Teli	0	2
Vesh	1	2
Dusad	1	5
Seunerine	0	1
Chamar	0	4
Total	34	94

of caste and varna endogamy, and suggests that caste matters a good deal more than most Hindus normally admit. The pejorative use of the terms *Kujat,* which means "outcaste," and *varanshankar,* which means "marrying outside the varnas of the twice-born," also indicate that exogamy, and especially varna exogamy, is not highly valued. A Chattri laborer who lives in Kakatwey expressed the conservative view in uncompromising terms: "Everybody should marry their own nation."

The high proportion of varna endogamy in San Fernando (73 per cent) compared with the varna endogamy which Schwartz (1964) has reported for the Trinidad village of "Boodram" (47 per cent), is partly to be explained by the larger size of the high varnas in San Fernando, the strength of their conservative views, and the inability of the Sudra to overcome prejudice against them. But above

all, varna endogamy has been reinforced by the high correlation between varna and class. Only one of the 26 males who married out of
varna belonged to social group I, and he was a Brahmin (Table VII).

TABLE VII. VARNA EXOGAMY FOR MALES BY CLASS, SAN FERNANDO

Varna	Social Group		
	I	II	III
Brahmin	1	3	5
Kshatriya	0	0	3
Vaishya	0	2	11
Sudra	0	0	1
Total	1	5	20

Five males belonging to social group II married out of varna; 3 were
Brahmins and 2 were Vaishyas. But 20 of the 26 males who married
out of varna belonged to group III and 5 were Brahmins, 3 Kshatriyas, 11 Vaishyas, and 1 a Sudra. Low-class status has frequently
been the common denominator where varna exogamy has occurred,
and high-class status has been an important basis for endogamy in the
two highest varnas. Class is frequently the common denominator in
hypergamous and hypogamous unions, and class endogamy is probably higher even than varna endogamy. The high degree of accordance between varna and class helps to explain why varna exogamy is
less frequent than caste exogamy. Nevertheless, most unions are both
class endogamous and varna endogamous, as were all the marriages
witnessed by the writer. No case was encountered of a low-class
Brahmin boy marrying a wealthy low-caste girl, although caste and
class may be traded in this way.

There is a tendency also for varna exogamous unions to be
associated with conditions of cultural breakdown, and this situation
obtains particularly among the lower class. The common-law union,
or consensual cohabitation, occurs in only 19 per cent of the unions
that have been analyzed. But one-third of these common-law unions
involve varna exogamy, and most of them are hypergamous. Among
Hindus, the common-law union is most frequent when parents either
object to a marriage, or when they or their children are either too
poor or too indifferent to their dharma (religious duty) or to society

to contract a religious or legal union. The case of hypogamy between the Teli and Brahmin woman (Table IV) results from the break down of the orthodox method of contracting marriages. The woman had been involved in a common-law union before she married the Teli in a legal, noncustomary ceremony. Change in one institution is frequently linked with change in another institution in this way.

Caste endogamy is not the basis of even an atrophied caste system in San Fernando. But varna endogamy or marriage between "approximately equal" castes both reflects and reinforces the social hierarchy of caste. However, it seems very much as though caste exogamy has increased during the last half-century. If the age of individual respondents is omitted and they are grouped as the "present generation" while their parents are grouped as the "preceding generation," it is found that the rate of caste exogamy is 50 per cent for the "present generation"; among the "preceding generation" the rate is 20.5 per cent and 15 per cent on the male and female sides respectively. Some of the endogamy attributed to the "preceding generation" may result from children's lack of knowledge about their mother's caste and from their assumption that it was the same as their father's. Furthermore, the increase in exogamy possibly reflects the urbanization of the "present generation," although it seems that this is not important. A similar pattern of change can be established for varna exogamy, the frequency of which is 27 per cent in the "present generation," compared to 12.5 per cent and 7.2 per cent in the "preceding generation" on the male and female sides respectively. The increase in caste and varna exogamy during the period covered by these "generations" probably indicates the extent to which class has successfully competed with caste as a determinant of social status among Hindus.

The great increase in varna exogamy between these "generations" has been due to hypergamy, and this has occurred when caste and class statuses are in opposition; in particular, it has involved low-class Vaishyas and Sudras. Hypergamy has not, however, provided a method whereby the varna "ladder" can be slowly scaled by members of the lower varnas. In the past, hypergamy has been characterized by one upward "jump" into a higher varna; the same is true in the history of the "present generation." But caste exogamy in the "preceding generation" does seem to facilitate caste exogamy in the "present generation." Out of the 96 men who have married and whose caste is known, 27 had fathers who married out of caste. According to the sample survey, at least 19 sons of these 27 fathers also contracted exogamous unions, and these 19 men were involved in 39 per cent of the exogamous unions in the "present generation." Marriage out of caste will continue in spite of the practice of village and town exogamy. Varna endogamy, however, will also continue in San Fernando as long as caste is valued as a pedigree and varna is in partial harmony with class.

Religion and the Priesthood

Brahmin control over the priesthood and the role of Brahminism in religion provide the best examples of the importance of caste in San Fernando. Recruitment to the priesthood of the orthodox Sanatan Dharma is controlled by the Pandits' Council of Trinidad and Tobago. About 500 pandits are members of the Council, and probably all are Brahmins. Both of the practising Sanatanist pandits who live in San Fernando are Brahmins. One, it is interesting to note, has a second wife who is an Ahir. No Brahmin pandit will teach the ritual of the puja (religious ceremony) to a non-Brahmin, and a non-Brahmin would find it impossible to obtain membership in the Pandits' Council. Unless he is recommended to the government by the Council, a pandit cannot become a licensed marriage officer. In 1961, a Sadhu from San Fernando, who has been given the pseudonym Goberdhan, attempted to prove before a specially constituted examining board that he was the son of a Brahmin father. The meeting was public, and was held in a cinema in a village just outside the town. The meeting was not a panchayat. Goberdhan did not succeed in his venture, but he nevertheless continues with his religious and magical work and is frequently mentioned in the Trinidad newspapers. It is significant that a meeting which resembled a panchayat was held recently, that it involved a public request for the recognition of Brahmin status, and that although Goberdhan lost his case, he has continued to work without any sanctions being taken against him. Goberdhan does not, however, officiate at public Sanatanist rites.

Caste is important in certain other religious contexts. The concepts of purity and pollution have largely disappeared from secular life, but they have been retained in an attenuated form in situations associated with ritual. It has been noted that priests raise their janeo over one ear when they have been temporarily polluted through self-contact, and that Sudras can become Vaishyas if they give up the polluting habit of pork eating. Furthermore, most Hindus refrain from eating flesh on the day when they are holding a private puja, although they may normally eat meat with the exceptions of beef and pork. The meal which accompanies the puja is always strictly vege-tarian. Commensality is normally practised at Hindu dinners, but some of the older and more conservative Brahmin pandits insist on being fed before, and separately from, the lower-caste people. Some Brahmins also raise objections when castes lower than "the twice-born," especially Chamars, and Muslims cook the food at Hindu weddings. These examples suggest that the idea of pollution is still attached to the preparation and serving of food at Hindu rituals, and that Brahmins, and pandits in particular, are most aware of it. The view is frequently expressed that "a Maharaj feels unhappy about cleanness in the home of a Chamar," but this probably refers more to hygiene than to purity in all but a religious context. Furthermore, some Hindus are still of the opinion that it is their religious duty to feed and give presents to Brahmins on the occasion of a family puja. One friend of the writer disapproved of this practice and always made a point of giving to a poor person any presents he received "because he was born the son of a Brahmin."

Hinduism is rapidly becoming "institutionalized," and corporate worship in the mandir is an important feature of the religion in San Fernando. The mandir is looked upon as a church, and is increasingly the center of Hindu activities. Since most members of the lower castes in San Fernando are not interested in organized Hinduism, this devel-opment has enabled the Brahmins to increase their control over the religion. For several years before 1955 the leaders in the mandir were an Ahir and a Chattri, but neither is involved with the Todd Street mandir which replaced their older building.

Brahmins are interested in filling leadership roles in the mandir and they donated most of the capital for the building and subsequent renovation of the Todd Street mandir, which was reopened in 1961. They provide most of the support for the organizations associated with the mandir and they account for at least 80 per cent of the congregation of 40 or 50 when the Sandhya Puja is held on Sunday mornings. Brahmin women hold all the offices in the Stri Sevak Sabha, a women's organization which arranges services in the mandir. Most of the members of the Sabha are Brahmins and Kshatriyas. On the occasion of Jhanam Astamie in 1964, the anniversary of the birth of Lord Krishna, a religious celebration in the form of a "show" was organized in the mandir. At least 80 per cent of the children who took part were Brahmin or Kshatriya. The activities of the mandir have provided an opportunity for the less wealthy Brahmins to exercise leadership roles. In the mandir they are given respect as Brahmins and are considered in the councils of the wealthier Maharajs. In this way, caste modifies class and makes it relatively easy for poorer Brahmins to have access to the social circles of the rich ones.

Until the end of 1963, the Brahmins maintained at least nominal control over the Gandhi Service League, an organization in which the running of the mandir is vested. At that time the president and treasurer were both wealthy Brahmins, but the secretary was a fair-skinned Chamar. Early in 1964, the Chamar, whose pseudonym is Nanan, was elected president. It is generally agreed among the Hindus that Nanan (who is a civil servant) is an able organizer, that the idea of building the new temple and starting the Gandhi Service League were both his, and that as secretary he had been in virtual control of the organization for several years. It is also common knowledge that the Gandhi Service League has done very little practical work in the community, that Nanan is a supporter of the Negro-dominated government, and that in the hope of receiving honors, he uses his apparent leadership of the Hindus to persuade the government that his political services are valuable to them. Although Nanan is a Chamar, he is one of the most able and best known members of the Hindu upper class. In theory, as a high-class member of a low caste, Nanan should mix less with Hindus than with members of the Negro community, who should accept him for his class status alone. In practice, Negroes and East Indians are mutually hostile, and Nanan's political standing depends on the support he gets, or appears to get, from Hindus. Nevertheless, Nanan mixes more widely in Negro circles than almost any other Hindu, and the functions with which he is associated are among the few multiracial events to be held in San Fernando. Because of this, he is despised by some of the

Hindus who complain that he is using them for political purposes. A middle-class Brahmin told the writer that Nanan was "a Chamar who does Chamar work." One or two of the Brahmins who are associated with Nanan are also known to be supporters of the government political party. However, they are not called Chamars. It is typical of the caste situation in San Fernando that Brahmins should be excused their faults, while even the high-class members of the low castes are upbraided for any misdemeanor.

The Brahmins are the most "Eastern" and "Western" of Hindus. The rich ones hold expensive weddings and own big American cars, and almost all of them hope, as do most East Indians, that their children will obtain higher education and remunerative jobs in the professions, commerce, and government. It is hardly surprising that very few young Brahmins are training for the priesthood. It is not essential for Brahmin pandits to be full-time priests. The writer knew one Brahmin who was a sugar chemist by profession and a part-time priest by inclination. However, all pandits have to be trained, and one of the wealthiest Brahmins in San Fernando has proposed that he should build a small seminary on his property so that young Brahmins can be educated in the philosophy of their dharam and the ritual of the puja. This scheme has been attacked by some non-Brahmin Hindus on the grounds that it represents a retrenchment to Brahminism. They welcome the proposal to set up a theological school, but argue that it should be open to interested youths of all castes. One man who is of this opinion is a middle-class Ahir who will be called Bisram. Bisram represents the views of the younger generation of non-Brahmins. In his opinion, the Brahmin pandits have used their position to make money from the Hindus; they have not taught the people about their religion; in fact, it has been in their interest to keep the people ignorant and superstitious. Bisram asks the questions: "Can't caste be achieved during a man's lifetime? Why should caste depend on a man's actions in his previous incarnation?" He argues that Hinduism needs rejuvenating, and that the Hindus cannot afford to allow energetic and earnest young non-Brahmins to be excluded from the priesthood.

Bisram is the head of a religious organization which he founded several years ago. It functions in several villages near San Fernando. Bisram also conducts the Sunday morning service in the San Fernando mandir, and has done so for the last two years, since one of the Brahmin pandits withdrew. The other Sanatanist pandit in town has made several attempts to stimulate Brahmin antagonism to Bisram, but without success. The Brahmins know that they cannot replace Bisram. On the other hand, Bisram's usefulness to them has enabled him to begin to penetrate the exclusive circle of Maharajs in San Fernando. In this he has been helped by the fact that his closest friend is a middle-class Brahmin who is interested in constructive religious work. However, Bisram is a strong character in his own right, and his behavior is impeccably Brahmin. He is a vegetarian and neither smokes nor drinks alcohol. Not only must he live like a Brahmin, but he must be seen to live like a Brahmin. Bisram has made a great impression on some of the Maharajs during the last year. But in spite of his conduct, his fluency in Hindi, and his knowledge of the Hindu scriptures, it is very unlikely that he will be given the office, or accorded the status of "pandit." Because Bisram has "sanskritized" his behavior and values, and lives more like a Brahmin than most Brahmins, he is respected as a good Hindu. But the final cachet of Brahminical status will be withheld from him because he was born a Vaishya.

Conclusion

The caste system has broken down in San Fernando, but some social, marital, and religious implications of caste persist. The concepts of purity and pollution have almost disappeared, and so, consequently, have the links between occupation and caste. However, purity is important at religious rituals, and the feeling still prevails that Chamars have unhygienic habits. Caste is partly mutable in secular life, and affects the individual and the family, but rarely a larger group. Castes are not internally organized and (except among some members of the Brahmin and Kshatriya varnas) are not characterized by exclusive cultures. Furthermore, some Hindus genuinely do not know what their caste is. Caste, therefore, does not affect all Hindus, and some Hindus, middle-class Vaishyas in particular, claim that it is of no importance to them. But caste is equated with prestige, and through varna is closely associated with class. In fact, while caste is less important than class or wealth as a determinant of social status, it still affects Hindus who are located at the extremities of the caste scale and ambitious Hindus who aspire to religious and political leadership in the community. Caste, however, affects only the small Hindu population, and although it may be felt in a residual form by some East Indian Presbyterians, it does not help to define the social stratification of the town as a whole.

Caste does not seem to have been especially eroded in the industrial, multiracial, and multireligious environment of San Fernando. The growth of the number of Hindus in the town through natural increase and migration has probably been slightly reduced through conversion to Christianity, but because some Hindu values have been retained in the family and in religion, the strength of what remains of caste is almost as great in San Fernando as anywhere else in Trinidad. In fact, Brahminism is probably stronger in San Fernando than elsewhere ; this strength may be attributed to the high proportion of Brahmins who live in the town. Caste values which are held by the family still influence varna endogamy and, to a lesser extent, caste endogamy. But since varna and class patterns are similar, varna endogamy may largely be attributed to class endogamy. Caste and varna exogamy and hypergamy have increased during the last half-century; the two highest varnas will remain relatively immune to intermarriage only as long as caste pride and parental control over marriage persist and caste and class statuses are fairly similar. However, the fact that a distinguished Brahmin who lives near San Fernando was recently approached by a married non-Brahmin woman with a view to his fathering a high-caste child for her, shows that caste consciousness is still strong.

The social and ritual dominance of the Brahmins have proved mutually reinforcing, and their leadership is widely accepted in the Hindu community. The orthodox Hindu priesthood is exclusively Brahmin and Brahmins control the affairs of the mandir. The only non-Brahmins who have challenged the leadership of the Brahmins in these fields are an intelligent Ahir and an able Chamar. The greater success of the Chamar may be explained by his social and political importance and by the fact that his interests are primarily secular, not religious. Caste modifies class, but class may also modify caste in this way. The operation of caste is most effective in the context of religious affairs, where the force of caste is brought to bear against ambitious non-Brahmins. The failure of the Sadhu Goberdhan to attain the rank of Brahmin contrasts with the success of the rich Kshatriya, and shows that mutability of caste is easier to effect in secular than in religious contexts.

In the wider field of Trinidad society, caste is of little importance. Most Negroes know nothing about caste, and the few who do assume that all East Indians are of low-caste origin. However, the Hindu community is highly segregated and ethnocentric. For almost a decade, between 1950 and 1960, there was a close link between the Hindu religious organization, the Sanatan Dharam Maha Sabha, and the Democratic Labour Party and its forerunner. The Democratic Labour Party, the opposition party in the House of Representatives, still draws most of its support from the Hindu population. The leader, deputy leader, and almost all the senior members of this party who sit in the House of Representatives are of Brahmin origin. It is therefore significant that the Chamar Nanan has aligned himself politically with the Negro government party and that he has done so partly because he was excluded on the grounds of caste from office in the Sanatan Dharam Maha Sabha. Even at the national level, and in its attenuated state, caste has a part to play as an expression of Hindu values. The situation has certainly not been reached in Trinidad, as it has in parts of India, where membership of the Brahmin varna can be a positive disadvantage.

REFERENCES

BENEDICT, BURTON
1961   *Indians in a plural society.* London: H.M.S.O.

CENTRAL STATISTICAL OFFICE
1963   Population Census 1960. Vol. II, Parts A and B. Port-of-Spain: Government Printing Office.

COMINS, D. W. D.
1892   *Note on the abolition of the return passage.* Calcutta: Bengal Secretariat Press.

CROOKE, W.
1896   *Tribes and castes of the North-Western Provinces and Oudh.* 4 vols. Calcutta: Office of the Superintendent of Government Printing.

1897   *The North-Western Provinces of India, their history, ethnology, and administration.* London: Methuen and Co.

CUMPSTON, I. M.
1953   *Indians overseas in British territories, 1834-1854.* London: Oxford University Press.

GILLION, K. L. O.
1956   "The sources of Indian emigration to Fiji." *Population Studies* X:2:139-157.

1962   *Fiji's Indian migrants.* Melbourne: Oxford University Press.

HUTTON, J. H.
1961   *Caste in India.* 3d ed. London: Oxford University Press. [1st ed. 1946, 2d ed. 1951, 4th ed. 1963]

JAYAWARDENA, CHANDRA
1963   *Conflict and solidarity in a Guianese plantation.* London: University of London Monographs in Social Anthropology No. 25.

KIRPALANI, MURLI J., MITRA G. SINANAN, S. M. RAMESHWAR, and L. F. SEUKERAN, EDS.
1945   *Indian centenary review, one hundred years of progress.* Port-of-Spain: Guardian Commercial Printing.

KLASS, MORTON
1961   *East Indians in Trinidad.* New York: Columbia University Press.

MARRIOTT, MCKIM
1960   "Social structure and change in a U.P. village," pp. 106-121 in *India's villages,* M. N. Srinivas, ed. London: Asia Publishing House.

MAYER, ADRIAN
1961   *Peasants in the Pacific.* Berkeley: University of California Press.

1963   *Indians in Fiji.* London: Oxford University Press.

MORTON, SARAH E., ED.
1916   *John Morton of Trinidad.* Toronto: Westminster Company.

NIEHOFF, A., and JUANITA NIEHOFF
1960   *East Indians in the West Indies.* Milwaukee: Milwaukee Public Museum Publications in Anthropology, No. 6.

RUBIN, VERA, ED.
1960   *Social and cultural pluralism in the Caribbean.* Annals of the New York Academy of Sciences, vol. 83, art. 5.

SCHWARTZ, BARTON M.
1964   "Caste and endogamy in Trinidad." *Southwestern Journal of Anthropology* 20:1:58-66.

SKINNER, E.
1955 *Ethnic interaction in a British Guiana rural community.* Unpublished
doctoral dissertation, Columbia University.

SMITH, M. G.
n.d. "A framework for Caribbean studies." In *Caribbean Affairs.* Jamaica: Extra-Mural Department, University of the West Indies.

SMITH, RAYMOND T.
1955 *A preliminary report on a study of selected groups of East Indians
in Jamaica.* Unpublished manuscript. Institute of Social and Economic Research, University of the West Indies.

1960 "Some social characteristics of Indian immigrants to British Guiana."
Population Studies XIII:34-39.

1962 *British Guiana.* Toronto, New York, London: Oxford University
Press.

SMITH, RAYMOND T., and CHANDRA JAYAWARDENA
1958 "Hindu marriage customs in British Guiana." *Social and Economic
Studies* 7:2:178-194.

1959 "Marriage and family amongst East Indians in British Guiana."
Social and Economic Studies 8:4:321-376.

SRINIVAS, M. N.
1952 *Religion and society among the Coorgs of South India.* Oxford:
Clarendon Press.

SRINIVAS, M. N., Y. B. DAMLE, S. SHAHANI, and A. BETEILLE
1959 "Caste, A trend report and bibliography." *Current Sociology* VIII:
3:135-156.

ZINKIN, T.
1962 *Caste today.* Oxford: Oxford University Press.

SURINAM

The Caste System and the Hindustani Group in Surinam

JOHAN D. SPECKMANN

In dealing with the problem of the extent to which the Indian caste system still exists among the Hindustani immigrants[1] in Surinam, it is necessary to elaborate the concept of "caste."

The phenomenon "caste" should first of all be viewed against the background of Hinduism, because Hinduism gives this system of stratification its social justification and specific character. In the words of Bergel (1962: 38-39):

> The three main features of Hindu religion are samsara, dharma, and karma, or in approximate Western equivalents reincarnation, correct ritual behavior, and causality. Reincarnation, the concept of being reborn after death, is, of course, no monopoly of Hinduistic creeds, but in Hinduism it has become the central theme beside which every-

---

[1] We are speaking here, naturally, about the Hindus. They make up the largest group in the Hindustani community in Surinam. Only about 20 per cent belong to Islam.

thing else becomes insignificant. The world is conceived of as an incessant process of transmigrations. Man is not created by any god; his soul has eternally existed and will eternally continue to exist. Death is not the end but a change to another life. Whether the next life will be better or worse depends solely on man himself. Neither faith nor prayer nor sacrifice, not even Brahmans, can help him, because the gods are powerless to influence man's destiny in future reincarnations. The real force is karma. Like our own notion of causality, it is thought of as an impersonal force, but with a peculiar twist. No divinity bestows awards or inflicts penalties; the retributory agent is karma, but its effects become manifest only in the next life, or more precisely, in the *status* of man in his next life. But karma functions as an automaton. Its effects depend on dharma. The term "dharma" indicates something like correct behavior in carrying out religious obligations, but in a rather anomalous way. Ordinarily, religious obligations are conceived either in terms of a moral code or as ritual duties. The moral obligations of Hinduism are similar to those of all advanced civilizations, but their observance has little bearing on dharma. Hinduism also knows very elaborate rituals, but again the meaning of dharma has very little to do with the performance of rituals. The main exception is the sacredness of the cow (including, at least for some castes, abstention from eating meat). Dharma consists mainly of two things: to respect the Brahmans and to fulfill the specific duties of one's own caste. Strictly speaking, there is not one dharma, but every caste has a different dharma of its own. But all forms of dharma have in common the supreme commandment that man must accept and live the life of the caste into which he has been born. If he neglects this obligation, he will be punished by being reborn into a lower caste; if he observes his dharma, his reward is rebirth into a higher caste. His future fate can thus be very bright or very dire. To use Max Weber's favorite example: it depends *only* on a person's behavior whether he will be reborn as a god or as a worm in the intestines of a dog. In the West the wages of sin is death; in Hinduism the wages of sin is life—in a lower caste. In other words, man is his own and sole savior.

The religious system indicates to the Hindu his relation to and place in the cosmos. The caste system is, as it were, a spectrum of that cosmos.

Pohlman (1951) has made a comparative study of the criteria for the caste system applied by more than thirty sociologists and anthropologists. He thinks one can speak of a consensus among these writers in relation to three characteristics: vertical immobility; endogamy; rigid isolation.

According to Pohlman, even with regard to these three characteristics many deviant cases are found in practice. It is difficult to give a clear definition of the concept of caste because the system always exhibits tension and incongruency between the precepts and reality. He writes (1951: 379):

> . . . commentators generally have assumed a conformity, throughout India's history, to either the Brahmanical precepts or to an academic ideal concept of caste, which apparently has not existed in actual practice.

Dumont, who has occupied himself greatly with the caste system, remarks (1961: 34) that all characteristics, that have been brought forward for the system, always have a single fundamental principle:

> . . . the opposition of pure and impure, an opposition of its nature hierarchical which implies separation and, on the professional level, specialisation of the occupations relevant to the opposition . . .

It is this principle that explains the precise regulation of the social contact between the castes. The prescriptions of purity in relation to food and the restrictions with regard to the consumption of meals with members of other castes are naturally connected with this. It is in this context that Hutton (1946: 62) remarks:

> Indeed, it seems possible that caste endogamy is more or less incidental to the taboo on taking food cooked by a person of at any rate a lower, if not of any other, caste, and in the view of the writer this taboo is probably the keystone of the whole system.

The opposition pure-impure, which in its most extreme form is manifested in the contrast Brahmin-"outcaste," not only leads to social isolation of the different castes but also implies a complementary function. This complementarism finds its expression in the so-called jajmani system, in which there is a dominant caste of landowners in relation to whom the other castes occupy a serving and dependent position. In the jajmani system all castes stand in a reciprocal relationship of duties and obligations.

Although it is evident that every enumeration remains arbitrary, we venture to summarize the following characteristics of the Indian caste system in the following way:

1. The fundamental principle of the caste system is the opposition pure-impure. The Brahmins on the one hand and the so-called "untouchables" on the other form the two poles of this continuum.

2. The pattern of relations between the castes is strictly regulated and anchored in the so-called jajmani system, whereby every caste is functionally incorporated into the entire social system of the village.

3. The caste is often an endogamous group.

4. The caste system is characterized by a high degree of vertical immobility; the position of the individual on the social scale is fixed. It is true, however, that a caste as a whole can achieve a higher status in the system.

5. The caste is a corporate body; some castes recognize a national caste council with jurisdiction extending over the whole country.

6. Many castes have specific religious notions and distinct religious and social customs as well.

Taking these criteria as a point of departure we shall subject the situation of the Hindustanis in Surinam to closer examination.

The recruitment area of the Emigration Agent for Surinam was located mainly in the United Provinces and Bihar. The main depot was established in 1872 in Calcutta. The recruited indentured laborers for the plantations in Surinam were transported to this depot through the subdepots set up in Benares, Allahabad, Muttra, and Patna among other places. A survey of the entire process of recruitment and care of the prospective emigrants indicates that the authorities were not very much concerned with caste. On board the emigrant ships the condition was even more difficult. The strict limitation of social contact between the castes, including such taboos as the ban on eating together or partaking of the same food, could not possibly be maintained. Very significant in this connection is the statement of an old Hindustani immigrant to Fiji, recorded by Mayer (1961: 157-158):

> One old woman told how she had set sail from Calcutta, and all on board had started to cook dinner, each caste with its own hearth. Suddenly a wave rocked the ship, and all the cauldrons of food over-

turned on to the deck together. It was a choice of eating food which had been mixed and so polluted, or of going hungry.

The first ship with indentured laborers from India arrived in Surinam on June 5, 1873. In that year five ships with a total of 2,449 immigrants, comprising 1,503 men, 556 women, and 390 children, were brought to Surinam. Due to a shortage of laborers on the plantations of Surinam, created by the abolition of slavery in 1863, the Hindustani indentured laborers were enthusiastically welcomed by both the Surinam government and the planters. Soon it became apparent, however, that the first transports did not come up to expectations. The insertion of these workers into the organization of the plantation proved to be a complicated matter because of the lack of familiarity of the staff with the customs and language of the group. Furthermore, it appeared that the immigrants were not apt to do heavy field work. The number of cases of disease was excessively large. It turned out that several immigrants were suffering from syphilis, anaemia, and sores. The mortality rate rose so high among these first transports that the English consul in Paramaribo saw himself compelled to inform his government of the situation. As a result the British Indian government decided to suspend the emigration of laborers to Surinam. In 1878 this decision was rescinded.

The disorganization among the first groups was very great indeed. Not only did the adaptation to another climate involve difficulties, but in addition the social system of the plantation was strange to them. The old relationships to which they had been accustomed in India no longer functioned in the new society. Normal family life was not possible because the number of men was much larger than the quota of women among the indentured laborers. In this period of social disintegration, with all the consequent feelings of disappointment, confusion, and insecurity, expressions of collective resistance emerged. Only in the course of the year 1875 and after did the situation ameliorate. The mortality rates decreased as did the number of cases of disease.

Due to the conditions during the first years of immigration, the Hindustani indentured laborers did not have the opportunity to achieve a social and cultural reconstruction of the caste system known in India; a total or even partial restoration was out of the question. The staff on the plantations, consisting of Creoles and Europeans, did not take caste into consideration. Even though the caste which the immigrant claimed was recorded in a register during the disembarkation process, it is interesting to note that general opinion in Surinam considered the Hindustani immigrant to belong to the lowest castes in British India. The argument behind this is relatively simple. The high castes are in a favorable social position, and because of this the urge to emigrate would not be particularly great among these groups. The low castes, on the other hand, are subjected to a discrimination that makes the mind willing to look for other and better circumstances. De Klerk (1953: 103-108) has, in this connection, determined to which caste the various immigrants from four ships with indentured laborers that arrived in Paramaribo belonged. He has compared this result with the relative numerical strengths of the castes in the population of the United Provinces, based on the census of 1931. In doing so, he came to the conclusion that while there were differences between the two sets of figures, the low castes in this contingent of immigrants were relatively no more numerous than in the mother country. For that matter, as long ago as 1896, Grierson carried out a similar sampling. The results (1896: 36) were:

> Two-thirds of the Hindus recruited belonged to castes of higher and medium social position, only one-third can be considered of decidedly low social position.

None of the above-mentioned characteristics of the Indian caste system could be found in the social structure of the first groups of Hindustanis in Surinam. Endogamy was impossible because of the great shortage of women; the number of women in the various transports was never more than fifty per cent of the number of men. Nothing remained of a social-economic interdependence of the castes; all the Hindustanis were field workers in the new country. The corporate character of the caste was also lost in Surinam. The indentured laborers left India as individuals and on the plantations they could find relatively few members of their own caste. The extensive prescriptions in relation to food and the contact with others could naturally not be maintained. De Klerk (1953: 172) describes the situation thus:

> The exceptional situation, to which, according to Manu, the *apād*

dharmāh—the rules of conduct in time of emergency—applied, has become the normal situation in Surinam.

The circumstances were not much different in the neighboring country of British Guiana. Jayawardena (1960: 67) writes thus:

> . . . managers did not give the caste hierarchy the consideration necessary to maintain it as a system. They divided the coolies into gangs, made them work next to each other, and appointed persons to positions of authority irrespective of caste. Coolies were housed cheek by jowl, in long barracks, and accommodated together in the hospital. They shared the same water supply, bathed in the same canal, and used the same latrine.

The first period, characterized to a large extent by anomie, was followed by a restoration. The group became more or less accustomed to the new living conditions and slowly tried to achieve a social and cultural reconstruction. It is evident that in this process the immigrants referred mainly to their country of origin. They tried to restore the well-known customs of India, as far as this was possible. The mother country also remained a reference group due to the regular arrival of new indentured laborers from India. The immigration was not completely stopped until 1916.[2]

Whereas the Negro slaves were forced to adapt themselves to Western values and norms, this requirement was hardly the case with the Hindustani group. First, the period on the plantation was of relatively short duration; the indentured laborer committed himself for a period of five years. Second, the prospect of a free voyage back to India imbued the stay in Surinam with a conditional character. Moreover, the attitude of the Creole population in regard to the Hindustani immigrants was generally negative; indentured labor was equated by the majority of the Surinamers with slave labor. The Hindustani group, therefore, continued to occupy a peripheral position in the society. It is understandable that under these circumstances the group showed very little inclination to adapt itself to the social system of the new land. This situation to a great extent further stimulated the orientation toward the mother country.

---

[2] In the period from 1873-1916 a total of 34,000 contract laborers were brought from India, of which approximately 30 per cent were repatriated.

The Brahmins present among the immigrants have played a very important role in this connection. Since they belonged to the local elite in India, they tried to restore the old customs and religious practices as much as possible. The restoration was necessarily undertaken in an improvising manner. It has been told that a Hindu priest performed a puja—a sacrificial ceremony—by reciting from an Indian railway timetable because there were no official religious texts available. The priests nevertheless succeeded in giving cult and ritual a place in the immigrant community. Because of these activities the priests regained, more or less, their traditional position as social and religious leaders. Based upon activities of this type, the elite of the Indian caste system formed themselves as a separate group again. As a consequence of this development the other immigrants came to determine their position in relation to the Brahmins, and in this way a new stratification system evolved. Life on the plantation, itself, did not give rise to status differentiation. All laborers performed a similar type of work and the staff consisted mainly of Creoles, especially during the initial stage of immigration. However, the new system of stratification was based mainly on criteria from the mother country; local status groups developed, deriving their prestige from their old caste affiliation. In this context, the crucial reference was not the caste proper (which did not always have a clear meaning for everyone in this "mixed" group), but to the varna to which a person belonged. Consequently, though the caste system did not survive the migration, the status differentiation in the new country was nevertheless founded on the basic pattern of the caste system in India.

It may be true that the division into four large groups—Brahmin, Kshatriya, Vaishya, and Sudra—is only of theoretical value in India, but it offers possibilities of reorientation in a situation where people from different parts of India are brought together. Stevenson (1953: 48), who otherwise attaches little value to the varna classification in an analysis of the caste system, remarks that:

> Srinivas (1952: 25) and Dube (personal communication), among modern Indian anthropologists, see in *varna* a classification which has value for the ordinary Hindu as a means of classifying status groups of regions other than his own in a broad relationship with those of his own area.

It is important to note that the opposition pure-impure, which is the basis of the Indian caste system, once again came to the fore.

Many Brahmins refused to assist the untouchables in their ritual obligations. Accordingly, the untouchables designated in Surinam as Charmars, have their own priests. As late as 1940, mention has still been made of a differentiation between Brahmins and the so-called "Chamar priests." The Indian caste system was reduced in the immigrant community to its two fundamental poles: Brahmins and Untouchables. The continuum in between had more or less disappeared.

The process of cultural and religious unification within the Hindustani community, resulting from (1) a common social position within the Surinam society and (2) continuation of the ideas of the higher caste groups ("Brahminizing" of the immigrant group as a whole), did lead finally to the acceptance of the Chamars. As the Hindustanis, in the course of their history in Surinam, were drawn into the social system of the society as a whole and as the group's social isolation was broken down (a development especially noticeable after 1940), the meaning of the internal stratification system decreased and a status differentiation based on education, profession, economic position, and political influence became important. For that matter, the supremacy of the Brahmins had already been challenged in 1930 by the rise of the Arya Samaj—a reform movement in Hinduism which, among other things, revolted against the caste system. With this development, the entire stratification pattern on the basis of varna affiliation came under fire. Nevertheless, varna consciousness continues to play a part even now. It is not uncommon for an informant to proudly remark that he is a Brahmin or that he belongs to the Kshatriyas. In the middle group, the Vaishyas, this consciousness is observed to a lesser extent. Even those people who, by virtue of their education and function in modern Surinam society, should have no need to derive status from their "caste," sometimes cannot resist the temptation to state that they belong to a high varna. Furthermore, the former distance with regard to the Chamars is still noticeable here and there. It has been told that a young Brahmin made the following remark about one of the members of his ethnic group: "He may have studied in the Netherlands and he may hold an important position here, he nevertheless remains a Chamar; you can always notice it by his way of life and his manners." In such cases, when one asks in what way these "Chamar characteristics" cleave to the person concerned, the most frequent answer given is: "A thing like that is in the blood." Similar reactions were obtained by Kuper in Natal. She reports such remarks as: "You know the group he comes from," or "The blood in him will show up" (1960: 37).

At times, importance is attached to the varna of the marriage candidate. This phenomenon is mainly apparent among the Brahmins and the Kshatriyas. However, this criterion is confused more and more with other considerations. Financial position, education, and profession play an increasingly important role in the selection of a marriage partner. On the other hand, the Brahmin father, when selecting a partner for one of his own children, will first of all limit his selection to his own "caste" group; marriage within the varna continues to enjoy a certain esteem in the community.

In our survey in Surinam during 1960 we tried to gauge the group's opinion of the significance of varna in choice of the marriage partner. The data based on a sample of 419 Hindustani household groups are given in Table I for the districts of Nickerie and Sara-

TABLE I. THE SIGNIFICANCE OF VARNA IN THE SELECTION OF MARRIAGE
PARTNERS ACCORDING TO RELIGION AND PLACE

Answer	Sanatan Dharma		Arya Samaj		Total	
	District	City	District	City	District	City
Marriage Partner for Children Must Be from Same Varna	29%	30%	3%	4%	25%	23%
Varna is Irrelevant in Choice of Marriage Partner	58	63	82	89	62	70
Other*	13	7	15	7	13	7
	100%	100%	100%	100%	100%	100%
	177	151	34	57	211	208

*In the category "Other" are included the reactions that corresponded to a middle position.

macca, and for the city of Paramaribo. Originally, a distinction was made between the demands of the parents in relation to boys and those applicable to Hindustani girls. It became apparent, however, that there was no significant difference between the results for the two groups; therefore, this differentiation has not been maintained. The table shows conclusively that even though a certain appreciation for the marriage within the varna exists (notably in the orthodox religious group of Hindus, the Sanatan Dharma), the majority no longer attaches importance to this criterion. Furthermore, it is interesting to note that there is no significant difference between the districts and the city regarding "caste" as a criterion in selecting a marriage partner.

Kuper reports from Natal that the Gujaratis still adhere to the caste system there. However, they did not, as did the other Hindustanis, come to South Africa as indentured laborers; rather they belonged to the category of free immigrants who undertook the voyage at their own cost. Based on a comparison of the Gujaratis with the other Hindu groups, Kuper comes to the conclusion (1960: 31) that the caste system survives migration only when the group satisfies the following conditions:

(1) can maintain a ritual exclusiveness from the time they leave India;

(2) hold a privileged position in the economic organisation and avoid proletarianisation;

(3) retain ties with a protected caste nucleus in India; and

(4) isolate their women from intimate cross-caste contact.

The Hindustani in Surinam could not satisfy these conditions. On the contrary, the common lot of the indentured laborers on the plantations, and later as small farmers, stimulated a sense of solidarity, which in many cases turned out to be stronger than the tendency toward segregation based on caste. One national Indian caste developed in Surinam to which all Hindustanis belonged. Within this group the differentiation based on varna and the distinction between the Hindus and the Moslems may be of some importance, but the Hindustanis often present themselves as a closed group to the outside world. The principle of caste endogamy, which could not be maintained for the caste proper, was now declared applicable to the entire Hindustani

212   JOHAN D. SPECKMANN

community. The ethnically mixed marriage is still rejected by the group.

Thomas writes in the framework of a consideration of Indian caste: "Pride of race and nobility of birth have still a fascination for Indians" (1956: 23). It can be said of the Hindustani in Surinam that these feelings of self-worth have shifted from the caste proper to the ethnic group as a whole. This development has, of course, important consequences for the acculturation process in the plural society of Surinam.

REFERENCES

BERGEL, E. E.
1962   *Social stratification.* New York: McGraw-Hill Book Co.
DUMONT, L.
1961   "Caste, racism and stratification." *Contributions to Indian Sociology* 5:20-43.
GRIERSON, G. A.
1896   *Report on colonial emigration.* Calcutta.
HUTTON, J. H.
1946   *Caste in India.* 1st ed. Cambridge: Cambridge University Press. [2d ed. 1951, 3d ed. 1961, 4th ed. 1963]
JAYAWARDENA, CHANDRA
1960   *Social structure of a sugar estate community in British Guiana with special reference to theories of social conflict and control.* Unpublished Ph. D. dissertation, University of London.
DE KLERK, C. J. M.
1953   *De Immigratie der Hindostanen in Suriname.* Amsterdam: Urbi.
KUPER, HILDA
1960   *Indian people in Natal.* Natal: Natal University Press.
MAYER, ADRIAN C.
1961   *Peasants in the Pacific: A study of Fiji Indian rural society.* Berkeley: University of California Press.
POHLMAN, E. W.
1951   "Evidence of disparity between the Hindu practice of caste and the ideal type." *American Sociological Review* 16:3:376-379.
STEVENSON, H. N. C.
1954   "Status evaluation in the Hindu caste system." *Journal of the Royal Anthropological Institute of Great Britain and Ireland* 84:45-65.
THOMAS, P.
1956   *Hindu religion, customs and manners.* Bombay: D. B. Taraporevala Sons.

FIJI

Caste and Endogamy in Fiji

BARTON M. SCHWARTZ

Patterns of marriage are frequently one of the several reliable indices which can be used to aid in ascertaining the degree to which particular social groups are perpetuated. While such patterns, in and of themselves, are never conclusive for measuring the effective structural and functional dimensions of a given social unit, they do provide certain insights into the differential degree of adherence by a community's members to a particular body of social prescriptions and proscriptions.

So it is with endogamous patterns of marriage and caste. While complete endogamy is not the equivalent of caste, it does indicate that at least one of the necessary criteria for perpetuating caste groups within the context of a caste system has been fulfilled. Endogamy is one of the mechanisms for achieving isolation and insulation of one caste vis à vis other castes, and as such, tends to reinforce the exclusiveness of each group while simultaneously contributing to the maintenance of the entire system. Similarly, the marital practices associated with a particular caste (or for that matter any other social unit) will reveal many of the more intimate contacts and relationships of its members, thereby suggesting the degree to which such individuals behaviorally subscribe to professed or ideal patterns of culture. In the case of Indians in Fiji, marital patterns not only demonstrate the degree of caste endogamy practised, but also provide some indication of the Indians' intimate contacts with members of non-Indian groups as well as among subgroups within the Indian community. Knowledge of such behavior is important in determining the actual social groups that the Indians recognize and the relative degree of importance attributed to each. As such, some idea of the contemporary values and attitudes of the Indians in Fiji is revealed, which in turn, aid in understanding: (1) the involvement of Indians in the general contemporary culture found in Fiji; and (2) the manner in which such involvement is contradictory to or compatible with the maintenance of traditional Indian culture in Fiji.

The information presented here constitutes the results of a survey investigation carried out among the rural Indian population in Fiji during February, 1965. No attempt was made to select a random sample of the population for this survey research, and the group of informants used is best described as constituting a scattered sample of the rural Indian population. One hundred respondents, each of whom are adult representatives of rural Indian households, were interviewed. The geographical extent of the survey encompasses the rural area west of Suva, the capital city of Fiji, continuing along the southern and western sections to the rural areas south of Nandi, the location of Fiji's international airport. None of the informants reside in towns included within the general area covered by the survey, and all respondents were selected from rural settlements only. Every effort was made to interview each informant either in his home or within the confines of his land holdings and to carry out the interview in the presence of other adult members of the informant's family. This intention was accomplished in most cases and proved to be valuable in two distinct ways. First, information which the respondent did not always remember was frequently supplied by the other adult members of the household. Second, the informant was less prone to deviate from actual facts in the presence of other household members than may have been the case had he been interviewed alone. Occasionally informants attempted to deviate in their response but were immediately corrected by other household members. In addition to this procedure for assuring reliability, an Indian aide and interpreter was present at each interview. His presence restricted individual informants from straying in their answers to the questions asked. The interviews were carried out in both Hindi and English, whichever was most applicable for each particular respondent.

Since the male is the traditional head of the Indian household and since he still retains a similar position in overseas Indian communities, most of the informants selected were men. However, it seemed desirable to include a small percentage of female respondents to ascertain whether or not any appreciable deviation based upon the criterion of sex could be isolated; none was detected. Distribution of the respondents by sex is given in Table I.

TABLE I. RESPONDENT BY SEX

Sex	Number
Male	86
Female	14
	100

Note: The ratio of males to females contained in this table is not intended to be indicative of the sex ratio for the total population.

The sample included India-born respondents. The proportion of these as opposed to Fiji-born informants is an approximate reflection of the numbers of each category found in the general rural Indian population.[1] The only exception to this is that no female respondents born in India are included in the sample. India-born females were contacted, but in each case their husbands or sons acted as informants. The exact distribution of the informants according to place of birth and sex is given in Table II.

TABLE II. RESPONDENTS' PLACE OF BIRTH

Birthplace	Male	Female	Total
Fiji	78	14	92
India	8	0	8
Total	86	14	100

---

[1] For more detailed analyses of the Indian population in Fiji, see McArthur 1958, Spate 1959, and Burns 1960.

To the extent that social action and cultural values differ among generations, the age of respondents is obviously an important factor which may bias the results of any interview survey similar to the one carried out. Consequently, the age of each informant was noted, and the age-distribution for all respondents is presented in Table III. This distribution compares favorably with the general age distribution of the Indian population in Fiji. Therefore, it is believed that the informant's age is not a factor which has biased the data in any significant manner, if at all. However, as will be shown later, the generational difference in values, attitudes and behavior, though not conclusive, remains an important consideration.

TABLE III. AGE DISTRIBUTION OF RESPONDENTS

Age Category	Number of Respondents
20-24	5
25-29	7
30-34	9
35-39	16
40-44	14
45-49	16
50-54	7
55-59	10
60-64	5
65-69	2
70-74	2
75-79	1
80-84	4
85-89	1
Unknown	1
Totals	100

In order to provide the reader with a summary chart of the relationship among the various criteria which characterize the sample population, Table IV combines the sex, place of birth, and age of all informants.

The total population represented by the 100 informants interviewed numbers 725, approximately 1 per cent of the total rural Indian population in Fiji. These 725 individuals are distributed in the household composition shown in Table V.

The relationship between age categories of informants and household composition (number of individuals in each household) is shown in Table VI. Table VI suggests what should be logically expected among this population: size of the household shows a general increase in accordance with the age of the head of the household

TABLE IV. AGE, SEX, AND PLACE OF BIRTH OF INFORMANTS

Age Category	Male	Female	Fiji-born	India-born
20-24	4	1	5	
25-29	3	4	7	
30-34	5	4	9	
35-39	12	4	16	
40-44	13	1	14	
45-49	16		16	
50-54	7		7	
55-59	10		10	
60-64	5		5	
65-69	2			2
70-74	2		1	1
75-79	1		1	
80-84	4			4
85-89	1			1
Unknown	1		1	
Totals	86	14	92	8

TABLE V. HOUSEHOLD COMPOSITION OF TOTAL SAMPLE POPULATION

Household Composition	Cases No.	Total Persons	
		No.	%
2	6	12	1.65
3	9	27	3.72
4	7	28	3.86
5	6	30	4.14
6	10	60	8.28
7	14	98	13.52
8	16	128	17.66
9	9	81	11.17
10	8	80	11.03
11	4	44	6.07
12	8	96	13.24
13	1	13	1.79
14	2	28	3.86
	100	725	99.99

Household Range: 2-14 individuals per household
Mean Composition: 7.25 individuals per household

TABLE VI. AGE CATEGORY AND HOUSEHOLD COMPOSITION OF INFORMANTS

Age Category	Household Composition													
	2	3	4	5	6	7	8	9	10	11	12	13	14	Totals
20-24	1	2	1	1										5
25-29	3			1	1		1	1						7
30-34	1		2	1	2	2		1						9
35-39		2	1	1	2	4	1	2	1	1		1		16
40-44	1	1			2	1	5	1	1	1	1			14
45-49	1	1	1	1	2	4	2		1	2		1		16
50-54						1	2	1	1		2			7
55-59	1	1	1			1	2	1	1		2			10
60-64	1					1	1		1		1			5
65-69					1				1					2
70-74						1				1				2
75-79	1													1
80-84					1	1			2					4
85-89	1													1
Unknown												1		1
Totals	6	9	7	6	10	14	16	9	8	4	8	1	2	100

until such time as the head of the household reaches old age, when the size of the household shows a general decrease. In cultural terms this sequence may be indicative of a repetitive cycle associated with the formation, dissolution, and subsequent reformation of the extended family organization.

Informants identified themselves by naming the following castes. The description of these castes was not given by the informants but was taken from the available literature, except where specified.

Ahir — Caste of cowherds, milkmen, and cattlebreeders (Russell 1916 II: 18).

Araiya — A subcaste of Telis in Bihar (Risley 1892 I: 22).

Bais — A trading caste of north Bhagalpur (Risley 1892 I: 51). Also possibly Vais, referring to a varna classification.

Bania — Occupational caste of bankers, money lenders, and dealers in grain, ghi (butter), groceries, and spices (Russell 1916 II: 111-112).

Barhi (Barhai) — The carpenter caste of Bihar (Risley 1892 I: 66).

Brahmin — The priestly caste of India (Russell 1916 II: 351).

Chamar	Tanners and menial laborers of north India (Russell 1916 II: 403).
Chattri	Local designation for Kshatriya.
Gareri	The shepherd, goat-herd and blanket-weaver caste of Bihar (Risley 1892 I: 271).
Gonda	A thar or sept of Mangars in Darjeeling (Risley 1892 I: 294). Mangars are described as one of the fighting tribes of Nepal (Risley 1892 II: 74).
Gawal	A gotra or section of Agarwals (Risley 1892 I: 275). Agarwals are described as a wealthy trading caste of Bihar and upper India (Risley 1892 I: 4).
Ghurki	A warrior and ruling group of Nepal.
Jalo	A title of Malos in Eastern Bengal (Risley 1892 I: 343). Malos are described as a Dravidian boating and fishing caste (Risley 1892 II: 64).
Jat	Cultivating caste of the Panjab (Russell 1916 III: 225).
Kahar	Palanquin bearers and watermen of northern India (Russell 1916 III: 291).
Kewat	Fishermen, boatmen, grain parchers, and cultivators, chiefly found in the Chhattisgarh districts of Drug, Raipur, and Bilaspur (Russell 1916 III: 422).
Koiri	Cultivating caste of Bihar and Chota Nagpur (Risley 1892 I: 500).
Kurmi	Cultivating caste of Hindustan (Russell 1916 IV: 55).
Kawar	A title of Chhatris (Chattri or Kshatriya) in Nepal (Risley 1892 I: 437).
Lunia	A synonym for Nunia (Risley 1892 II: 25). Nunia is described as a Dravidian caste of Bihar and Upper India engaged in cultivation, saltpeter making, and various kinds of earthwork (Risley 1892 II: 135).
Madrassi	Regional classification for an individual who comes from Madras in South India, or whose ancestors were shipped through Madras as indentured laborers.
Mali	Caste of vegetable and flower gardeners (Russell 1916 IV: 159).
Maraj	Local designation for a Brahmin caste.
Misra	A title of particular Brahmin groups in Bihar, Bengal, Orissa and Nepal (Risley 1892 II: 92-93).

Morai	Described by local informants as a caste of individuals whose traditional occupation was selling vegetables.
Nair	Possibly Naiar, a section of the Bahannajati subcaste of Khatris in Bengal (Risley 1892 II: 122); or Nayar, an aristocratic matrilineal caste of the Malabar coast whose traditional occupation is fighting (Hutton 1961: 289).
Nau	Local designation for an occupational caste of barbers (Russell 1916 IV: 262).
Nepali	Designation of an individual who comes from Nepal. May also refer to a subcaste of Brahmins in Nepal (Risley 1892 II: 132).
Pandit	A title given to a learned man. Locally is usually indicative of a Brahmin practising as a religious specialist, but not always.
Panjabi	An individual who comes from the Panjab.
Pasi	A Dravidian caste of Bihar, whose original occupation is believed to have been the tapping of the palmyra, date, and other palm trees for their sap (Risley 1892 II: 166).
Pile	Described by local informants as a caste of individuals engaged in cultivation.
Rajwar	A Dravidian cultivating caste of Bihar, western Bengal and Chota Nagpur (Risley 1892 II: 192).
Redas	Described by local informants as a caste of cultivators.
Rikhi	A section of Rajwars and Ruatias in Chota Nagpur (Risley 1892 II: 210).
Tamil	A linguistic and cultural category of south India.
Telegu	A linguistic and cultural category of south India.
Thakur	A landowning and martial caste of north India.

Some of the groups given by the respondents are not traditional caste groups found in India, but reflect regional, linguistic, religious, and subcaste categories. Nevertheless, such social categories are recognized as important in Fiji and with certain exceptions refer to a relationship similar to but not identical with traditional caste groups. Including these categories, endogamous and exogamous marriages in relation to caste occur in the proportions shown in Table VII.

TABLE VII. CASTE ENDOGAMY AND EXOGAMY

	Number of Cases	Per cent
Endogamy	45	44
Exogamy	41	40
Incomplete*	17	16
Totals	103†	100

*The category "Incomplete" refers to those cases where the caste of one or both of the spouses was not known.

†The total number of cases is increased by three (3) in this context because 3 of the respondents interviewed had been married more than once. There were two cases of polygyny and a single case of a widower remarrying.

In order to show the specific marital patterns that occur among each of the groups, the endogamous and exogamous marriages are given for each caste in Table VIII. In addition, exogamous marriages are further specified by showing the caste and the frequency with which they occur.

TABLE VIII. ENDOGAMY AND EXOGAMY BY SPECIFIC CASTE

Caste	Endogamy		Exogamy			
	No.	%	No.	%	Caste	Frequency
Ahir	11	34	21	66	Barhi	2
					Bania	1
					Brahmin	2
					Chamar	1
					Chattri	2
					Ghurki	1
					Kahar	1
					Kewat	1
					Koiri	1
					Kurmi	3
					Lunia	1
					Maraj	1
					Morai	1
					Nau	1
					Thakur	2
Araiya	1	100				
Bais	1	100				
Bania	1	20	4	80	Ahir	1
					Kurmi	1
					Pile	1
					Rajwar	1

[continued

Table VIII, continued]

Caste	Endogamy		Exogamy			
	No.	%	No.	%	Caste	Frequency
Barhi			2	100	Ahir	2
Brahmin	7	58	5	42	Ahir	2
					Chattri	2
					Mali	1
Chamar	2	50	2	50	Ahir	1
					Kurmi	1
Chattri	5	45	6	55	Ahir	2
					Brahmin	2
					Jat	1
					Nepali	1
Gareri			2	100	Kahar	2
Gawal	1	100				
Ghurki			1	100	Ahir	1
Gonda	1	100				
Jalo	1	100				
Jat			2	100	Chattri	1
					Kurmi	1
Kahar			4	100	Ahir	1
					Gareri	2
					Madrassi	1
Kawar			1	100	Koiri	1
Kewat	1	50	1	50	Ahir	1
Koiri			2	100	Ahir	1
					Kawar	1
Kurmi	2	18	9	82	Ahir	3
					Bania	1
					Chamar	1
					Jat	1
					Mali	1
					Rajwar	1
					Rikri	1
Lunia			1	100	Ahir	1
Madrassi	1	33	2	67	Kahar	1
					Maraj	1
Mali			2	100	Brahmin	1
					Kurmi	1
Maraj			2	100	Ahir	1
					Madrassi	1
Misra	1	100				
Morai	1	50	1	50	Ahir	1
Nair	1	100				
Nau			1	100	Ahir	1

Caste	Endogamy		Exogamy			
	No.	%	No.	%	Caste	Frequency
Nepali			1	100	Chattri	1
Pandit			1	100	Panjabi	1
Panjabi			1	100	Pandit	1
Pasi	1	100				
Pile			1	100	Bania	1
Rajwar	1	33	2	67	Bania	1
					Kurmi	1
Redas	3	100				
Rikri			1	100	Kurmi	1
Tamil	1	50	1	50	Telegu	1
Telegu			1	100	Tamil	1
Thakur	1	33	2	67	Ahir	2
	45	52	82 (41)	48		82

Note: N = 86. To arrive at the total number of respondents reported in Tables VII and IX, add 17 cases "Unknown," not reported here.

In order to show whether a relationship exists between age and marital practices, Table IX presents the distribution of exogamy and endogamy in accordance with the age category of the respondent.

TABLE IX. ENDOGAMY, EXOGAMY, AND AGE OF INFORMANTS

Age Category	Endogamy		Exogamy		Unknown		Totals
	No.	%	No.	%	No.	%	
20-24	2	40	2	40	1	20	5
25-29	1	14	3	43	3	43	7
30-34	3	33	4	44	2	22	9
35-39	8	50	5	31	3	19	16
40-44	8	50	5	31	3	19	16*
45-49	8	50	6	38	2	12	16
50-54	2	25	4	50	2	25	8*
55-59	6	60	4	40			10
60-64	1	20	4	80			5
65-69			2	100			2
70-74	1	50	1	50			2
75-79	1	100					1
80-84	3	75	1	25			4
85-89	1	100					1
Unknown					1	100	1
	45	44	41	40	17	17	103*

*These categories are increased by the number of cases involving multiple marriage as explained in Table VII, Note. Hence the discrepancy between the totals shown in Tables III and IX for age categories.

Similarly, to expose any possible relationship which may exist between household composition and marital practices, Table X presents the distribution of exogamy and endogamy in accordance with household composition.

TABLE X. ENDOGAMY, EXOGAMY, AND HOUSEHOLD COMPOSITION

Household Composition	Endogamy No.	Endogamy %	Exogamy No.	Exogamy %	Unknown No.	Unknown %	Totals
2	1	17	4	67	1	17	6
3	7	78	2	22			9
4	3	43	4	57			7
5	2	33	2	33	2	33	6
6	5	50	3	30	2	20	10
7	6	43	5	36	3	21	14
8	5	31	6	38	5	31	16
9	6	67	1	11	2	22	9
10	3	37	5	63			8
11	3	75	1	25			4
12	3	37	5	63			8
13					1	100	1
14			1	50	1	50	2
	44*	44	39*	39	17	17	100

*The number of cases of endogamy is reduced by 1 and of exogamy by 2. These are the cases of multiple marriage previously indicated in Table VII. The reduction is made here in order not to duplicate the number of households.

The following tables show the relationship for India-born informants among age, endogamy, and exogamy (Table XI), and among household composition, endogamy, and exogamy (Table XII). The distributions in these tables demonstrate that India-born informants have not skewed the data in any significant manner. Exog-

TABLE XI. ENDOGAMY, EXOGAMY, AND AGE CATEGORY OF INDIA-BORN INFORMANTS

Age Category	Endogamy No.	Endogamy %	Exogamy No.	Exogamy %	Totals
65-69			2	100	2
70-74			1	100	1
80-84	3	75	1	25	4
85-89	1	100			1
	4	50	4	50	8

TABLE XII. ENDOGAMY, EXOGAMY, AND HOUSEHOLD COMPOSITION OF
INDIA-BORN INFORMANTS

Household Composition	Endogamy		Exogamy		Totals
	No.	%	No.	%	
2	1	100			1
6			2	100	2
7	1	50	1	50	2
10	2	67	1	33	3
	4	50	4	50	8

amy and endogamy occur in equal proportions (50 per cent each), household composition is scattered over four categories, and the age distribution is an accurate reflection of the age distribution for all India-born individuals in Fiji and is consistent with the details of the indenture migration.

Informants were asked to indicate their preferences in selection of marital partners for their children. These responses are grouped into a limited number of meaningful categories as shown in Table XIII. If a specific caste was indicated, or if all but a single caste was excluded, the response is placed in the category "Specific Caste Indicated." Where the informant felt that more than one caste was acceptable but excluded castes from a particular varna, or where he

TABLE XIII. ATTITUDES AND PREFERENCES OF INFORMANTS RELATING TO
SELECTION OF MARITAL PARTNERS FOR THEIR CHILDREN

Attitude	Number of Cases
Specific Caste Indicated	12
Specific Varna Indicated	44
All Castes Acceptable	39
No Response	5
Totals	100
ETHNIC GROUPS ACCEPTABLE:	
No Other	75
All	16
European	3
Fijian	1
Muslim	—
No Response	5
Totals	100

indicated that only castes from a particular varna would be acceptable, then the answer is included in the category "Specific Varna
Indicated." If the informant answered that all castes were equally
acceptable, the response is incorporated in the category, "All Castes
Acceptable." In the case of ethnic groups, the category "No Other"
indicates that no other ethnic group is acceptable for marriage to the
informants' children; "All" means that representatives of all other
ethnic groups would be acceptable as marriage partners; "European,"
"Fijian," and "Muslim" suggest that only these ethnic groups are
acceptable, but no others. While it is realized that the single most
basic distinction between Hindus and Muslims is one of religion,
certain other important cultural differences exist together with nationalistic overtones which lead us to include the category "Muslim"
in this particular context as a social unit comparable to that of other
ethnic groups.

These attitudinal and preferential responses are further specified
by showing the response given by those (a) involved in endogamous
unions (Table XIV), those involved in exogamous unions (Table
XV), and those involved in "Unknown" or incomplete unions
(Table XVI). While one may logically expect important differences
between the responses given by informants involved in caste-en-
dogamous unions as compared with those given by informants who
are in unions characterized by caste exogamy, Tables XIV and XV
show that no significant difference occurs. The responses are further
specified within each table by distinguishing those informants whose
families have a history of previous exogamy from those whose families
have not previously engaged in exogamous marriages. In Tables XIV,
XV, and XVI, the category "Previous Exogamy" refers to informants
whose familial kin have previously been part of an exogamous union
at least once; "No Previous Exogamy" refers to informants whose
familial kin have never been involved in exogamous unions; and
"Unknown" refers to those informants who do not know or are not
sure whether their kin have been involved in previous exogamy.
Familial kin is used here to include only the informants' mo., fa.,
mo.mo., fa.fa., wi.mo., wi.fa., wi.mo.mo., and wi.fa.fa. Information
reflecting exogamous and endogamous patterns among informants'
siblings is incomplete and is not included; so also those kin of the
grandparental generation not listed above.

TABLE XIV. ATTITUDES AND PREFERENCES OF THOSE INVOLVED IN ENDOGAMOUS UNIONS

Attitude	Previous Exogamy			No Previous Exogamy			Unknown			Totals	
	No.	%	% of Total No. of Cases	No.	%	% of Total No. of Cases	No.	%	% of Total No. of Cases	No.	%
Specific Caste Indicated	2	15	5	4	13	9				6	14
Specific Varna Indicated	7	54	16	12	40	27				19	43
All Castes Acceptable	4	31	9	12	40	27	1	100	2	17	39*
No Response				2	7	5				2	5
	13	100	30	30	100	68	1	100	2	44	101*
ETHNIC GROUPS ACCEPTABLE:											
No Other	10	77	23	24	80	55				34	77*
All	2	15	5	4	13	9	1	100	2	7	16
European	1	8	2							1	2
Fijian											
Muslim											
No Response				2	7	5				2	5
	13	100	30	30	100	69	1	100	2	44	100*

*Discrepancies in per cent totals by reason of rounding.

TABLE XV. ATTITUDES AND PREFERENCES OF THOSE INVOLVED IN EXOGAMOUS UNIONS

Attitude	Previous Exogamy			No Previous Exogamy			Unknown			Totals	
	No.	%	% of Total No. of Cases	No.	%	% of Total No. of Cases	No.	%	% of Total No. of Cases	No.	%
Specific Caste Indicated	3	17	8	3	15	8				6	15*
Specific Varna Indicated	11	61	28	8	40	21				19	49
All Castes Acceptable	4	22	10	8	40	21	1	100	3	13	33*
No Response				1	5	3				1	3
	18	100	46	20	100	53	1	100	3	39	100
ETHNIC GROUPS ACCEPTABLE:											
No Other	15	83	38	15	75	38	1	100	3	31	80*
All	2	11	5	4	20	10				4	10
European	1	6	3							2	5
Fijian										1	3
Muslim											
No Response				1	5	3				1	3
	18	100	46	20	100	51	1	100	3	39	101*

*Discrepancies in per cent totals by reason of rounding.

TABLE XVI. ATTITUDES AND PREFERENCES OF THOSE INVOLVED IN UNKNOWN UNIONS

Attitude	Previous Exogamy No.	%	% of Total No. of Cases	No Previous Exogamy No.	%	% of Total No. of Cases	Unknown No.	%	% of Total No. of Cases	Totals No.	%
Specific Caste Indicated											
Specific Varna Indicated							6	38	35	6	35
All Castes Acceptable				1	100	6	8	50	47	9	53
No Response							2	12	12	2	12
	0	0	0	1	100	6*	16	100	94	17	100
ETHNIC GROUPS ACCEPTABLE:											
Other							10	63	59	10	59
All				1	100	6	4	25	24	5	29*
European											
Fijian											
Muslim											
No Response							2	12	12	2	12
	0	0	0	1	100	6*	16	100	95*	17	100*

*Discrepancies in cross per cent totals by reason of rounding.

229

Analysis

I choose to discuss nine generalizations that can be derived from the data presented.

First, and most pertinent to the major focus of the paper: Endogamous practices among rural Indians in Fiji do not occur in a frequency sufficient to maintain or perpetuate caste as a system of organization. The ideal pattern would be complete caste endogamy, and the necessary and sufficient frequency would approximate 80 per cent endogamous unions for any and all castes if such social groups are to maintain themselves as distinct and closed social units vis-à-vis other castes. Endogamy occurring in lesser frequencies would be indicative of possible changes in the structure and the function of the caste. For example, a caste which had previously practised complete caste endogamy and which is now participating significantly in patterned or limited exogamy has broadened the scope of its intimate relations and has altered its previous organization.

Compared to the suggested endogamous frequencies for maintenance and perpetuation of castes is the fact that only 44 per cent of the marriages among rural Indians in Fiji are caste endogamous. This ratio is opposed to an almost equal ratio (40 per cent) of exogamous unions (Table VII). If the number of incomplete cases (those where the caste identity of one or more of the spouses is not known) is added to the exogamous category, the relative frequency of exogamous unions becomes even more significant.

The basis for combining these categories (exogamous unions and those labeled "incomplete"), is a logical one. The fact that an individual is not aware of his caste identity or that of his spouse may be a strong indication of his lack of concern with caste as a major, even important, cultural institution. The alternative explanation centers around the idea that the informant is concerned with disguising his own caste identity or that of his spouse for reasons of social status, or merely that he is unwilling to divulge cultural information of this type to an "outsider" asking questions. For those cases reported here, I am of the belief that the informants and their families genuinely lacked a knowledge of their caste identity. This belief is justified by the fact that in several cases respondents contacted neighbors in an effort to identify their castes or those of their spouses. More, these same informants were willing and able to give information of a similar nature, such as religious affiliation, rituals, type and frequency of practicing them, reasons for the failure to engage in basic religious practices, attitudes toward other ethnic groups in Fiji, and the like. Added to this evidence is the response by these same individuals to questions eliciting their preferences and attitudes for selection of their children's spouses. Of the 17 cases categorized as "incomplete," 8 indicated that all castes provided equally acceptable marriage partners, and 2 others had no preferences. Only 6 of the 17 preferred marital partners from a specific varna, and none of the informants indicated that a specific caste was preferred (see Table XVI). Such preferential and attitudinal response for selection of children's spouses is consistent with a lack of awareness of the parent's own caste identity. This consistency is reemphasized by the dissimilar responses given by those informants who were involved in both endogamous (Table XIV) and exogamous (Table XV) marriages.

Second: Exogamous marriages among rural Indians in Fiji do not occur between members of particular caste groups in a frequency which is necessary or sufficient to indicate, much less achieve, patterned or structured exogamy or modified group endogamy. Table VIII specifies the caste for exogamous marriages. Where the number of cases are sufficiently meaningful, no pattern of exogamy appears. For example, individuals who identified themselves as Ahir entered into 21 exogamous marriages which involved 15 different castes. Similarly, persons who identified themselves as Kurmi entered into 9 exogamous marriages which involved 7 different castes. While the sample is small, one could logically expect a higher frequency of marriage among members of particular castes if patterned exogamy or modified group endogamy did exist.

Third: A lack of caste consciousness or a lack of concern with particular caste practices exists among a significant segment of the rural Indian population in Fiji. This lack is demonstrated by several factors:

1. The relatively high frequency of exogamy that occurs among this population (40 per cent).
2. The incomplete category (17 per cent) (Table VII).
3. The attitude and preferences in selection of marital partners for

their children given by the informants. Only 12 informants indicate a preference for a specific caste, 44 prefer a specific varna, and 39 are willing to accept all castes as eligible marriage partners for their children, while 5 informants give no stated preference (Table XIII).

4. The failure to consider caste identity as a major criterion in the selection of marital partners.

Fourth: A simultaneous concern with caste and an awareness of caste consciousness is present among a numerically important part of the population. This presence is suggested by the frequency of endogamous unions that have taken place among the informants interviewed (44 per cent), together with the preferential and attitudinal response given by all informants. Twelve per cent preferred their children to marry into a specific caste and 44 per cent preferred a specific varna or excluded a specific varna (Table XIII). No significant preferential or attitudinal difference exists between those informants involved in endogamous unions (Table XIV) and those involved in exogamous unions (Table XV).

Of those involved in endogamous unions, 14 per cent specified a particular caste and 43 per cent a specific varna, while 39 per cent felt all castes were acceptable (Table XIV). This pattern is to be compared to the preferences of those involved in exogamous unions, where 15 per cent specified a particular caste, 49 per cent a specific varna, and 33 per cent felt all castes were acceptable. The greatest differences of this comparison are in the "Specific Varna" and "All Castes Acceptable" categories. A higher proportion of those involved in exogamous unions stated a preference for a specific varna in selecting marital partners for their children than those informants involved in endogamous unions—49 per cent as compared to 43 per cent—(Tables XIV and XV). Of those informants involved in exogamous marriages a smaller percentage felt that all castes provided equally acceptable marriage partners for their children than did those informants involved in endogamous unions—33 per cent as compared to 39 per cent (Tables XIV and XV).

Fifth: The relatively high degree of exogamous and incomplete unions, together with the preferential and attitudinal responses which occur among the rural Indian population of Fiji, suggests certain modifications of more traditional caste behavior: (1) caste is no longer a major institutionalized criterion for selection of marriage partners; (2) pollution through physical contact is not a major deterrent for action by members of a caste group; and (3) the ability to enforce rules of caste conduct is not present. By contrast, breach of caste endogamy in rural India would probably lead to pollution of both partners, sanctions by the caste panchayats involved, serious objection by the families of the individuals concerned and severe loss of social status, among other possibilities.

Sixth: Birth in India has no significant influence upon endogamous practices among rural Indians in Fiji. Of those informants born in India 50 per cent are engaged in exogamous unions and 50 per cent adhere to endogamy. This observation affirms the greater marital latitude possible in Fiji. (See Tables XI and XII.)

Seventh: Caste endogamy is not a function of age among rural Indians in Fiji. One might logically expect a significantly higher percentage of younger persons indulging in caste exogamy to a greater extent than those of older generations, and the reverse. A generalization of this type is not fully supported by the data (see Table IX). For example, the age category 20-24 shows an equal number of cases of exogamy and endogamy, whereas the age category 60-64 indicates only 20 per cent endogamy but 80 per cent exogamy. If the data concerning age and caste endogamy are regrouped at a more general level (20-year categories) this point becomes somewhat clearer (see Table XVII).

TABLE XVII. ENDOGAMY, EXOGAMY, AND GENERAL AGE

Age Category	Endogamy		Exogamy		Unknown		Total
	No.	%	No.	%	No.	%	
Young (20-39)	14	38	14	38	9	24	37
Middle (40-59)	24	48	19	38	7	14	50
Old (60-89)	7	47	8	53	0		15
Unknown					1	100	1
	45	44	41	40	17	16	103

Eighth: Household composition is not a major factor which influences the adherence to more traditional caste practices, either by fostering or detracting from such action. Table X shows the relatively even distribution of endogamy and exogamy for most household compositions. The exceptions to this consistency may very well be a function of the small sample for some of the categories. The comparison between endogamy and exogamy as related to household composition becomes more even if all households are grouped into two major categories: small households, those with a composition of 2 through 5 individuals; and large households, those with a composition of 6 through 14 persons. This categorization yields the distribution shown in Table XVIII.

TABLE XVIII. ENDOGAMY AND EXOGAMY FOR SMALL AND LARGE HOUSEHOLDS

	Endogamy	*Exogamy*	*Unknown*
Small Households (2-5 persons)	13	12	3
Large Households (6-14 persons)	31	27	14
	44	39	17

Ninth: More important than adherence to caste endogamy is the apparently greater concern among the rural Indians in Fiji for maintaining ethnic-group endogamy. Not one of the informants was engaged in an ethnic-group exogamous union; none had married Fijians, Europeans, or Muslims. In addition, the expressed attitudes and preferences of the informants for selection of marital partners for their children indicate that only 20 out of 100 were willing to allow a marriage where another ethnic group was involved, while 75 felt that no other ethnic group was acceptable. (See Table XIII.)

In conclusion then, the data presented indicate that (a) endogamous marriages among rural Indians in Fiji are not sufficient to allow the maintenance or the perpetuation of caste; (b) caste is not an effective organizational system in Fiji; (c) caste is not essential for determining cultural success in contemporary Fiji but may be used toward such goals; (d) caste is of little or no concern to a large segment of the same population, but simultaneously, caste or the concepts related to caste are of some concern to an important but different part of the rural Indian population; (e) adherence to caste practices appears to coincide most closely with individual preferences and action rather than those of any specific group; and (f) ethnic-group endogamy is of greater concern to the rural Indian in Fiji than continuing caste endogamy.

It is recognized that the sample used is a relatively small one, and extensive generalizations based upon such data would be weak. However, many of the results of the investigation appear to be fairly consistent with the more intensive study made of rural Indians in Fiji (Mayer 1961). Consistency of this kind lends a greater degree of reliability to the quantitative data presented here, but more extensive reliability is still dependent upon further research involving additional quantitative data.

REFERENCES

BURNS, ALAN, T. Y. WATSON, and A. T. PEACOCK
1960   *Report of the commission of enquiry into the natural resources and population trends of the Colony of Fiji.* Suva: Legislative Council of Fiji, Council Paper No. 1 of 1960.

HUTTON, J. H.
1961   *Caste in India.* 3d ed. London: Oxford University Press. [1st ed. 1946, 2d ed. 1951, 4th ed. 1963]

MAYER, ADRIAN C.
1961   *Peasants in the Pacific.* London: Routledge & Kegan Paul.

1963   *Indians in Fiji.* London: Oxford University Press.

McARTHUR, NORMA
1958   *Report on the census of the population, 1956.* Suva: Legislative Council of Fiji, Council Paper No. 1 of 1958.

RISLEY, H. H.
1892   *The tribes and castes of Bengal.* 2 vols. Calcutta: Bengal Secretariat Press.

RUSSELL, R. V., and BAHADUR HIRA LAL RAI
1916   *The tribes and castes of the Central Provinces of India.* 4 vols. London: Macmillan and Company.

SCHWARTZ, BARTON M.
1964   "Caste and endogamy in Trinidad," *Southwestern Journal of Anthropology* 20:1:58-66.

SPATE, O. H. K.
1959   *The Fijian people: Economic problems and prospects.* Suva: Legislative Council of Fiji, Council Paper No. 13 of 1959.

SOUTH AFRICA

Changes in Caste of the South African Indian[1]

HILDA KUPER

The Republic of South Africa is a plural society characterized by a major "racial" or "color" cleavage which overrides cultural similarities. Control of power in all fields—politics, wealth, education, and entertainment—is held by the self-styled Whites who accord differential recognition to several non-White groups classified as Africans, Asians (mainly Indians) and Coloureds. Though this paper focuses on the Indians, each group has its identity defined primarily by its position in the wider South African polity.

The total South African population was enumerated in the 1960 census as 16,002,797 of whom 3,088,492 (19.4 per cent) were Whites; the non-Whites included 10,927,922 (68.2 per cent) Africans, 1,509,258 (9.4 per cent) Coloureds, and 477,125 (3 per cent) Indians. Through historical and political processes 82 per cent of all Indians have become concentrated in the province of Natal, the smallest of the four provinces of the Republic. Natal is bounded on

[1]This paper includes sections already published in my book *Indian People in Natal* (Natal University Press: 1960). I would like to thank Ed Leddel and Lyle Steadman for their critical suggestions in the draft of this paper.

the east by the Indian Ocean, and it was at Natal's Durban harbor that the first shipload of Indian immigrants arrived in 1860. A century later there were roughly 150,000 Indians in the Durban city limits, and 16,000 Indians in Pietermaritzburg, Natal's provincial capital.[2] Of the Natal Indians 74 per cent were Hindu, 16 per cent were Muslims, 6½ per cent Christians and the remaining 3½ per cent unclassified.

Caste is generally considered the most important traditional social characteristic of India, and was part of the background of Indian immigrants to South Africa. As the vast literature on the subject shows,[3] caste is difficult to define, but it can, for our purpose, be crudely described by six criteria: first, a jati (the general Hindi term translated as *caste*) is a distinct and exclusive social unit, membership of which is acquired by birth and retained for life unless members are outcaste through breach of caste laws; second, membership imposes limited in-group marriage, either through caste endogamy or prescribed hypergamy; third, caste laws impose restrictions on social contact through eating, touching, or association; fourth, caste members claim a common origin and/or common traditional occupation(s); fifth, in any locality castes have positions of relative prestige, "higher" or "lower"; sixth, and finally, the caste system includes a religious rationalization expressed through the dogma of karma (moral causation) and dharma (righteous conduct), which are reflected in the social position of the individual in his different incarnations. A mystical criterion, expressed in the concept of ritual pollution, underlies the entire structure and delineates each part. Caste, as I have described it here, is thus a system of both relationships and of ideas.

The number of jati has been estimated at about 3,000, but the names, distribution, and ranking vary with locality; thus two functionally similar jati may have different names in separate parts of India. Only a limited number of jati are locally represented and even

---

[2]For discussion of this type of pluralism, see Leo Kuper 1965: 107-131; and Smith 1960: 763-777.

[3]See particularly Blunt 1932, Thurston 1909, Hutton 1951, Risley 1915, Bhattacharya 1896, Desai 1936, Dube 1955, Dutt 1931, Ghurye 1932, Roy 1937, Srinivas 1952.

jati with the same name may be differently rated according to the wider local composition.

Forming a framework for caste and subcaste classification throughout the vast area of India are four hierarchically graded varna caste categories. The varna structure is symbolically represented by the Brahmins (priests) as the head, the Kshatriya (warriors and rulers) as the arms, the Vaishya (traders) as the body, the Sudras (menials) as the lower limbs; falling outside the varna are the Exterior or Scheduled Castes, the Untouchables.

The first three varna cover the "twice-born" castes which have special privileges, while the Sudra and the Scheduled Castes are greatly restricted in their interaction with other caste Hindus—for instance, they may not be served by "clean Brahmins," nor use the same barbers or water carriers that serve the higher castes; they may not enter Hindu temples as equals, nor use the same community facilities such as wells or schools. While the detailed behavior restrictions and obligations are prescribed by the local jati hierarchy, the fourfold varna division extends conceptually across local boundaries.

In theory, jati and varna gradings are rigid, but in fact some degree of flexibility is recognized as inevitable. And while the varna value scale is fixed, there is, and apparently has always been, considerable competitive mobility of jati, the functioning corporate units.[4] Complete rigidity would require a uniform rate of reproduction and replacement plus the exclusion of all outside personal contact. Subdivision of some castes and amalgamation of others have taken place through the centuries. Some castes admit new members and some permit marriage to outsiders. There is limited mobility of individuals through the custom of hypergamy. Moreover, caste gradation is based on certain standards of behavior related to cleanliness, purity, occupation, and knowledge of sacred writings; upward imitation of these standards has improved the status of some groups while relaxation of standards has lowered the status of others.

Despite this flexibility, we can apply the six criteria of caste as crude indices of change to social relationships in South Africa. In

---

[4] This traditional framework is being further modified as a result of legislation and industrialization. See Cohn 1955, also Srinivas 1955.

India, caste endured in principle for some twenty centuries, despite the Moslem invasions, the European occupation, and sporadic anti-caste movements by religious sects in the country. Legislation against caste discrimination is contained in the 1948 Constitution of Independent India, but Srinivas, writing in 1952, states that caste still governs the lives of 300 million Hindus in many important respects (Srinivas 1952: 24). It persists most tenaciously in the villages and least in the mixed population of the cities.

When we look at South Africa in the middle of the twentieth century, the caste system presents certain striking differences from its classical prototype or even from its modern Indian counterpart. Contact with different cultural values always affects societies unequally, particularly societies already highly differentiated, and the extent to which caste survives varies with different religious and interest groups in South African Indian society.

The six criteria of caste are not all of the same order: the first, second, and fifth (relationships by birth, marriage, and rank) could be considered to constitute structure; and the third, fourth, and sixth (social contact, occupation, and ritual) culture.[5] But this is clearly an arbitrary division, in much the same way as the enumeration of characteristics is an arbitrary analytic device. No single characteristic constitutes caste, and structure without the specific content is not caste as perceived by Hindus. Caste is meaningful in a particular universe, a universe conceptualized by such beliefs as karma and dharma, purity and pollution. Without these concepts, expressed in sacred literature and ritual as well as in daily life, caste becomes simply another rigid system of secular stratification. To define caste as a hierarchical arrangement of closed groups, membership of which is determined by birth and maintained by "correct" marriage, appears to me to be but one more attempt to impose a classification based on a belief in universal cultural behavior, instead of trying to understand caste as a distinctive meaningful system.

The process of change in caste involves both time and place, with variations taking place among Indians outside of Africa as well

---

[5] I am using structure as defined by Radcliffe-Brown (1952: 11) " . . . an arrangement of persons in institutionally defined relationships." Structure is related to social position; culture is expressed in manipulation of things and persons.

as in India itself. The situation in South Africa may be unique, for, as I indicate at the end of this paper, the caste system of Hinduism may find its closest parallel in the Republic's apartheid society dominated by the Afrikaner Calvinists.

The Indians who came to South Africa were classified by the South African government into two distinct categories—the indentured and the passenger. The indentured were recruited in the first place for work on sugar plantations, and later, as the system was seen to be profitable, for work on railways, in coal mines, and in domestic service. Apart from a period of eight years, indenturing continued from 1860 until 1911, when the Indian government stopped further recruitment mainly because of the refusal of the South African colonial government to recognize Indians as permanent citizens after the expiration of their indenture. The majority of indentured were Hindus who spoke Tamil or Telugu and came from villages and towns in Madras Presidency which, until 1954, included the Telugu state of Andhra.[6] There were also Hindu speakers of Hindi and other Indo-European languages from the northern and northeastern districts of Bihar, the United Provinces (Uttar Pradesh), Central Provinces (Madhya Pradesh), Orissa, and western Bengal. Included among the indentured from both South and North India were a few hundred Muslims and Christians.

The recruiting agents in southern India sent their "catch" from Madras and those in northern India from Calcutta. The terms "Madrassis" and "Calcuttias" were commonly applied to people irrespective of culture or ethnic origin—the port of embarkation was used to indicate their new identity. Migration was a selective process (see Kuper 1960, Ferguson-Davie 1952), and while to the recruiter caste as such was irrelevant, the occupations for which the indentured were required led to an emphasis on certain castes and also to a deliberate exclusion of others. It appears that less than 20 per cent were non-Hindu, and of the Hindu roughly 60 per cent were of the Sudra and Scheduled Castes, about 25 to 30 per cent were Vaishya, and the remaining 10 to 15 per cent mainly Kshatriya with a small

---

[6]The main Madras districts for recruitment were Trichinopoly, Tanjore, North and South Arcot, Salem, and Chingleput. The main Andhra districts from which most recruits were recorded were the eastern districts of Vizagapatam, East and West Godavari, Kistna, Guntur, Nellore, and Chittoor.

percentage of Brahmins. Occasional reference is made in the Reports of the Indian Immigration Agent to rejection of men of certain occupations and castes, including "Poojaries," toddy drawers, shopkeepers, beggars, policemen and "palanquin" bearers.

Among 3,200 indentured, coming on eight boatloads (as listed in records selected at random in the Office of the Protector of Indian Immigration, Durban), approximately 2 per cent were Brahmins, 9 per cent Kshatriya, 21 per cent Vaishya, 31 per cent Sudra, 27 per cent Exterior Castes; of the remaining 10 per cent, 3 per cent were Christian, 4 per cent Muslim, and the remainder not possible to classify.[7]

The "passengers" (approximately 10 per cent of all Indian immigrants) entered South Africa at their own expense and came specifically to trade and serve in commerce. They were mainly Urdu-speaking Muslims from north and central India and Gujarati-speaking Muslims and Hindus from Kathiawad and Porbandar in Saurasthtra and from Surat in Bombay Presidency. Minority groups of passengers included Parsee Zoroastrians and Jains. Except for a few Shiah the Muslims were predominantly Meman and Bohra who belonged to the Sunni sect. Many of the Gujarati-speaking Hindus

---

[7]Other sources support this general distribution. Thus Ferguson-Davie (1952: 13) wrote: "Of the first group from Madras, twelve per cent were Moslems, five per cent Christian, one per cent Rajputs, and some were Pillais (traders), but the majority were of the lower and more numerous castes who would do labourers' work in India. Of those who came from Calcutta, five and a half per cent were Brahmins, five per cent Rajputs, others were Lohars (blacksmiths), Koris (weavers) and so on. The Natal Mercury, describing the first shipload, says that the first arrivals were not so much field labourers as mechanics, household servants, domestics, gardeners, and trades people, and adds that there were barbers, carpenters, accountants, and grooms amongst them."

The caste composition of Indians leaving from Calcutta in 1875-1876 was reported as follows:

		Persons	*Percentage*
a.	High Caste Brahmans, etc.	1,628	21
b.	Middle Castes: Agriculture	2,518	32
	Artisans	746	9
c.	Lower Castes: Labourers, etc.	3,055	38
		7,947	100

(Report No. 1 of 1877, Emigration. Department of Revenue, Agriculture and Commerce.)

came as accountants to Muslim traders. The term *Baniya* is extended locally to all Hindu traders, money lenders and shopkeepers, though within the Vaishya varna they keep their own separate distinctions such as Lohar, Sonar, and Kumhar.

While the indentured were initially desired because they satisfied the demand for laborers and menials, the passengers and later "free indentured" were seen as dangerous economic competitors. Immigration of passenger Indians was restricted in 1897 and virtually stopped in 1913. Since about that time South African governments have been trying by all means short of direct compulsion to get Indians to return to India. But for reasons which will become apparent the majority remained in South Africa; 99 per cent of the Durban Indians are third-generation South Africans.

The Indians who came to South Africa could not maintain, even had they so desired, the variegated and yet interlocking social patterns which had been built through the ages on the Indian continent. Caste is a social and ideologically hierarchical system which could not be transported by the Indian immigrants into a new society where a small number of self-conscious Whites were establishing their rule over a vast population of tribal Africans. The Indians as a minority group of laborers, not lords, could not impose (nor even continue) their traditional values and social structure. Caste developed in the preindustrial period of Indian history; it was manipulated by priests and warrior princes and supported by a feudal agricultural economy. The system changed when village boundaries were broken by migration, peasants were drawn into industrial cities, and the authority of caste priests was challenged by other political leaders.

Urban living, or "urbanization," is not sufficient to destroy caste, for, as we shall see, in Durban the group that adheres most closely to caste is the small Gujarati-speaking Hindu trading community concentrated in the center of the city. Urbanization as a process covers a wide range of possible social interaction, and it is in the interplay of particular relationships and beliefs that we must seek an answer to the uneven survival of caste, both structurally and ideologically.

We can state categorically that in no section of the contemporary South African Indian population is the traditional caste system rigidly maintained, but at the same time its influence cannot be ignored by sociologists working in South Africa. The idealogy of caste affects many interpersonal relations, even when it does not operate as a clearly defined system of structured social relationships. These facts were brought home to me early in my field work when I was taken by my Indian assistant to meet several leading personalities in a working-class district in Durban. Among them was Mrs. N. E. Maharaj, who was introduced as a Brahmin, and promptly expounded on the importance of caste in dealing with people. She had lived in the area for twenty years and knew every one of her neighbors and had placed them all on a social scale. Her husband, a third-generation South African, practised as a priest over weekends and in his spare time, though he derived his main income from tailoring in the city. They had three children—two daughters, Latchmi and Pulgari, aged 22 and 16, and a son aged 10. I learned later that Latchmi, the older daughter, had been married for four years, but her marriage had proved unsuccessful for reasons which in Durban are by no means unique. At high school she had fallen in love with a Tamil boy, and when this was discovered her parents arranged her marriage to a Hindi-speaking boy of the "right" (Brahmin) caste. The choice was made with considerable care; full attention was paid to his education, stars, age, and appearance as well as his caste. Despite all these efforts at "correct matching" of the qualities of the young couple, the marriage proved so unhappy that Latchmi returned to her family. The boy followed, and for nearly a year both lived under her parents' roof, but the young bride continued to detest him and finally he left her; since they had never registered the marriage, he was free to take another woman as legal wife.

Latchmi's behavior had caused a deep rift between her and her mother. At my first visit mother and daughter openly expressed two hostile and opposed points of view—the traditional and the Western —on caste. Mrs. Maharaj criticized all cross-caste marriages and lamented that her daughter would "lower the family turban" by her behavior, while the Western-educated daughter reported that caste was "out-of-date nonsense." She argued that the essential thing was "love," but conceded that a couple should both be of the same religion, whether Hindu or Muslim or Christian (the Tamil boy was also Hindu). Mrs. Maharaj referred to the glories of ancient India as part of the flowering of a society built on caste, and described the present period as one of degradation and immorality through the breaking down of caste. Conservative in her attitude to caste, Mrs. Maharaj had a strong sense of public responsibility. She was one of the few women who had joined a passive-resistance campaign and served a period in prison. She was also a member of three women's associations active in welfare work on a nonsectarian basis.

But despite her "good deeds," she was not popular. Several informants commented on her "snobbish attitude." She would not mix freely with the neighbors, so that when she offered her house for meetings of different associations many of the women were reluctant to come. These women were not prepared to accept her patronage, though there were others who treated her with conspicuous deference. While she made a point of going to homes where there were misfortunes, she kept her distance from all but the few whom she regarded as equal in birth, and frequently took the opportunity of delivering a short lecture on "right" behavior. Even those who disliked her did not contradict her openly. At the funeral of the mother of a prominent man who, I later learned, was one of her strongest and most hostile critics, she was the only woman given a chair in the family kitchen. At such visits she would deign to take tea, but no other food. Similarly, if she participated in temple ceremonies, she kept aloof from other devotees.

Mr. Maharaj shared his wife's opinion on caste but was regarded as a virtuous, singularly good-natured, and patient man. He was active in several Hindu religious associations and also served on the Ratepayers' Association of the area and other local secular associations. Moreover, he was a vegetarian; surprisingly, Mrs. Maharaj was not, and of the children only Latchmi followed her father's "high examples" in this respect.

Latchmi, however, was criticized for wearing Western dress after marriage, talking too loudly, "showing herself" on the front veranda too much, and speaking to men, even though she knew them, in the street. When her husband left her he had the sympathy of the people, not she. To add to her unpopularity, she decided to take a job and later to study shorthand-typing. Her father threatened at one stage that he would leave the house from shame, if she did so, but in the end Latchmi won.

Even when caste is a focus of emotional interest and is recognized as giving a family status in the local community, it regulates only a limited range of social life. In this Brahmin family Mrs. Maharaj, the main upholder of caste, was drawn by her political and welfare activities into alignments with people not only of different castes but opposed to all that caste stands for. Mr. Maharaj was partly associated with caste through his role as (part-time) priest, but his main activities were in nonreligious commercial associations. The daughter Latchmi was the product of a Western school system; she had no patience with traditional values and only limited knowledge of them, identifying herself as far as possible with the Western intellectual. Her husband was not sure where he stood. Until his trouble with his wife he had supported education for women and greater equality between the sexes. Later he began to assert the rights claimed by the most conservative of Hindu husbands, while he himself led a life of relative independence associated with the young men of the West—attending sports meetings, races, and other amusements.

I would like here also to emphasize that the caste system was not a cause of the troubles of the Maharaj family, since in fact it was not accepted by most of those directly involved and did not exist as a coherent universe of behavior; at the same time ideas about caste were used at different points and by the several persons to justify certain behavior which was condemned by others. Whereas in many situations of change the structured units of social relations appear to persist though the underlying concepts have altered, in South Africa the units have changed but some of the ideas persist.

From the time of embarkation both the structure and the ideology of the traditional caste system of the indentured Indians were affected by external physical circumstances. Conditions under which they traveled to South Africa made it virtually impossible for them to maintain social distance, and ritual "pollution" was inevitable, especially of the higher castes. Members of different religions, as well as Hindus of varying sects and a medley of castes, were crammed together in the same boat. The number of passengers (ranging from 200 to 700) was calculated on the basis of "at least twelve superficial feet and seventy-two cubic feet" per adult, half that amount for a child under 10 years. The journeys lasted from three weeks to three months, and the appropriate rituals could not be performed for those who were born or for those who died on the way. Food was provided from a common kitchen, though the cooking was in the hands of the immigrants themselves and efforts were made in selecting special cooks to avoid offending caste scruples. On arrival at their destination the indentured were housed in barracks, with no special accommodation for unmarried women, no privacy for the married, and no consideration for caste. The territorial basis of the system—the spatially visible distribution of a functional hierarchy of complementary jati —was irrelevant.

Radical demographic changes in the Indian migrant population as a whole and of its constituent subgroups resulted in major structural adjustments. The high ratio of men to women (roughly 100 to 40) and the remoteness from the restraining influence of the caste elders altered caste foundations. Even when caste endogamy was retained as the ideal, the absence of women of the "right" caste and the scarcity of women of any caste made it frequently impossible in practice. Had the indentured come in family units with sufficient members of their own castes, or had they retained active contact with kin in India, caste endogamy might have persisted. But apart from a few exceptions, the indentured came mainly as isolated individuals from scattered villages, and if they could not marry into their own castes the alternatives were to return to India, or to be celibate, or to marry across caste barriers. Many of those who returned to India found themselves aliens and were regarded, in Gandhi's words, as "social lepers."[8] The majority remained in South Africa and chose to marry across the caste line. However, and this development will be shown later, most marriages took place within religious and language units which are loosely and imprecisely described by a number of words, including "caste" and "race" and "nation."

The indentured who had served their period of labor and settled in South Africa were faced with the problem of finding homes outside the plantations and of building up new associations. A few hundred were fortunate enough to receive free plots of land. There is evidence that among these people, the founders of various small Indian settlements along the coast, attempts were sometimes made to recreate a village caste structure. Thus, I was told of one village on the North

---

[8]Mahatma Gandhi, *Young India,* June, 1931. He based remarks on an investigation carried out by Swami Bhawani Dayal and Pandit Benarsidas Chaturvedi in 1931.

Coast that was occupied entirely by Hindi-speaking Hindus from different parts of Bihar; they included a nucleus of Singhs (Kshatriya varna) who built close to each other. They established a local panchayat (council), with a chowdree (headman) and padhan (vice-head), which controlled the village activities. A special Brahmin was used as village purohita (priest), a Nao family acted as barbers, a Kohar made the clay pots and lamps required for the festivals, a Dhobi family did all the laundry, Barhais built the homes and made the furniture and Sonars made the jewelry, and they all cultivated cane and other crops. There appear to have been no "Untouchables." The community, however, gradually merged with the wider, noncaste organized society of South Africa. Traditionally those members of any caste who could not operate their specific caste occupations were able to enter agricultural services, and in this way excess persons from nonagricultural castes were absorbed while occupational caste specialization was stabilized. With difficulties in the acquisition of land and limited opportunities for developing the land inside the village boundaries, the younger people sought new avenues of employment in outside areas. Furthermore, the caste basis or organization became subordinate to a Local Health Board, and the panchayat then had no legal power to enforce or counter the laws enacted by the new bureaucratic government.

The majority of the formerly indentured Indians became peri-urban dwellers, or, more recently, drifted into urban barracks and subeconomic housing schemes. An analysis of jati and varna in the so-called "Indian areas" would bear little relationship to actual social interaction between the inhabitants at the present time—a century after the arrival of the first indentured laborers.[9] A common language is a more usual symbol of unity in urban areas than are varna and jati. Thus Puntans Hill and Stella Hill are two suburbs in Durban described as "nearly 100 per cent Telugu," and non-Telugus living

---

[9]Thus of the 25 heads of Hindi-speaking households in three streets of Merebank, we listed 10 Sudra, 4 Kshatriya, 1 Vaishya, 2 Brahmin, and 8 "don't know" or who refused to answer the question of caste. Scattered among the Hindi were 16 Tamil-speaking family heads, of whom 1 was a Padayachee (Kshatriya), 6 possibly Vaishya (2 Koli, 2 Chetty, 2 Reddi), 9 possibly Sudra or Scheduled (3 Pillay, 1 Moonsamy, 2 Naidoo and 3 "unknown"). The associations in these areas—sports clubs, orchestras, debating societies, Ratepayers' Associations, and religious societies—have no direct reference to caste.

among them are distinguished as "the Tamil family" or "the Hindustani family." Again, Newlands is predominantly Hindi-speaking and Springfield mainly Tamil. But inevitably there are many mixed areas—particularly in the town—where predominance of any particular linguistic group is largely accidental and linguistically homogeneous enclaves are not rooted in caste.

There appears to be a general tendency for newcomers to any city to live in areas where they are more "at home," that is, with people of similar cultural, particularly linguistic, background. Provided no obstacles to assimilation or integration are put in their way and provided they participate in a common system of education, later generations may merge increasingly with members of other subgroups and lose or give up their specific identity. Any local concentration of particular Indian cultural groups is not unique and cannot be attributed to caste.

Apart from conditions of indenture and subsequent residence which contributed to weaken caste ties, there were deliberate acts by a few individuals to improve their status by changing their caste name or by dropping a caste name altogether. It would be misleading, and virtually impossible, to trace caste affiliations of many South African Indians from the present confusion of names. On arrival each recruit was issued a so-called "pass," containing as a rule a "calling name," but not the caste of the holder. The names of children were later entered on the pass of the mother; and when they grew up and required separate passes, their names, usually without the caste names of either parent, were recorded. Later, some returned to their caste names, a few adopted new names, and others kept their own names as surnames.

Children of the same parent frequently hold different surnames, some taking the father's calling name and some the caste name. Thus the name Maharaj, which in north India is usually a title of address, has been generally adopted in South Africa as a family and caste name by any Hindi-speaking family which claims to be of the Brahmin varna.

Individuals who climb the economic ladder of South African industrialization find it possible to take on names, not necessarily caste names, in different environments; if registered with caste names, they are able—at a small cost—to change to another and noncaste registered name. To have no caste name gives an anonymity; a low-caste name is a perpetual stigma; a high-caste name is a potential advantage. People born into the higher castes may, and sometimes do, resent the "upstarts," but can do nothing about them.

One might ask why more, if not all, South African Hindus of the lower castes did not promote themselves by way of name. The answer lies in the nature of effective social relationships. The status of the individual was frequently known at the time of embarkation, or ferreted out on arrival. It then became fixed vis à vis South African Indian associations which were not easy to avoid in a society dominated by interpersonal relationships, and in which the opportunities to break away were restricted. It would seem that deliberate changes in caste identification were made by a very limited number of people who were regarded as low in caste but had made enough money to establish themselves in respected occupations in areas where they were not known and could, under a changed name, receive a higher social rating.

There are, on the other hand, a few leading intellectuals who have deliberately dropped high-caste names to mark their individuality or exclusiveness, and in some cases to indicate their disapproval of the caste system as such. For caste, by the illogic of analogy, has been used as a favorite argument by South African politicians to justify enforced inferiority and exclusion of non-Europeans, especially of Indians.

A number of Hindu reform movements that originated in India also express disapproval of caste discrimination and state that all men are equal in spiritual potentiality. Of growing importance, drawing a membership from many of the more educated, are the Arya Samaj, Ramakrishna Centre, Saiva Siddhanta and the Divine Life Society, whose broad ethical nonsectarian doctrines cut across caste differences. Buddhism in South Africa has about a hundred adherents of mixed origin.

Caste is associated with Hinduism, but in South Africa other religions and sects, with different systems of control and a more egalitarian ethic, converted a number of orthodox Hindus and influenced others. Christianity, the religion of the dominant Whites and of approximately 6.7 per cent of the Indians in Durban, does not recognize the Hindu caste system. Some of the early Christians are accepted by the South African Indian elite; others, especially the more recently converted, are known to have been drawn from the lower castes and are despised as such. Most Indian Christians deliberately drop caste names and usually assume biblical names for surnames as well as for first names. Almost one-third of the Indian Christians in Durban belong to the Protestant churches, about one-quarter to the Roman Catholic church, and the remainder are members of minor sects. The strongest proselytizing influence is at present exerted by the Holy Gospel Bethesda Mission, whose leader (a European) has deliberately adapted his teaching to Hindu symbolism and theology but has eliminated all reference to caste. The claim of the convert to equality is not of course acceptable to the most conservative, and in some cases is not even made.

Caste is not operative within the Muslim minority. Accepting the religious authority of the Koran, Muslims in South Africa profess the equality of all Believers irrespective of race and class. In 1960 the Muslims of Natal included, in addition to the 23,429 Indians, 13 Europeans, 954 Coloureds, and 335 Africans. While ignoring caste, South African Indian Muslims evaluate in-group differences by sect (Sunni or Shiah), place of origin, and local dialect. Among the Sunni Bohra of Durban there are Kathorians (from Kathor), Surti (from Surat), Gamadia (from Gam), Meman (from Porbandar). The Kathorians were the first to acquire wealth and at one period were very exclusive. The Gamadia, as their name implies, are drawn mainly from a number of villages (Gam) and are considered less sophisticated. Intermarriage between Muslims and Hindus is extremely rare, and social intercourse is limited.

The Hindu section that adheres most to traditional caste practices and ideas is the Gujarati, but in Durban, Gujaratis (Hindu and Muslim) totaled less than 9,000 persons.

There is also a small caste-conscious enclave of Telugu-speaking Naidus.

It is necessary to reiterate here a theoretical distinction between caste structure and caste ideology or consciousness. The Maharaj case mentioned earlier illustrated that caste consciousness may exist when the caste structure is absent; it is expressed in arguments over the system and the concept of pollution through breach of caste laws. A few informants who were in favor of the traditional Indian system did not follow the practices; they were influenced by the wider social environment and unable to withdraw into the exclusive yet integrated world prescribed by caste.

The relative persistence of caste among the Gujarati Hindus flows from their passenger status, their greater economic security. They did not come on the ships with the indentured; they could afford to bring their families with them, or to them, and they retained contact with their own caste members in villages in India through business and/or marriage. Though described by other Indians in Durban by the general label *Baniyas* (traders), they are very conscious of jati (Patel, Desai, Amin, and the like) within this broad Vaishya varna. Confronted with the difficulty of finding suitable mates for their children in South Africa, many Gujarati Hindus sent their daughters to husbands selected in India (tradition demands that a girl accept the domicile of her husband) and they imported "correct" wives for their sons. The Gujaratis are most affected by the Immigration Amendment Act of 1960 prohibiting the entry of Indian wives.

In addition to endogamy, many Gujaratis retain other characteristics associated with caste. They are exclusive in their eating, selective in occupation, explicit in their evaluation of status, conservative in ritual. They show that a caste structure can survive as a group among urbanized immigrant groups under the following conditions; namely, if members

(1) can maintain a separate identity from the time they leave their home country (India) either
  (a) by retaining ties with a protected caste nucleus in India, or
  (b) by isolating their women from intimate cross-caste contact;
(2) hold a privileged position in the economic organization and avoid proletarianization.

This survival is explained by the fact that a sufficient number of people from the same jati (especially Vellamar, Kappar, Kammar and Gavra) and from the same districts of Andhra migrated at much the same time, and were able to set up small "islands" when they had completed their indenture. They became market gardeners and hawked their products in kin units, and married into similar units.

In exceptional cases, and usually among people who rate themselves as "high" caste, caste endogamy may be the most important factor in a parent's choice of a child's marriage partner, but family background, health, economic standing, appearance, and level of education are also considered.

In South Africa endogamy is determined primarily by "race" (White, Asian, African) and then by different divisive principles (such as religion and language) within each "race." Among Indians, religion and language are broader and more clearly recognizable divisions than varna or caste. Most Hindu marriages take place between people who belong to a single linguistic-cultural category. Marriages between people of the same jati name are frequent but, as we saw, those names are somewhat arbitrary. In the collection of genealogies many individuals were (deliberately?) "forgotten," perhaps supporting what Barnes described as "structural amnesia" (Barnes 1947: 52).

Ranking of families as "higher," "lower," or "equal" is important in most Hindu marriage negotiations, and some informants distinguished "high" and "low" families within a single caste category, using the criteria of dialect and social habits; they spoke, for example, of "high" Chetty or "low" Chetty, "high" Pillay and "low" Pillay. The "high" Chetty or "high" Pillay were then described as Vaishya and the "low" Chetty or "low" Pillay were put into the Sudra or Scheduled castes.

Hypergamy for women is generally approved, but there have been cases where a girl's parents reject a high-caste suitor because of his poor character or because of his family's reputation. For a woman to "marry down"—to a man considered her social inferior—is widely condemned, but perhaps no more so than in societies where status is based on criteria other than caste; the main difference is that the South African Hindu still sometimes expresses this type of snobbery in terms of caste. Examination of a few cases of women marrying "down" in caste indicated that they tended to marry "up" in terms of economic or occupational status.

Material collected by B. Rambiritch and Pierre van den Berghe from Caneville, a small coastal community in Natal, documents these general findings in greater detail. In only 25 out of 318 cases was varna endogamy not observed. In 19 of the 25 cases the woman married "down" contrary to the traditional rule of hypergamy, but in 8 of the 19 cases the husband had a higher occupational standard, so that it seems "new western criteria of status such as occupation can effectively override traditional considerations" (1961: 217-225).

Ceremonies ordained for different occasions in the life cycle of the individual are seldom controlled by caste; they depend primarily on the degree of westernization, irrespective of caste, of the individual as well as his family. Among the North Indian Hindi speakers, traditional ceremonies should be performed by priests of the Brahmin caste, but among the Telugu and Tamil this is usually not necessary. Even the sacred-thread ceremony (upanyana in Sanskrit, janeo in Hindi and Gujarati, punul in Tamil), traditionally the most important ceremony for the "twice-born" castes and one which still reflects caste differences, is enacted in very abbreviated form if at all. In Durban, Brahmins generally wear the sacred cord on special occasions; they find it impossible to wear it regularly because of the inevitability of pollution through contact with the "unclean" and the elaborate precautions required to maintain its purity. There is no annual gathering of Brahmins for the purpose of "renewal of the cord," but each Brahmin usually performs a ceremony on his own or with a couple of colleagues.

Overt symbols of caste are few and are becoming fewer. Informants stated that both fellow workers and European employers poked fun at those who retained caste hair styles, ornaments, and local costumes. Today men have their hair cut at public barbershops except for special rituals when a Nao is specially sought, and they conform to Western dress except at special ceremonies when officials don the dhoti and various traditional garments (for example, the turban). Children (apart from Muslims attending private and government-aided schools) wear Western dress. There is no restriction on the ornaments or dress of the various castes. The younger generation of married men and women have abandoned caste tattoo marks. The varied range of women's fashions reflects differences between Muslims and Hindus; but the style of sari and ornament of Hindus is related to the division into North and South, not caste.

The religious sanction behind caste is seldom expressed. The belief in karma and dharma is generally accepted by Hindus, but rebirth into a higher caste is not formulated as one of the highest rewards of virtuous conduct. In response to a questionnaire submitted to 450 school children between the ages of 13 and 16, 390 stated they were Hindu, 30 Muslim, and 30 Christian. To the question "Do you believe in reincarnation?": of 160 Tamil-speaking Hindus, 80 said yes, 80 no; of 114 Hindi-speaking, 100 said yes, 14 no; of 27 Telugu-speaking, 17 said yes, 10 no; and 49 did not answer. All the non-Hindus replied no.

Individuals who have broken fundamental caste laws are seldom required to perform any traditional purification ceremony; this was required once during our years of study when a Hindi-speaking Hindu who had been converted to Islam returned to Hinduism. We were told of two other cases: in the first, a Hindi-speaking Hindu in a rural area killed a cow and had to be purified before he was readmitted by his family; in the second, a high-caste Tamil Hindu family drove out one of the sons because he lived with a "loose woman of low caste," and would not readmit him till he had undergone a ritual purification, after which his people married him to a girl of their own choice.

Elaborate dietary rules have fallen away almost entirely and, in the sharing of the common meal, the invitation of friendship generally replaces the credential of caste. Many Brahmins, though not all, dine at the houses of members of various castes as long as they are provided with only vegetarian dishes. For services performed by them, Brahmins are frequently given siddha—reward in uncooked foods—but this is not strictly related to caste structure. Nor is the traditional caste distinction drawn between food cooked with ghee and food cooked with water. Traditional utensils, designed to maintain caste purity, are replaced by Western crockery. Only at ritual meals, especially at weddings and funerals, the portion for each guest is still often served on separate banana leaves and these are thrown away when the meal is over; but the usual explanation given me for the use of the leaf plate (pattal) was that it "costs nothing to hire" and "can't break." Some families have a number of brass drinking vessels from which liquid can be poured into the mouth without the vessel touching the lips, but these are now regarded as ornaments and heirlooms, china cups and glasses being in common use. There are, however, a few families who use special crockery for guests and outsiders, and metal (tin or aluminum) vessels which are cleaned with sand or ash for people of the home. Bars and restaurants introduce further contact and pollution. There are not very many Hindus who will eat only in the homes of people whom they consider "caste" equals. Nor is there clear social separation on a caste basis at weddings, funerals, and temple ceremonies.

Certain customs associated in India with the Brahmin castes—more especially their food habits and social manners—tend in South Africa to become symbols of a particular individual outlook irrespective of caste. Priests in Durban are generally vegetarian, but members of their own families living under the same roof are sometimes "flesh" eaters, obeying only a general injunction against eating meat of the sacred "cow mother." On "fast days" and special feast days all South African Hindus abstain from "flesh."

Participation in communal ceremonies formerly regulated by caste is now on a voluntary, personal basis, and responsible positions in temples are attainable by the learned or the wealthy. In one of the main orthodox temples, the honored position of trustee is held by a member of a Sudra caste. No person is officially disqualified by lowly birth from entering any South African temple, though I have been told of one case in Durban where there is a "freezing out" of "undesirable low castes." The players of wind instruments required in certain ceremonies have been described as "low" (or pariahs) because they "must have alcohol" (to give them energy) and "don't mind spittle": they usually remain in the yard of the temple and do not try to come inside.

Generally speaking, caste and occupations no longer have any significant correlation. Many caste names specifying occupations (as Lohar—smith, Vannya—oil presser) have become functionally meaningless. Members of the same caste follow a variety of occupations. Only small numbers of the Brahmin caste carry on the traditional occupation as priests and scholars, full- or part-time; others are tailors, furniture dealers, estate agents. There are Singhs (Kshatriya) who are doctors, lawyers, butchers (but dealing only in mutton), market gardeners, and hawkers.

At the same time, certain occupations still tend to be practised by people of particular jati. Among south Indians, the jewelers are Pathers, and among the Hindi-speaking, priests are Maharaj, goldsmiths Soni, washermen Dhobi, potters Kumhar, barbers Nau. I would in fact suggest that this persistent association between jati and occupation contributes to the general awareness of caste.

Several informants voiced the opinion that "high-caste" people are found in "clean" (upper-status) occupations—the professions and white-collar jobs—and "low-caste" people are mainly in jobs considered physically and spiritually dirty—leather working, hair cutting, street sweeping, washing other people's clothes, handling dead bodies. There appears to be something to this opinion, but it would be difficult to examine statistically because of the ambiguity in many of the present names ; it is clear that high-caste families object to their sons' taking on manual and poorly paid jobs, but the question of earning power and general prestige of occupations is as relevant to this outlook as is their caste. A typical text by a Brahmin states:

> I will always give my son the freedom to choose his occupation for himself but I would not like him to be a shoemaker. I will not object to his becoming a carpenter. Some fathers would like their children to become doctors or lawyers, and force them into it, but it is not right to do this to another. For my son-in-law, I will look first to see that he is not one who walks about the streets associating with anyone and everyone, and that he does not drink. Yes, I would look also to caste, and would not go below a Singh; but most I want a good man and I would not mind any clean occupation.

It is also clear that the conditions prevailing in South Africa since the time of the first immigration opened new and sometimes preferable occupations for Sudras and Untouchables, and undermined the retention of any rigid occupational stratification, except for a few specialized crafts (such as goldsmithing or pot making) and trade in the passenger group.[10] There was no demand for the specialized labor of castes such as Oil Pressers, Palanquin Bearers, Welldiggers, Land Surveyors, Shepherds. Since occupational openings in South Africa operate irrespective of caste, the occupational interdependence of castes, including the Untouchables, has virtually disappeared. In a random sample of 84 men, 64 had taken on occupations different from their fathers. Parents acknowledge that they

---

[10]See H. Kuper and Meer 1956 and H. Kuper 1960.

may direct their children into a particular profession, but cannot force them.

There is in many circles—especially among conservatives—a strongly held belief that a person of a high-caste family will be decent and honorable, and that relatively little can be expected from a person of a low-caste family. On this point a university-educated Telugu commented:

> If someone from the high Naidoos—Yellama, Kappar or Kammar —did something bad, people will try to think in his favour and find excuses or an explanation, but if he was a low Naidoo—a Gavra, or an Odde Chetty [low in the Chetty caste category]—it is considered understandable, and people will say 'You know the group he comes from' or 'We should have known what to expect' or 'The blood in him will show up.' The individual who goes beyond his family status is regarded with suspicion, and the ability to use only acquired techniques is always dangerous.

It is significant that most of the social and political leaders in the community are from "good families" with high-caste names, and that their outstanding qualities are often attributed not to their individual ability or intelligence, nor even to special economic or social advantages given them by the family background, but to "their blood." At the same time it is only the closer kin who benefit because of their association with these leaders; no specific privileges can be claimed by others simply on the basis of belonging to the same castes.

Attacking the foundation of caste is the "democratic" schooling system of the country in which Indians are admitted to schools on a noncaste basis. The qualifying factor is "race" (Indians may only attend segregated Indian schools) and, in some schools, the ability to pay an entrance fee. Once educated, the future of an Indian in the total society depends not on caste but on opportunity and ability. Vernacular schools are open to all members of a particular language group, and caste does not enter into, let alone determine, the system and syllabus of education.

The caste panchayat (council) does not exist and so cannot operate. Authority and control are vested in leaders selected for various noncaste qualities. Though in some cases the trustees of a school or a temple or the members of a Ratepayers' Association have been referred to as panchayat, they include men of different sects and castes. Caste associations such as those developed by Indians in East Africa are significantly absent.

The ultimate sanction of caste rules is outcasting. Where the caste is the social world, outcasting cuts off a man and usually his family from all communion with his fellow men. In South Africa the caste had no power to impose this drastic punishment. In the field of law the courts of the country have control, and though the family, in its widest form, may ostracize a member it cannot excommunicate him. The man who breaks from his caste is neither an exile nor the nucleus of another "caste."

The changes that have taken place, and are taking place, in the concept of caste can be understood only as part of the general process of adaptation of Indians to the wider South African milieu.[11] In India there appears to have been a constant process of segmentation of castes through increased occupational specialization, the rise of new religious sects, and local peculiarities, while fusion of a number of castes into a single unit for political or social prestige was a less frequent occurrence. In South Africa, the process as expressed through caste is reversed—fusion of subcastes, not fission, is the overriding tendency.

I have shown that attitudes to the caste system vary with informants;[12] members of the same family may, and often do, hold different opinions, and there are members of high-caste families that condemn it and of low-caste families that defend it. The majority of young South African Indians are ignorant of the intricacies of caste,[13] but they are conscious that it is a system of discrimination and hence it is an embarrassing subject.

---

[11] See also van den Berghe 1964.

[12] I originally wrote that, "With a few exceptions, it is the older [generation] Hindus in South Africa who are prepared to speak openly in support of caste." On reexamining my data I find this statement is not correct. Many of the older generation condemn caste, and my quantitative material is not adequate to make any sharp distinction in terms of generation differences. It is also important to remember that the "older generation" is already second-generation South African.

[13] A question on caste affiliation to the above-mentioned group of 450 school children elicited the following responses: 244 replied "none," 79 gave a linguistic, cultural, or ethnic group (as Andhra, Telugu, Dravidian [sic]) and 107 gave a more specific caste name (as Chetty, Singh, or the like). The remaining 20 left the answer blank.

Terminology in South Africa reflects a change in structural units. Some informants had never heard the word *jati* or *jat*. Those Hindus who recognized it usually applied it to more inclusive units than the traditional castes or even classes of castes. It is used predominantly for large religious-cultural categories (as Muslims, Christians, and Hindus), and for linguistic-cultural groups (as Gujarati, Hindi, Tamil, and Telugu), and is frequently translated without discrimination by South African Indians into English as "nation" or "race." These new categories, rather than the traditional subcastes, are endogamous, self-conscious, and exclusive; but they are not put into a rigid hierarchy of values—an essential of the caste system.

The intensity of prohibition of contact between these large categories, even when expressed in "caste" terms, varies with cultural affinity and ethnic identity. Prohibition is least between South African Tamil and Telugu, whose language and religion and culture are very similar; in case of marriage, if the families of the young couple are considered equal in status, there is usually no opposition. Reaction is stronger between North Indian (Hindi- or Gujarati-speaking) and South Indian (Tamil or Telugu), though the bond of a common religion (Hinduism) coupled with social equality sometimes mitigates disapproval of intermarriage. Hinduism, however, is such an amorphous bond and between "Hindus" there are such cultural distinctions that as a rule the differences in language and culture between northern and southern Hindus dominate over other considerations. There are cases in which a Hindi-speaking Hindu boy fell in love with a Tamil girl and both parents refused permission, not on grounds of caste but of "custom." Sometimes the couple eloped, and sometimes one party was quickly married off to a person described as "the same kind."

Different customs are not necessarily judged inferior or superior, though an ethnocentric cultural bias is generally evident. Thus when a Tamil boy wanted to marry a Hindi-speaking girl, negotiations went smoothly until the girl's people learned that the boy's parents were cross-cousins—a type of marriage "preferred" by Tamils and many southern Indians but prohibited by Hindus of the North. The girl's people considered the custom "not clean" and immediately broke off negotiations and married her to a Hindi-speaking boy.

The linguistic-cultural categories are, however, not castes: I

repeat—they are not graded into an accepted social hierarchy; moreover they are not functionally interdependent, and they do not claim
divine sanction for difference. The concept of caste is equally inapplicable to the separate and distinct religious groups—Hindu, Muslim, and Christian. In India, Muslim and Christian minorities tended
to be treated as castes in the total structure defined by Hinduism; in
South Africa they are classified in the total structure by "race"—
they are all "Indians" or "Asians." Though the facade of solidarity
imposed through sharing in anti-Indian discrimination cannot elim-
inate the distinctiveness of the three religious groups, the complex of
caste characteristics is absent. Their interrelationship is very similar
to that of Catholic and Protestant, where endogamy alone does not
create caste.

In a number of instances parents refused permission for marriage because of differences in language, religion, caste or race, and
though as a rule the young people obeyed, there are said to be an
increasing number of cases in which they have married by civil law.
Moreover, disapproval may not be general or equally intense even in a
circle of close kin. Diagram 1 indicates the type of interaction arising
in the current urban setting.

P.S., a Singh (Kshatriya) and an orthodox Hindi-speaking
Hindu, lived in a single house with his old father A.B.S. and older
married brother R.S. He had two sons (C. and D.) and one daughter
(L.). P.S. and his brother R.S. had married two sisters (V. and Y.)
of the "right caste," and planned that their children do likewise.
P.S.'s older son C. conformed to family tradition and accepted in
marriage a girl (T.) chosen by his kin.

The second son D. had fallen in love with a girl (H.) whose
father (N.S.) was also Hindi-speaking and of good caste but whose
mother (M.) was Coloured. D.'s family (that is, P.S.) opposed the
marriage because of the "race" of the mother, but H.'s parents (N.S.
and M.) accepted the boy and eventually the young couple married
by civil rites without any of P.S.'s family attending. The girl's older
sister (I.) had previously married an upper-caste Hindi-speaking boy
(T.S.) with full ritual; J., another sister of H., was eager to marry a
Tamil (M.K.) whose parents (K.K. and J.K.) were opposing the
marriage on the grounds of differences in language, culture, and
"race" of the families; the only son (V.S.) had married a Coloured

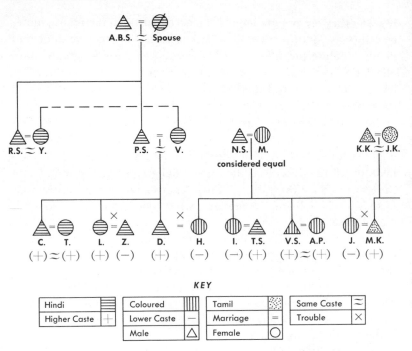

DIAGRAM 1. MARITAL INTERACTION. *See text for explanation.*

girl (A.P.) in the Catholic Church (both being so light-skinned that they pass as "Whites" when they wish).

P.S.'s daughter (L.) was a teacher who wanted to marry a fellow teacher, thus a professional equal, but a man of low caste; the whole family expressed their disapproval, but eventually her parents "could not resist their beloved daughter's tears and threats of suicide" and gave their consent. But P.S.'s brother and sister-in-law (R.S. and Y.) remained adamant, and there was a strong rift in their relationship. However, P.S. won his old father (A.B.S.) over to his side, and the marriage date was settled. On the morning of the marriage the old man died suddenly. The marriage took place "in an atmosphere of mourning." Then the girl (L.) died in childbirth. At L.'s funeral her parents and their second son (D.) were reconciled, but though five years have passed they still do not speak to P.S.'s brother (R.S.) and his wife (Y.). (the bereaved mother's own sister).

If the term *caste* is applied analytically rather than descriptively, it is more clearly embodied in the South African social structure as a whole than in the Indian community in particular. Nearly all characteristics of the traditional caste system are evident in the relationship of the so-called "races"—"Europeans" (Whites), Coloured, Indians, and Africans, graded in that order. Definition of "race" is by fiat of the White rulers, and the concept is primarily political and mystical, not genetic and scientific. Maintenance of Whites at the top is explicit in government policy. The relative position of every citizen and his dependents is fixed "for all time" by a Population Register classified into racial categories. Breach of race endogamy for Whites and non-Whites is a criminal offense under the Prohibition of Mixed Marriages Act.

Contact between Whites and non-Whites through other channels—living in the same neighborhood, sharing the same schools and universities, enjoying the same civic amenities—is restricted, and the restrictions increasingly carry penal sanctions. Apartheid demands the minimum of interracial mixing.

The breakdown of caste within the Indian population reflects the heterogeneity of the South African population and the effect of new bases of stratification. Even within the Hindu community the majority find the social cost of the traditional caste system too high and the rewards too low, and have developed other associations and values more in keeping with the contemporary milieu. Individuals shift alliances according to a wide range of alternative and contrasting situations, and in their roles as employers or employees, landlords or tenants, traders or peasants they cannot be confined within the narrow bounds of caste. In the White-dominated society the Indians are, in Weber's terms, a "pariah-people"; but among themselves they are heterogeneous and stratified by religion, language, education, occupation and wealth. Cutting across these lines, which are not parallel, are numerous voluntary associations, and these associations, not caste, draw leading officials from various groups and express the dynamic and changing interests, alignments and ideas of Indians in the plural society of South Africa.[14]

---

[14]Elites and Associations are discussed in Kuper 1960, Chapters III, IV, and V.

REFERENCES

BARNES, JOHN A.
1947   "The collection of genealogies: human problems in British Central Africa." *Rhodes-Livingston Journal* V: 48-55.

BHATTACHARYA, J. N.
1896   *Hindu castes and sects.* Calcutta: Thacker, Spink & Co.

BLUNT, E. A. H.
1932   *The caste system of Northern India.* London: Oxford University Press.

COHN, B. S.
1955   "The changing status of a depressed caste." pp. 53-77 in *Village India,* McKim Marriott, ed. Chicago: University of Chicago Press.

DEPARTMENT OF REVENUE, AGRICULTURE AND COMMERCE
1877   *Report No. 1 of 1877, Emigration.* Calcutta.

DESAI, N. C.
1936   *Report on the Hindu joint family system.* Baroda.

DUBE, S. C.
1955   *Indian village.* London: Routledge and Kegan Paul, Ltd.

DUTT, N. K.
1931   *Origin and growth of caste in India.* London: Kegan Paul, Trench, Trubner & Co., Ltd.

FERGUSON-DAVIE, C. J.
1952   *The early history of Indians in Natal.* Johannesburg: South African Institute of Race Relations.

GANDHI, M. K., ED.
1931   *Young India,* June, 1931.

GHURYE, G. S.
1932   *Caste and race in India.* London: Kegan Paul, Trench, Trubner & Co.

HUTTON, J. H.
1951   *Caste in India.* London: Oxford University Press.

KUPER, HILDA
1960   *Indian people in Natal.* Natal: Natal University Press.

KUPER, HILDA, and FATIMA MEER
1956   *Indian elites in Natal.* Durban: Institute for Social Research.

KUPER, LEO
1965   "Some aspects of pluralism in urban African societies." pp. 107-131 in *The African World,* Robert A. Lystad, ed. New York: Praeger.

RADCLIFFE-BROWN, A. R.
1952 *Structure and function in primitive society.* London: Cohen and West.

RAMBIRITCH, B., and PIERRE L. VAN DEN BERGHE
1961 "Caste in a Natal Hindu community." *African Studies* 20:217-225.

RISLEY, H. H.
1915 *The People of India.* 2d ed. Calcutta: Thacker, Spink & Co. [1st ed. 1892]

ROY, S. C.
1934 "Caste, race and religion in India," Part I. *Man in India* XIV:39-63; 271-311.

1937 "Caste, race and religion in India," Part II. *Man in India* XVII: 147-176; 212-254.

1938 "Caste, race and religion in India," Part III. *Man in India* XVIII: 85-105.

SMITH, M. G.
1960 "Social and cultural pluralism." pp. 763-777 in *Social and cultural pluralism in the Caribbean,* Vera Rubin, ed. Annals of the New York Academy of Sciences. Vol. 83, Art. 5.

SRINIVAS, M. N.
1952 *Religion and society among the Coorgs of Southern India.* London: Oxford University Press.

1955 "The social system of a Mysore village." pp. 1-35 in *Village India,* McKim Marriott, ed. Chicago: University of Chicago Press.

THURSTON, E.
1909 *Castes and tribes in Southern India.* 6 Vols. Madras: Government Press.

VAN DEN BERGHE, PIERRE L.
1964 *Caneville: The social structure of a South African town.* Middletown, Conn.: Wesleyan University Press.

EAST AFRICA

Caste among the
Indians of Uganda

The East African territories of Kenya, Tanganyika, Uganda, and Zanzibar had in the years immediately before and after 1950 a population of just over 18½ million people. Of these a little under 18 million were African and some 83,000 were of Arab extraction and Muslims but no less indigenous to the country than the Africans, some of whom had been converted to Islam. The exact number of these converts was unknown. Indian and European immigrants into East Africa numbered about 190,000 and 50,000 respectively. Of the total number of Indians approximately 111,000 (57 per cent) were Hindu and about 79,000 (43 per cent) were Muslim.[1]

---

[1] *A Report on the Census of the Non-native Population of Uganda Protectorate* (1948), Nairobi, 1953. *Report on the Census of the Non-native Population of Kenya Colony and Protectorate* (1948), Nairobi, 1953. *A Report on the Census of the Non-native Population of Tanganyika* (1952), Dar-es-Salaam, 1953. *Notes on the Census of the Zanzibar Protectorate* (1948), Zanzibar, 1953. *Annual Report (1952) for Kenya, Tanganyika, Uganda, and Zanzibar.*

After the partition of India and Pakistan it was the custom in East Africa to speak of "Asians" instead of "Indians." The word *Asian* covered a miscellaneous category of nationalities and included Indians, Pakistanis, Arabs,

In 1948 Indian immigrants to Uganda numbered 33,767, constituting a minority of .71 per cent of the whole population. About 20,000 were Hindus belonging to various castes and 11,000 were Muslims divided among Shia and Sunni sects. Most derived from Gujarat, Kathiawar, and Cutch on the North West Coast of India. Gujarati was the predominant language, but Punjabi, Urdu, and Hindi were also spoken. The majority of the Indian population (79.2 per cent) was engaged in trade and manufacturing occupations.

Indian traders had been settled in Zanzibar and the coastal cities of East Africa for many centuries before the arrival of Europeans; but the opportunities provided by the British establishment of the East African Protectorate in the late nineteenth century, together with the building of a railway from Mombasa to Lake Victoria Nyanza at the turn of the century, brought many new immigrants from India to fill the demand for trade, and thus to stimulate agricultural production among the African population and make traffic for the newly built railway and a revenue for the administration. Unlike the migration of Indians to many other parts of the tropical world, such as South Africa, Mauritius, Fiji, or the West Indies, this was a spontaneous movement using connections with settlers already established on the coast. It was not a migration of plantation laborers; for though the railway was built by Indian "coolies" under indenture, only a small number of these remained as settlers in Africa. Most of the migrants came as skilled artisans and traders and never settled on the land as farmers or agricultural laborers.

Caste in India

In coming to Africa the immigrants had necessarily to alter much that had distinguished their social system at home. One of the

---

Chinese, Mauritians, and sometimes even Somalis. I have therefore preferred to retain the older term, and in speaking of Indians to mean immigrants from the whole subcontinent of India.

The field work on which this article is based was undertaken under the auspices of the East African Institute of Social Research from 1952 to 1955. In 1955 Uganda was granted a constitution which ultimately led to self-government as an independent country; but the structure of Indian society up to and after independence did not appreciably alter, and this article refers mainly to the period before 1955.

more important features of society in India, particularly the Hindu section of it, was that the component groups, the castes and sub-castes, were arranged in a hierarchy with Brahmins at the top and the Untouchables at the bottom. Each subcaste was an endogamous group with prescribed behavior and certain symbols which set it apart from similar groups in the hierarchy. Correct relations between the groups were maintained and validated by religious rules, espe-cially the rule that improper contact between the castes produced a state of impurity which entailed religious, legal, and other penalties. In describing a caste system care needs to be taken not to confuse the traditional division of all Hindus into castes (varna) with the division of people into subcastes (jati). Traditionally caste or varna divided the population of India into four or sometimes five categories—priests, soldiers, businessmen, laborers, and those outside this ranking system. These ranked castes were categories of value against which an individual or a subcaste could evaluate position in a local system of stratified subcastes; if a man went to another part of the country he could use the varna system to place himself in that new district. The varna, which were uniform throughout India, were not stratified social groups which imposed obligatory behavior, rights, and duties upon their members (Srinivas 1952).

In practice Indian society was made up of many small local hierarchies of subcastes, each of which was a social system largely independent of those adjacent to it. In contrast to the varna the constituent jati were corporate social groups which imposed very definite rules of behavior on their members. Traditionally the sub-castes in such a local system were organized so that social labor was cooperatively and complementarily divided among them, each jati holding a monopoly of a particular service. All Shoemakers, for example, though not bound to practise that occupation, could pre-vent others from doing so. To a greater or lesser degree Muslims were also related to and caught up into this Hindu scheme (Leach 1960).

Although most of the immigrants to East Africa came from Gujarat, Kathiawar, and Cutch, these provinces are large and it frequently happened that the districts of origin of groups living side by side in East Africa were widely separated in India. More-over, as we have just seen, a hierarchy of subcastes in one district was distinct from that in another, and even though the jati in two such systems carried the same names their local ranking was not necessarily the same. Consequently groups in Africa, coming from different parts of India, were not easily able to relate themselves to one another. No representative cross-section of society from any district in India was transplanted to East Africa since members of certain subcastes did not migrate at all. Therefore if a man became rich and influential abroad, he could not use his wealth to gain honor and position for himself or his subcaste in traditional ways until he returned to India. Eventually everybody would hope to go back there with a fortune, but in the meantime both men and women were obliged to live in Africa among people whose ideals and ways of living were not those of orthodox Hindus or faithful Muslims at home.

Before considering the adjustments which Indians in East Africa made in caste arrangements it would be wise first to examine the term *caste* a little further than we have already done. In Indian studies the English word *caste* is used to refer to four types of social grouping, and much muddle is caused by writers who do not make it clear in what sense they are using the word.

The term *caste* is often used in the first place by writers for two traditional social groupings which we have already mentioned:

(I) *Varna*, that is, *caste* as one of the fourfold divisions of Indian society into categories of value and prestige. In theory these comprised the whole population of India.

(II) *Jati*, here called *subcastes*, are frequently referred to in the literature as *castes*. Unlike the varna they are not, as we saw, simply categories of the population, but are groups[2] which impose clearly specified rights and duties on their members. When the word

---

[2]For the sake of clarifying the argument it is worth making plain the distinction which is used in this essay between a social *group* and a social *category*. By a *group* is meant an aggregation of people recruited on clear principles, who are bound to one another by formal institutionalized rules and characteristic informal behavior. Unless a group is to be no more than a temporary aggregation, it must, in addition, be organized for cohesion and persistence; that is to say, the rights and duties of membership must regulate internal order and relations with other groups. Members usually identify themselves with a group and give it a name. In practice, social groups vary in

caste is used it is usually one of these jati in a local hierarchy which is referred to. Each varna includes a large number of separate jati within it, and two jati bearing the same name but in different districts may be rated as belonging to different varna.

The word *caste* is also used in the literature to refer to two other types of grouping:

(III) *Jati* as *subcaste categories* in distinction to *jati* as *subcaste groups*. A subcaste category consists of people who have the same jati name, but who live in different local hierarchies. In traditional circumstances they did not as a rule form an interacting social group but were merely people who had ancestral or other not very well defined connections with one another. With modern developments of communication and large-scale migration to towns, these categories of people have tended to become real social groups with common obligatory behavior demanded from members. In East Africa members of jati with the same name but from different districts, that is to say members of one subcaste category, have in some instances slowly emerged as a unified group locally known as a "community" which bears the common subcaste or jati name.

(IV) *Caste associations.* A caste association is a modern voluntary association recruited either from a subcaste group (jati), a subcaste category (jati), or even in a few instances from a varna (caste) category for welfare or political ends. In East Africa such bodies, which seldom include all members of the group or category settled in Africa or even in one territory, are known as *castes* or *community associations* or *communities.* Through the governing or organizing body of such a community the leaders of the group or category approach the Administration, and through it, too, the more marginal members of the group or category are able to attach themselves to the local "community." Thus the leaders of such an organized jati or varna are able to persuade the more old-fashioned

---

the degree to which they are corporate; and in certain situations one of the principal difficulties of analysis may be to decide whether a particular social entity is in fact a social group or a mere category of the population, such as red-haired people, selected by a criterion which in the context is socially neutral and which does not prescribe uniform behavior. For any study of group relations the distinction is essential.

members to enlarge the boundaries of the "caste community" for the sake of greater numbers and effectiveness in the African scene.

In the analysis of "caste" in East Africa it is clearly most important to distinguish these four types of social grouping (all locally referred to as "castes") ; for any one of them may form the basis of an emerging "caste community."

Caste in East Africa

The fact that the immigrants to East Africa failed to transplant any representative cross-section of their traditional society was of capital importance ; but, as we have also noted, the failure was hardly surprising. Not only did the nature of the immigration make the establishment of local subcaste hierarchies unlikely in Africa, but the immigrants themselves also came with the intention of being only traders in a society subject to laws and economic customs which were in conflict with Hindu and Muslim rules and regulations. Large numbers did in fact abandon traditional practices and began to model their behavior not on Hindu or Muslim ideals but on those they believed to be held by Europeans or the westernized classes in the larger cities of India.

An outsider might have predicted, therefore, that eventually a single Indian community would emerge, different in language and culture from that of the Africans, the Arabs, or the Europeans, but having an over-all similarity in wishing to remain separate and in being stratified perhaps in terms of economic wealth and social class. Hindu caste and Muslim sectarian differences, it might have been thought, would become relatively unimportant. What in fact emerged was something quite different.

In 1955 the Indian community in Uganda was divided between Hindus and Muslims, but in addition there were also, as we have just seen, a number of what were locally known as Hindu caste and Muslim sectarian communities, groups such as the Hindu Patidar caste community, the Muslim Shia Imami Ismailia sectarian community, and other groups such as the Sikh and Goan communities, one of which was founded on its own particular religion and the other on immigrants from the former Portuguese colony of Goa. The organization of these communities differed slightly from one to another, but since they had emerged as communities in order to further the political, economic, and social welfare of their members, they essentially resembled one another in form and function, both of which were conditioned by the society within which they had developed. By 1955 they had become some of the most important institutions of Indian life in East Africa. For most practical purposes the fact that a man was a member of the Patidar caste or a Goan or a follower of the Aga Khan's Shia Imami Ismailia sect was more important to him than being either a Hindu or a Muslim or even a member of the Indian community (Morris 1956).

Africans and Europeans were, of course, aware that there was great diversity among Indians but in most circumstances found it convenient to ignore the divisions which marked off one Indian from another and to speak of an Indian or Asian community as if it were a corporate group organized to defend Indian interests. In course of time various pieces of legislation, the founding of separate schools, and administrative practice all combined to reenforce the view. In the same way the categories of Hindus and Muslims were often treated as if they too were united groups with responsible leaders able to answer politically, legally, and socially for their members. While their numbers were small it was also convenient for Indians to acquiesce in this view. All-Indian organizations were created to negotiate with the Administration; but, with the growth of numbers and wealth, separate caste and sectarian communities emerged and new leaders replaced the older men who had spoken on behalf of all Indians. Hindus and Muslims never in fact effectively organized themselves as united associations, and by the end of the Second World War the Indian community as such had little reality as a united corporate body. This arrangement of groups and categories—comprising castes, sects, Hindus, Muslims, and Indians as a whole—was, of course, only one element in the complex multiracial society found in the East African territories. There were also the African, the Arab, and the European communities, each made up of its own characteristic groups and categories, embedded in a network of relations that extended far beyond the boundaries of the ethnic and cultural groupings.

Until the end of the Second World War, all members of the

public in Uganda, whether African, Indian, or European, were more or less excluded from seriously participating in political decisions. The Protectorate was administered by a Governor appointed in Britain, assisted by an Executive Council nominated by him, and a permanent civil service, the senior members of which were also appointed in Britain. Legislative measures were enacted by the Governor on the advice of a Legislative Council, the majority of whose members were nominated by the Administration. The effective ruling of the country was therefore in the hands of a European civil service which, to the best of its abilities, consulted and used a limited section of the population in making political and administrative decisions. During the period before the introduction of representative government, advice was requested from an increasing number of people, and those who were thus consulted often acquired great influence.

It was within this political framework that the structure of Indian society in Uganda developed. Most Indians were traders, and to a trader his most important dealings with an administration concern his legal status and his rights to trade. Hindu and Muslim law were often incompatible with the system of English-based law administered by the courts in East Africa, and when a trader fell into difficulties he tended to go to a patron for help rather than face the hazards of a court of law or of direct dealing with a civil servant. For a man to set up as a patron in and leader of a community he needed to establish good relations with the administrative services. It was to this situation that Indian society was adjusted.

Although the African and European inhabitants of the East African territories believed that the Indian community was tightly organized, at no stage had this belief ever been in real correspondence to fact. With the emergence of caste and sectarian communities, associations speaking for Indians as a whole became increasingly less effective. The Indian community as a body of people united by common interests became even less of a reality than in earlier days when small numbers and the hazards of their social environment had to some extent held them together. Nevertheless the ideal of an Indian community which, it was felt, ought to unite people within a common civilization still remained; and if circumstances ever arose which might make it necessary to band together once more for self-defense these rather tenuous links did exist. The structural units which significantly guided the lives of Indians were the caste and sectarian communities. These were in unending rivalry with one another in a political situation where Indians did not as of right share the real powers of making decisions, and where ultimately they could safeguard their economic interests only by attracting the favorable opinion of officials. Within a caste community, power and influence were mainly secured by election to the committees and councils which controlled it. A man had to achieve position on these before he could hope to become a leader of the community and in that capacity enter into relationships with the Administration and other sections of the wider society. In no sense, however, were such caste and sectarian leaders trying to gain leadership of the Indian community as a whole. Even less were they competing with one another to take hold of the state organization of Uganda, or any other territory in East Africa, in order to speak and act for the country as a whole (Morris 1957).

The nature of these caste and sectarian communities and the way in which they developed and maintained relations with one another and the rest of society in Uganda need more discussions. As we have seen, the Indian immigrants to East Africa came mostly from small rural caste systems in which the behavior of subcastes and (to some degree) of Muslims sects was regulated by their place in a hierarchy. Sometimes there were councils with jurisdiction over the members of the subcaste within the local system; sometimes there were not. The more important factors which inhibited the emergence of local caste systems in East Africa have already been touched on: the immigrants were a minority in a large non-Hindu population and they came from districts in India that were often widely separated. Even if a sufficient number of members of the full range of jati needed to set up a traditional local caste system had emigrated to Africa, the immigrants would still have found it difficult to agree upon a hierarchy, for nobody was willing to accept any position for his own group except that which it held in his own home district. Moreover, the economic and legal systems in East Africa did not permit division of labor according to the rules of caste. A man who did not want to practise his traditional occupation was not allowed to stop others from following it. Indians came to Africa to trade in a modern large-scale economic system and not to engage in traditional occupations, some of which were essential to the caste system (for example, washing clothes or acting as priests) but which had to be neglected or performed by non-Hindus who were by definition outcast and polluting.

The ease with which India could be visited and the frequency with which people in fact went to and from their homes meant that although they were not able to construct a caste system in Africa, they were obliged to maintain the identity and a large part of the exclusiveness of their jati. In particular they dared not fail to arrange correct endogamous marriages, so that on their permanent return to India—a hope cherished by all though achieved by few—they could once more assume their proper place in the local system. This need for caste exclusiveness was so strong that, in spite of an environment almost wholly unfavorable to it, caste exclusiveness was one of the most important structural principles in organizing Indian social life in East Africa. In this respect East Africa contrasts with other areas of overseas settlement, where the links with India were not so close and where caste barriers in course of time were relaxed.

Nevertheless, though exclusiveness was built into the structure of Indian society in East Africa, its application was not the same as in the local caste hierarchies of India. In Africa it was an exclusiveness of caste and sectarian communities, of caste categories and caste associations, rather than of jati, though within these larger new formations traditional restrictions, especially on marriage, might still be maintained in the interests of an eventual return to India. As long as the population in a trading settlement anywhere in East Africa remained small and the men were engaged in occupations which necessarily meant that they shared common interests, the Indians were willing, with some reservations, to act and to be treated as a united community. It would, they felt, have been unwise in the face of the many legal, cultural, and physical difficulties which confronted them to let disunity appear. Furthermore, the restricted choice of friends in a small settlement drove them to associate with one another, since most, in spite of differences, spoke the same language, ate the same kinds of food, and had many memories of India in common.

Whenever the members of a particular caste grouping or sect grew large enough for the members to consort mainly with one another, it was not long before they began to emerge as a distinct communal group—a caste or sectarian community. The organization set up to further this process also began to take over tasks formerly undertaken by united Indian organizations. Institutions peculiar to a caste, such as councils or feasts for its members or specific rituals, might have been brought from India. These gave a foundation for organization, but in Africa if money was collected from the public a registered association had to be formed ; and it would be around such a caste association that the new community crystallized.

In the beginning often only the members of one jati from one district would organize in this way, for example the Patidar subcaste of Kaira district in Gujarat ; but it sometimes happened that people carrying the same jati name wished to associate formally, even though they came from different areas in India, as did the Lohana of Kathiawar. In such a case, the basis of the new community was a caste category. Sometimes, too, as with the representatives of several Brahmin jati who settled in Uganda, the new community was founded on a varna category. Developments of this kind were not, of course, special to East Africa: they could also be found in every large city of India itself.

The emergence of communities was facilitated by the relatively favorable political atmosphere of East Africa. In Uganda what are usually called race relations were superficially cordial, a state of affairs which was warmly appreciated by the immigrant traders who depended on the good will of the rest of the population for their livelihood. There were few occasions, especially in Uganda, when they had to close their ranks against outside hostility; hence the tendencies towards separation latent in the structure of Indian society as it had developed in Africa could be safely allowed to go unchecked. So much was this so that the followers of the Aga Khan (the Shia Imami Ismailia sect) felt sufficiently secure to look for allies in forwarding their interest both within and without the Indian section of society. This favorable political atmosphere, then, encouraged the multiplication of communities for yet other reasons. The larger the number of such communal organizations, the more positions there were open to ambitious men—positions from which they could advance their own interests as well as those of their community. In the light of these circumstances it is not hard to see why the development of caste in the form of caste associations and caste categories became so important in the organization of Indian society in East Africa. What is not so clear is why communities did not crystallize around Hindu sects as they did around those of Muslims.

Associated with the failure to develop local caste systems in East Africa was the failure to develop much of the public part of Hindu religion. The lack of a caste system meant that those sections of the religion which were connected with the maintenance and welfare of traditional groups also fell into disuse. For the same reason, too, many domestic rites and beliefs were neglected. Only a few of the many Hindu sects which flourished in Gujarat and other parts of India were taken to Africa, and, perhaps because communication with India was easy and frequent, centers of pilgrimage did not appear in East Africa. Indian migrants to Mauritius, Fiji, and South Africa (Benedict 1961; Mayer 1961; H. Kuper 1960), in contrast with those to East Africa, arrived with virtually no material possessions and small likelihood of returning home. Unlike the traders of Kenya, Tanganyika, and Uganda, these other immigrants lived in agricultural settlements and they and their children cultivated land as had their ancestors before them. Among their immaterial possessions were their gods and their habits of worship. In their new environment, with risks and dangers similar to those they had left at home in their villages, the gods were, if anything, more needed. For most of the indentured, it would have been useless to vow a pilgrimage to the Ganges, and it was not long before new saints and shrines were discovered. But in Uganda a man could safely vow a pilgrimage to India, knowing that it was not impossible. He could also safely ignore his gods for the duration of his stay abroad, if he believed that he could make amends in later years in a real emergency. For reasons of this kind an elaborate public religion was not urgently needed in East Africa and did not appear.

Nevertheless, religious cults and sects were taken to Africa and maintained themselves. But even had Indians wished to support large religious establishments, the rules and regulations of immigration would have made the task difficult. No alien was permitted to enter East Africa unless he could fill a post that was for the benefit of everybody. Officials did not find it easy to appreciate the value of priests and of ascetics and of a life spent in contemplating without a commercial occupation; most professionally religious men in India hesitated when confronted by the ritual impurity of Africa. But the critical factor making caste rather than sect the basis of community among the Hindus of East Africa was that traditionally exclusiveness was institutionalized in the caste system and not in religion. The leader of a Hindu sectarian movement could never rely on the undivided loyalty of ordinary members. Unlike their Muslim counterparts, Hindu religious leaders were not able to offer exclusive religious salvation to their followers or everlasting damnation to unbelievers. For a Hindu, salvation depended on correct caste behavior and the discovery of religious leaders suitable to his station in life.

Caste-Community Relationships

In Uganda the relationship of caste and sectarian communities to one another was primarily one of competition in contrast to the ideal of cooperation between complementary jati in a local caste system in India. A community usually emerged as an organized corporate group because some vital interest was threatened or because it saw that another community which had organized was able through its leaders to obtain advantages that the leaders of the older all-Indian bodies were either unable or unwilling to obtain. Probably the easiest way to show how caste and sectarian communities worked in relation to one another, to the Indian community as a whole, and to the wider society is to ask the question: How did an Indian in Uganda obtain influence and power?

Immediately before and after the Second World War there were two main ways in which an Indian could obtain influence in the wider society of Uganda. Both required a man to be rich, westernized, and able to establish personal relationships with members of the Administration, so that he could approach them on behalf of his community as a whole or of individual members. The earlier of these two routes was to gain office and respect in the old all-Indian associations which had the respect of the Administration. After 1945 this method became uncertain in its results. The position of the older inclusive Indian councils had been undermined by the development of caste and sectarian associations, and the more usual route to influence then came to be the gaining of power within the communities.

The emergence of caste and sectarian communities was accompanied by the rise of many new leaders who maintained their places only if they were successful as patrons and able to negotiate satisfactorily with the Administration. The part played by such a communal leader had two aspects. He could hope to succeed in a career of this kind only if he had sufficient wealth to attract followers, either by giving them commercial credit or by being able to help them through his contacts. His position in the community and its councils turned directly on the success with which he could attract and hold a following. The second aspect of the part played by a communal leader was that he handled extracommunal relations explicitly on behalf of the community and implicitly on behalf of his clients. The most important of these relations was with the civil service. Once a caste or sect had emerged as a corporate group it was necessarily in competition with other similar groups for favors from the Government. It could function only as a pressure group demanding preferential treatment or proffering advice. In a situation of this kind, if the members of a community wished to succeed in making their views heard, they were obliged to see that their leaders reached positions close to the seats of power where their opinions would be heard and their requests perhaps be granted; for here the interests of the leaders and the led coincided.

In a political system of this kind, where power is not obtained through election, there is a premium on selecting leaders for their abilities in what may be called the politics of persuasion. In the structure of Indian society in Uganda there was also a high premium on castes developing themselves into efficiently organized caste communities. Relations between them were routed, as it were, not along traditional lines, but principally through the Administration, in the sense that the leaders of the communities were competing with one another to establish themselves favorably in the eyes of civil servants. The greater part of their dealings with one another was in this context. The same was even more true of relations between Africans and Indians, except in part for economic relations and those arising out of them, especially in rural areas. The leaders of the different sections of society—African, Indian, and European—therefore met regularly and frequently at formal dinners and parties which were ultimately intended only to attract the attention of members of the Administration.

This phenomenon, which is common in colonial societies, is not, however, confined to them. As the territories of East Africa became independent self-governing countries with the formal machinery of voting and election to political office, the situation of the Indians did not alter. Their small numbers meant that they could never hope to achieve real power in the society and that consequently their economic safety still lay in ingratiating themselves with the holders of power. So far they have not been threatened merely because they are Indians and thus forced to close their ranks and become a united group at the expense of caste and sectarian communities. Many indeed argue that it would now be exceedingly dangerous to unite in this way. Caste as the basis of communities is therefore likely to retain its importance in organizing Indian society in East Africa for a considerable time to come. In 1955 it was possible to watch the leaders of these communities in process, so to speak, of rerouting their lines of communication from a primarily European Administration to leaders of the potential African state. Personal links with India are not likely to be discarded quickly; and for those who regard India as a place of refuge should their position in Africa become untenable, the importance of maintaining a minimum of caste observance, in the traditional sense as well as in the sense which has developed in Africa, becomes all the greater.

REFERENCES

BENEDICT, BURTON
1961   *Indians in a plural society.* London: H.M.S.O.

KUPER, HILDA
1960   *Indian people in Natal.* Natal: Natal University Press.

LEACH, E. R.
1960   *Aspects of caste in South India, Ceylon, and North-West Pakistan.*
        Cambridge: Cambridge University Press.

MAYER, ADRIAN C.
1961   *Peasants in the Pacific.* Berkeley: University of California Press.

MORRIS, H. S.
1956   "Indians in East Africa." *British Journal of Sociology* VII:3:194-211.

1957   "Communal rivalry among Indians in Uganda." *British Journal of Sociology* VIII:4:306-317.

SRINIVAS, M. N.
1952   *Religion and society among the Coorgs of South India.* London: Oxford University Press.

EAST AFRICA

Ideology and Content of Caste among the Indians in East Africa[1]

AGEHANANDA BHARATI

This article employs the structure-content dichotomy (Hsu 1959, 1963) as its major analytical referent for examining caste among Indians in East Africa. Hsu juxtaposes the relatively permanent matrix of any social order with the events that rest upon the matrix. Though the events (in the widest possible sense of the word as covering persons, families, sibs, clans, rituals, and the like, all the things ethnologists write about in a specific society) are fairly variable within their matrix, they do not usually fall outside its scope. If they do, the situation is a deviant one. For parallel models to further exemplify this type of analysis, I would think of a chessboard

[1]This contribution is the result of a seven-month field trip to East Africa, India, and Pakistan, which was financed by the Overseas Center of the Maxwell School of Public Affairs and Citizenship, Syracuse University, New York, and the National Institute of Mental Health (Department of Health, Education, and Welfare), Bethesda, Md. The author is indebted to both organizations for their munificent support.

and the rules of chess. These two provide the structure of chess. All possible chess games and chess moves, a virtually infinite number, are the content of chess. Or, to provide a terser model from mathematical logic, the constants in any function, together with the function, provide the structure. The variables replacing the nonconstant items in the function would be their content. Some mathematical logicians actually use "structure" and "content," and it is conceivable that Hsu was inspired by the mathematical and/or logical model.

Approaches to the Inquiry

In India, then, the matrix of jati (caste) is part of the structure of Indian society; endogamy, commensality, and trade exclusiveness are the fundamental configuration of the structure irrespective of the proportionate strength or weakness of any of these three parts. As soon as relative weightings (strengths and weaknesses) are discussed, we have moved into the realm of content. For example, as soon as conjugality is shown to be significantly more crucial than commensality or occupational exclusiveness, or (as in the case of East African Asian society) that trade exclusiveness has been almost entirely abandoned, we have begun to talk about the content of caste. Quantitative statements are statements of content, just as the variable in a mathematical function is a statement of content. The constants (structure) are nonquantitative and are therefore not significantly involved with matters of degree, intensity, proportion, or the like. It must be made quite clear at the outset that in East African Indian society, conjugality is the only facet of caste remaining intact; noncommensality is complete and occupational exclusiveness applies only to the very lowest and least numerous people and jatis. But endogamy is so complete and its workings so unchanged from those in the Indian sister communities in South Asia that it remains the *only* criterion of caste (jati) among East African Asians. Therefore, for both descriptive reasons and pedagogical reasons, I shall isolate endogamy as the only completely valid criterion of jati in East Africa; inclusion of commensality and occupational exclusiveness as coordinate or even subordinate criteria in defining jati would be grossly misleading. (It would be like trying to equate descriptively fauna of Africa and India by saying "There are elephants, buffaloes and lions in Africa just as there are elephants, buffaloes and lions in India." There are indeed a few lions left in the Junagarh district in western India, but listing them just like lions in Africa is misleading.) For these reasons I equate, discursively, jati (caste) with endogamy *only* in East Africa throughout this study. In other words, jati and endogamy are functional synonyms in Asian East Africa.

While greater emphasis is placed upon content, structure as the complementary pole must be kept in mind continuously. Justification for treating structure less intensively is based on the conviction that there has been no important change in the caste structure among Indians in East Africa, whereas the ideology and content of caste in this area have been unduly neglected. Truly ideological statements and judgments refer to content alone, and this is all we are concerned with here. By ideology we mean the sum total of positive and negative value judgments about the *nos*.[2] More specifically, the term "ideology" is used in a metalinguistic sense: a set of statements *about* value statements of any sort. Such usage removes the emotive tone of "ideology." To do so is particularly important to our study, since the word has a politically loaded, negative flavor for intelligent Indians in present-day East Africa. When they hear "ideology," they understand communism, capitalism, racism, nationalism, or the like. Indeed, Indian discussants since Vivekananda inveigh against "isms" as the wrong, misleading, or disturbing factor in human thought and human relationships. For the Asian audience, insofar as it participates in social discourse, "ideology" means "isms" and only that. The word "casteism" has been used, due to Gandhian literature, and is understood as an *ideology* by the Asians: casteism is bad, it must be overcome, it is an ideology that must be transcended for the benefit of the Asian minority. But this is precisely the kind of meaning that *caste* must not have in a study like ours. *Caste* as we use the word, however, is value-free, analytic, and an ideology in the only permissible sense— a set of notions and pronouncements based on the historical accident of a particular social structure in a societal content. In this sense, Hinduism, Islam, ritual, and antiritual are ideologies like caste.

---

[2] I am using the plural instead of "ego" where a modal self-image of a social group requires a term of reference: "ego" would hardly do for more than one individual.

Particular problems are inherent in an analysis which makes use of ideology and content. Many of these difficulties are directly related to collection of field data and to the rapport of the field worker with his informants. Consequently, the reader should be explicitly aware of them. The sociologist or anthropologist who studies caste in Africa, or for that matter in India, is obliged by the reaction of his informants to disguise his intent. This whole book, perhaps, is an opus compiled largely against the wishes of the subjects. The sophisticated Indian who reads this anthology might feel offended or at least annoyed by its very aim. "Caste does not exist today" and propositions to this effect are the common summary statements among groups within and outside of South Asia. They proceed from the idea that since caste (in a wide, nonsociological, political sense) ought not to exist, it ought not to be mentioned let alone studied. It is beyond the modern Indian's comprehension why sociologists and anthropologists keep harping on an outmoded idea when there are so many more fascinating and important things to be studied about Indians everywhere: river-valley projects, education, participation in democracy, their role in the United Nations and international organizations, Indian religions and philosophy, Gandhi and Nehru, and so on. The modern Indian attitude is reflected in the official policies of the Indian government: anthropologists are suspect *because* they are known to study caste. The feeling is that such studies will perpetuate rather than diminish caste feeling.[3]

The criticism of an Asian leader in Nairobi is highly representative of this attitude. When I explained to him that the purpose of my visit to East Africa was to study culture change and stagnation among the Asian minorities in the area, he became quite upset: I ought not to conduct such a study at all—and if I persisted, I ought to be asked to leave the country; Asians in Africa are Africans; even referring to them as Asians or as a minority is harmful; "if you mention Lohanas and Patels and Ramgarhias, these people will say, Oh, see, a foreign scholar mentions us! They will be prouder of being Lohanas and

---

[3]Many anthropologists who do not have a Commonwealth passport have been and are being refused visas to India (Commonwealth citizens do not require visas), and it is hoped that this book may help Indian authorities to realize that the objective analysis of a basic phenomenon in the structure of a society neither increases nor decreases its workings.

Patels instead of forgetting this nonsense and of being Kenyans and Africans *like all of us.*"[4] When I remonstrated that my mentioning these groups and castes was nothing commendatory, he refused to accept the argument. The very mentioning of a caste name by any-one of status outside the caste makes its members happy and proud of their "fissiparous" attitudes.

The leader in question is a radical on all counts; but even a person who is known to be both a lenient liberal and a scholar among the Asians thought that the sort of study I was making would harm the Asian community: "Why do you not write about caste among the British and the Americans? Why are the Asians always singled out for this harmful interest?" The implied charge against some social scientists is not entirely unjustified. There is a tendency to hope for perpetuation of structures that are interesting to the anthropologist and a somewhat obtuse insistence, among some, that caste *must* last. This hope, of course, is nonsense, for both structure and content may change, as they have, say, in the Caribbean and in Fiji.

But it must also be said that Indian audiences are highly and unnecessarily sensitive to any outsider's inquiry about caste. Swami Vivekananda, one of the founders of the Indian Renaissance, com-pared this sort of interest to the Egyptologist's love for Egypt—a censure from his viewpoint. Yet, if we bear in mind that some element of caste study will always remain obnoxious to people who live in caste, we can proceed with due apology to them, trying to show that there is merit in descriptive analysis. This is a difficult task and in-volves long discourse between anthropologists—including Indian-born anthropologists—and Indians; but this discourse is a duty that India-centered anthropologists still have to fulfill.

The ideology of caste among the Asians in East Africa is one of radical denial and latent admission. To the student of India this paradox is only apparent. The psychocultural hallmark of the modern Indian intellectual[5] is what I call a systematic confusion between the social "is" and the social "ought." The confusion is not cognitive; it is unconscious or psychocultural. "There ought to be no caste" is

---

[4]Interview with Mr. Makhan Singh, Nairobi, June 29, 1964.

[5]The best, albeit a short treatise on the problems of the Indian intellectual is that of E. Shils, *The Intellectual between Tradition and Modernity: the Indian Situation.* The Hague: Mouton & Co., 1959.

formulated "there is no caste" or "there is no caste any longer." The modal attitude for the Indian intellectual in India is shared by all Asians in East Africa who are now younger than age fifty. If we look for a standard distinction in the style of social parlance between the young and the old, caste-language provides quite a clearcut demarcation: The "young" are those in East Africa who claim that there is no caste, that it has broken down, that everyone does as he pleases, that there is free intermarriage, and so on. The "old" are those who although they *now* say that caste is getting weaker actually believe that it is still very strong—they make their kin-oriented decisions on caste lines and they view their caste as the corporate unit wherewith they identify themselves.

These are statements of a mutual alter-image. It remains for us to see how the situation stands objectively, how ideology of caste diverges from content of caste in East Africa. To begin: it so happens that the "old" are as yet closer to the facts. Caste in the properly defined sense has not broken down. It is showing signs of weakening, but this weakening is one of ideology, not one of content in a quantitatively significant degree. And, as was indicated earlier, there is no change in caste structure. This statement requires substantiation of a purely empirical kind.

Whenever young Asians in East Africa speak about caste, they consistently use the English word, regardless of whether they are speaking English, Gujarati, Panjabi, or Hindustani. They *never* use the Indian terms. The reasons for this practice are diffuse. In the first place, very few Asians are quite clear about the proper vernacular word. The correct Indian term is jati (literally "birth"). A jati is an endogamous unit and, as already stated, endogamy is its only unexceptional trait. In India until the turn of the century, and to a small extent in rural India today, a jati was also occupationally exclusive and commensal. In the past a jati had the economic features of a guild, to a degree, and the ritualistic feature of eating food cooked only by members of the same or of a higher caste. In East Africa, the commensal and occupation-exclusive aspects of the Indian caste system have disappeared almost entirely. Transcaste commensality is virtually complete—the cooks in the wealthier houses are almost all Africans, who would rank lower than the lowest in an Indian caste-

culinary setting. One minor exception involves some 200 members of the sweeper caste among the Panjabis in the larger East African cities —Panjabis refer to them as "Valmiks."[6] Valmiks would not usually be invited to share a meal with other Panjabis. At the annual function of the Arya Samaj, the most aggressively reformist parochial group in Hindu East Africa, Valmiks and some parallel Gujarati Untouchables are fed conspicuously and the fact that they are fed is pointed out emphatically—obviously a very definite compensatory device. But apart from the numerically insignificant exception of the Valmiks, commensality is complete.

Ishmailis "eat together" with other groups outside their homes, and they make a point of stressing commensal liberality. However, it seems to me that their case is one of enhanced esoterism rather than of caste-group feeling: just as no one but an Ishmaili can participate in their formal prayers at the Jamatkhana, the Ishmaili mosque, no outsiders or few outsiders would be called in frequently for a meal. Yet I do not think that this meal-taking exclusiveness instantiates non-commensality, because the notion of ritualistic purity which is paramount in the Indian commensality structure does not obtain with the Ishmailis in East Africa.

There is some degree of trade exclusiveness, but in a special unilateral sense only: fund[7] people, who do the jobs originally restricted to their castes, may and often do perform a variety of other jobs—in fact many Ramgarhias, Sutarias, and Mochis, all classical Panjabi and Gujarati fundi castes, have gone into the professions and some of the most brilliant lawyers, judges, and physicians hail from them.

---

[6]"Valmiks" is a euphemism for the Panjabi-speaking former Untouchables: Valmiki, the mythological author of the *Ramayana,* the more popular of the two great Hindu epics, was a low-caste or outcaste in the mythological tradition. The number of Valmiks has shrunk in the past five years, as the menial jobs of house and street cleaning have been taken over by indigenous Africans.

[7]"*Fundi*" is the Swahili word for any skilled artisan, carpenter, mason, joiner, or the like. The word has completely diffused into the three Indian languages spoken in East Africa, as well as into Konkani. When a Gujarati speaker refers to an Indian carpenter in Gujarati, he will use the word *fundi,* not the equivalent Gujarati term; the same holds for Panjabis and Goans when speaking their language.

But no person of non-*fundi* caste does (or has done so far) *fundi* jobs except for a hobby. In other words, though *fundis* participate in all jobs, including the professions, persons of the higher castes do not do carpentry, masonry, cobbling, tailoring, or the like. A young Jain lad was sawing a bench which he had constructed ; his mother said with a frown: "Why are you doing this—are you a *fundi?*" It is conceivable that some individuals from groups higher than *fundi* castes would have taken to carpentry or masonry, because these jobs are often much more lucrative than petty shopkeeping—and though there would have been no objection to such a change of trade in the East African setting, it just has not happened at any time. With the present uncertainty about the survival of the Asians in East Africa as a whole, no such experiment seems to be in prospect. Thus, vestigial trade exclusiveness is upward unilateral, just as it has been in urban India for at least five decades.

I return to the fact that Asians in East Africa use *caste,* and not jati or an Indian vernacular equivalent when they talk about caste in English, Gujarati, Panjabi, or Hindustani. Whenever it is pointed out to them that caste is not an insidious menace encroaching from the past into the present nor a political stratagem of reactionaries, but simply an anthropological fact—specifically, that of endogamy— and really nothing else, such clarification is taken with considerable dismay. Somehow, the feeling is ubiquitous that caste is something one has to fight against, to supersede, and to explain away as nonexistent or no longer existent and no longer important. A dry, uninspiring disquisition on the sociologically actual function of caste causes a traumatic reaction, or reactions. The Asian confronted with it may change the topic, but more often, he or she will take up the issue and go to great pains to show that even endogamy is not a significant factor: "Everyone marries whom he or she pleases." To substantiate this claim the speaker will then adduce a few cases "from my own family" or "a good friend of mine" who has married a girl or a boy of his or her own choice and from another caste or religion. How much such responses are subjective fancy, and how often they are true—or rather, how large the number of friends shared by the people who married across caste lines may be, the fact is that in 1964 the percentage of intercaste marriages in all communities together

—Hindu, Jain, Muslim, Sikh, and Goan—was about 0.2 per cent.[8] When this fact is pointed out, it is not usually denied—but the parlance then shifts to forecast: even though there may be few intercaste marriages yet, there will soon be more and more and within a few years (ranging from 2 to 20 generations in the prognostication by different subjects), all Asians will marry without reference to caste boundaries.

This ideology is not specific to East African Asians; it is shared by almost all Hindus in India under the age of fifty insofar as they are verbal and critical about social matters. In rural India the situation is different—rural Hindus in India tend to be indifferent to the perpetuation or the discontinuation of the jati system, though the very young, who have gone to school since independence, are at least theoretically opposed to its continuance. This does not necessarily mean that they will themselves marry across caste lines in great numbers during the next few generations. However, East African Asians are all urban Indians, and whatever rudimentarily rural background some of the groups have had (the Patels, the Visa Oshwals, and certainly the very few Sikh Jat families in East Africa hail from purely rural backgrounds), they now have no knowledge of the ways of the village. With the exception of about 200 Jat farmers in the Highlands of Kenya, all Asians in East Africa are urban people, with urban tastes—not sophisticatedly urban, but decidedly urban—and with urban aspirations. It is probably very largely due to this fact that the cognitive part of their caste ideology is negative and critical, with

---

[8]There are absolutely no statistics relevant to intercaste or non-Asian intermarriage. This figure, which is very crude, was arrived at by personal investigations of the following sort: Leaders, mostly executives in the various parochial service societies, were consulted for a numerical estimate of intermarriages in their communities. In each community, such persons were approached independently at three different places without mutual knowledge of the query. The median of each estimate was then determined for each community. In this manner, the average estimate among the Ishmailis was 200 cases, among the Goans 100 cases, among the Panjabis (Sikhs and Hindus) 100 cases, among Lohanas and Patels 50 cases, and a cautious 50 cases are assumed by myself for the other Gujarati communities, all of which are much less likely to intermarry. The total Asian population of East Africa being roughly 360,000, 0.2 per cent emerged as the total percentage of intermarriage. This figure includes marriage liaisons with Whites.

the above-mentioned semantic specification—all "young" East African Asians are against caste, though very few really knew what caste is. Their invectives are a bit quixotic: caste does not really exist as they see it, that is, as a set of noxious rules to be broken away from.

The Structure of Caste

The structure of caste among the Asians in East Africa is stagnant. The infrequent intercaste marriages, the verbal criticism of "caste" as an ideology, and the symbiosis with non-Indian people have not changed caste structure as they did, say, in Trinidad (Klass 1961, Niehoff 1960), or in Fiji (Mayer 1963). The situation is closest to that in Natal (Kuper 1960), and most divergent from that in Fiji and the Caribbean. There may be a suggestion that the Sikhs in British Columbia and California are equally or more stagnant in matters of caste: however, these two groups do not really come into a comparative purview as do the people in East or South Africa.

Stagnation, of course, has to be defined in a modified manner in different areas. When we claim that the Asian caste structure in East Africa is "stagnant," we mean these things: rules of endogamy, hypergamy, and intercaste ranking are unchanged with reference to the original situation; marriages are arranged within the traditional limitations, that is, caste (jati-) endogamy, occasional hypergamy, and infrequent deviation. There are probably more intercaste alliances, both arranged by parents and by individual choice, than in the sister communities in India, but "more" can at best mean 2 to 3 per cent more. The "modern" Asians' statement to the effect that things have completely changed are largely make-believe or to put it more mildly, are instances of a culture-endemic confusion of the "is" with the "ought."

Caste structure is not entirely stagnant, however, when compared with the rural parts of the Indian sister communities. In the latter, there is, by and large, village exogamy—of which there is hardly any trace left in East Africa. About 4 out of 10 older people—Lohanas and Patels—who were asked whether their children's marriage had been arranged with village exogamy in mind said they had been so arranged. The other six either did not seem to know, or only knew the mere historical fact that there was such a rule as village exogamy in their Indian sister or parent communities. Hardly any young people are cognizant of village exogamy, and where the houses—this holds mainly for Gujarati Hindus and Jains—are most conservative, village exogamous choices made for the children are not communicated to them. Obviously, this is done with a view not to aggravate possible discontent among the young about conventional structures. Village exogamy, however, does not mean East African location exogamy; it is totally beside the point whether or not the bride's and groom's family have settled in the same or in a different East African locality. The reference is to the original villages in India. But as the majority of Gujarati-speaking Asians in East Africa hail from an urban, or at least not from a purely rural background, village exogamy is a very weak factor and most likely to disappear completely within this generation. Urban Gujaratis in the Indian sister communities—in Porbandar, Jamnagar, or Baroda, for example —have not adhered rigidly to the village-exogamy rule if their ancestors had been urbanized before 1800.

One point is important here from the contemporary anthropological scene: the floating notion that change in ecology may affect social structure (Steward 1955) is just not applicable here, simply because East African Asian society was too complex even at the time of its first settlement. All its members were traders with a considerable literary background, and all of them were cognitively conscious of caste rules and strictures. Also, they foisted their own ecological setting on their environments and were not the least bit impressed or affected by the indigenous settings surrounding them.

The process of "sanskritization-westernization," as described by Srinivas (1956) and Staal (1963), was uniquely manifest in the East African Asian milieux. The retention of caste structure during the first generation of Asian settlement was part of the prestige complex which was adhered to because it perpetuated the sort of identification that made the Asians a strong, self-contained populace which needed no cultural standards outside itself. It is not too important whether or not the early Asians knew that African society had its own elaborate caste structure along tribal lines, and whether or not the British ruling minority had a parallel set of social institutions. Viscerally and cognitively, the first-generation settlers knew that their jati and varna system was unique and that it helped them to be Indian and to communicate among themselves. This value was all that mattered, for the Indians desired no noncommercial intercourse either with the Africans or with the Whites.

Now in the present generation (people between 20 and 45) the ideology is pointedly opposed to "caste," but then "caste" is used as a token in the analytical sense: a word to indicate something that has to be handled without further analysis, as analysis would arrest manipulation. Once it is pointed out to the modern Asians that caste (jati) means nothing but endogamy, the momentum of ideological opposition lapses. This is indeed a local version of sanskritization and westernization, though it is a good deal subtler than in the Indian sister communities. Sanskritization means a cognitive devaluation of ritual by way of a philosophical-ideological reinterpretation or reval-uation—a process that has been at work in India since the Upanishads (900-400 B.C.). Ritual remains, but its content has moved up: the Vedic horse sacrifice became a process of exalted inner contemplation in the Upanishads ; and the traditional workings of jati are challenged by defying, dialectically at first, caste—the defiance being couched in terms of nationalism, social integration, Indian-ness. These, how-ever, are rarefied ritualistic themes in themselves, for *India, nation, spirituality, Indian culture,* and the like are not anthropological or historically descriptive terms in modern Asian usage; they are rather, like *caste,* emotive tokens harnessed for a shift from lower to higher, to a more rarefied, ritualism. It is quite irrelevant whether one of these tokens is lauded (like Hindu culture) or denigrated (like caste).

Invective against a lower ritual in the event of institutionalizing a higher one, one more rarefied and intellectualized, is not only a time-honored device in the Indian tradition, but has canonical sanc-tions. The technical term is the Sanskrit word *samanvaya,* which can be interpreted as reconciliation of opposing views about the same (ritualistic) matter. One of the hallmarks of the Hindu Renaissance in India, which began near the opening of the nineteenth century and which seems to have reached its zenith at this time, has been the denigration of sacerdotalism, of ritual, *and* of caste. The sanskritic high ritual having been the exclusive domain of the Brahmins, its contents were rejected by the teachers of the Renaissance—Dayan-anda, Vivekananda, Gandhi, and others. The rejection gestalt covers sacerdotal ritual. Performance of ritual is not restricted to the Brahmin alone, but each person should be his own priest and philosopher. Still, in certain rituals (marriage and other life-cycle rites), the Brahmin-by-birth is essential and is treated as a paid functionary. In this respect the situation provides a corollary to occupational exclusiveness. This rejection also includes nationalism as against caste and village particularization (criticism of the modern political Renaissance uses the term "fissiparous tendencies"), so much so that the officially acceptable Indian is one who denies, dialectically that is, the existence of caste, denies also the reality of gods and goddesses (except as aspects of the one pervasive divinity of the Upanishads, the Brahman),[9] and asserts the existence of one India, one Hindu or Indian society, as well as caste by achievement and not by birth. The latter notion was powerfully upheld by Gandhi and, before him, by Tilak. Thus a Brahmin is a person who acts wisely and scholarly, a Kshatriya is a person who is a good soldier or ruler, and so on—a notion which is not borne out by the scriptures but which has now become part of the official Indian credo.

Objections which I have heard from fellow anthropologists that this complicated syndrome does not extend to Indian groups outside South Asia are quite unwarranted. East African Asians are not only fully cognizant of these ideological developments, but furthermore their leaders and a large number of sophisticates actively participate in the official ideology of the Indian or Hindu Renaissance: almost all Hindus in East Africa, as well as many Khoja Ishmailis and other non-Hindus, read and admire the late Swami Shivananda Sarasvati who was the most popular and least sophisticated figure of the Hindu Renaissance in the last two decades. Quite a few Gujaratis are ardent followers and admirers of Sri Aurobindo and the Pondicherry movement—particularly, however, some Patels, because one of their lead-

---

[9]Very few East African Hindus ever use the term *Brahman,* this being too scholastic a word. However, they all understand it when it is used. The universal being is usually referred to by theologically less ambitious terms, like *Bhagavan* or *Ishvar;* but almost all East African Hindus are aware of the personal-impersonal dichotomy of Hindu theology, a fact that comes out clearly in temple and other frequent religious meetings. The awareness is shared by women, very many of whom are actively interested in religious discourse quite apart from the simpler litanies *(bhajan, kirtan)* which are almost daily conducted by the Hindu women in the East African cities.

ers moved physically to Pondicherry for good after having propagandized the Aurobindo cult in East Africa. Here we have an interesting encroachment of the jati pattern into anticaste teaching, for Aurobindo claimed complete universality and probably meant it. In East Africa, where his first active follower was a Patel, the Patels have virtually monopolized the Aurobindo cult for their community as the most sophisticated form of modern Hindu ideology. This has become a prestige symbol which reinforces ideological cohesion on a visceral level, very typically in the manner of the old Indian model.[10]

It would not be astonishing at all if the East African Patels could at some future time be said to be followers of Aurobindo just as the Iyengars have been followers of Ramanuja for about six centuries. If the Asians' stay in East Africa can continue into the future, the Patels who follow Aurobindo might well become an endogamous group distinct from the non-Aurobindite Patels. This, however, is sheer speculation, for the model-particularization of Indian social history is not likely to remain unaffected in this and the next century.

Perhaps the main difference in the caste and philosophy (ideology) relation between the Asian groups in East Africa and the Indian sister communities is precisely of this quantitative sort. Newly accepted Hindu ideologies have not created endogamous groups in East Africa. There simply has been no time for them to form, the Asians being only in their third generation in East Africa. Thus, the Swaminarayani sect (mostly Patels but also other Gujarati groups of similar caste ranking) shows definite signs of becoming an endogamous group in the Gujarat and even in Bombay; not so in East Africa, where Patels marry according to their traditional pattern. On the other hand, the Panjabi Arya Samajists in India have not become an en-

---

[10]A tribe or a *jati* follows one or several types of cult, with one or several over-all theological doctrines known to its specialists; some prominent man within the caste fold creates or takes to a specific doctrine of the "great tradition"; largely because of his proselytizing the doctrine and of his being accepted by the monastic or ecclesiastical heads outside of his caste, the more perspicacious within it tend to get interested in the doctrine, which becomes the standard "philosophy" of the particular caste in due course. Thus, the Smartas of south India have the monistic Vedanta of the Samkārācarya variety as their basic "philosophy," the Iyengars the qualified dualistic teachings of Ramanuja.

dogamous group in spite of the fact that many followers in the last generation took on the name "Arya" in the manner of a caste designation, especially when they were of non-Brahmin and non-Khattri descent. In the Panjab, there seems to be a slight preference for an Arya Samaji boy to be married to an Arya Samaji girl. In East Africa there is no such feeling. Arya Samajis and Sanatani and even Sikh Panjabis of the same caste intermarry quite freely, although the ideological-sectarian provenance of the couple's families is taken note of and mentioned in a purely nonevaluative fashion.

The Panjabi groups keep marrying in the traditional jati pattern (Khattris marrying Khattris, Suds marrying Suds, Baniyas Baniyas) with little sectarian consideration if any.

In content, the main shift in caste in East Africa seems to proceed from a close-kin, village-exogamous group to a wider, basically linguistic type. It is a subtle shift, and cannot be analyzed without taking into account the alter-image of the various groups, and, to a much smaller degree, the alter-image of non-Indians toward the Asian minority. An aspect of these images is the names that are applied to the Indians. The indigenous Africans refer to the Asians by a strictly limited nomenclature: they would call *all* Asians Cutchi or Banya with the occasional exception of the Sikhs. The sophisticated, radio-television and newspaper term in Swahili is *Wahindi,* based on the model of tribal nomenclature, the prefix *wa-* designating a tribal name in Bantu languages; but this term is not used in ordinary African parlance.

The Sikhs are referred to as *Singa* or more frequently *kala Singa* ("black Singh"). The original model was provided by the Asians themselves, in all cases.[11]

The designations "Cutchi" and "Banya" are much more complicated. We do not know how the term "Cutchi" got such enormous vogue in East Africa, because the Cutchi speakers proper do not

---

[11]The Sikhs themselves have a legend that during the days of the building of the Railway, many Asians were picked off and killed by lions. The Indian word for lion is *simha (singha, singh,* and variants), and to distinguish the zoological lion who was white or yellow from the Panjabi lions, the Sikhs, the latter started calling themselves *kala-singha*—"black lion," which term got into vogue with non-Asian groups, both African and European.

really constitute a majority of the Gujarati speakers if Cutchi is to be taken as a Gujarati dialect.[12] The amazing thing is that all Asians except the non-Cutchi Gujaratis, for reasons to be adumbrated, refer to all Gujarati and Cutchi speakers as "Cutchi," a practice that gives chronic annoyance to the Gujarati Hindus who are *not* Cutchi-speakers. It is conceivable that this designatory habit set the example for the African's usage.

With respect to "Banya," very few Asians who are not Gujarati speakers (as Goans and Panjabis are not) know that the Patels and the Lohanas are not Banyas at all in the Gujarati-Cutchi caste ranking. Yet they tend to refer to all Gujarati-Cutchi speakers as Banyas unless they have a more specific reference for the person or group they are talking about—as Patel, Lohana, or the like. Again, it is quite probable that this Asian use spilled over to the Africans, through domestic servants or more likely through the clientele at the duka.[13] But the function of the dukawala (shopkeeper) is that of a Banya (Merchant) regardless of whether he belongs to the actual Merchant caste (Vaishya, Banya), or not. In fact, not more than about 10 per cent of all the dukawalas in East Africa are Banyas by caste: about 70 per cent are Patels, Lohanas, members of some "small" Gujarati castes, Visa Oshwal, and Navnit Vanik Jains[14]; about 15 per cent are Khoja and some other Muslims; the rest belong to other communities, including Goans and Panjabis. Yet functional

---

[12]In India, with its far greater proliferation of languages and dialects, Cutchi can be safely referred to as a separate speech-form, although it is not recognized by the Government of India as a language distinct from Gujarati; the Gujarati script is used for Cutchi writing. Linguistically, Cutchi stands somewhere between Gujarati and Sindhi, analogous to the position of Galician between Spanish and Portuguese. But as Cutchi and Gujarati speakers in East Africa overlap and as the present generation does not make the linguistic distinction in that territory, we must refer to the two as one language in this context.

[13]The duka (shop) being the proper domain of the Banya (Trader, Merchant) jati in the functional sense, the word *banya* is often used and heard in and around the location, where the speakers themselves know the difference.

[14]Jainism—probably the oldest living religion of the subcontinent—has about 15 million followers in India, the vast majority of whom are Banya by caste; Jainism is strict about diet and other taboos; its doctrine is archaic, complicated, pluralistic, and atheistic. A more detailed account of the East African Jains is to be found in Bharati 1965.

rather than caste-ascriptive identification seems to diffuse more read-ily to extraneous groups. Most Indians themselves tend to refer at times to all trading people as Banyas, although most of those who use the term in this functional manner are perfectly aware of the fact that the Banya proper are a caste. Not so, of course, the Africans —for short of two or three African sociologists or anthropologists no one knows or is interested in the distinction between functional and ascriptive Banya-hood. The genesis of the African use of Banya for all Indians (except again for the Sikhs) could now be easily traced, provided the initial argument is accepted. Consistently for over 50 years, Asians have been referring to Gujarati traders as "Banya" in a generic functional sense in front of Africans. Although they were aware of the difference between Banya-by-caste and Banya-by-trade, the Asians did not spell out the difference to the Africans (why in-deed should they) and this ambiguity may explain the African ap-pellatory extension of "Banya" to all Asians.

The reasons for most Asians referring to all Gujarati speakers as "Cutchi" are historical rather than linguistic. The first settlers in Zanzibar and Mombasa were predominantly Cutchi speakers; the Khoja Ishmailis, the most different and outstanding community in an all-over view, were converted Cutchi-speaking Lohanas. The Gujar-atis proper—Lewa and Kharwa Patels and other castes—did not initially mind being called "Cutchis" because the former were well established, and also because the cultural and linguistic distinction between Gujaratis proper and Cutchis is negligible when juxtaposed with other South Asian groups (Goans, Panjabis, and the like), and it tends to disappear as the Asian community stays on in East Africa. The long-persisting common designation of *Cutchi* and *Gujarati* must have aided the blurring of the original distinctive self-image of the two linguistic groups. Lastly, the very young and the present "schooling" generation of Cutchi provenance tend to hear and speak Gujarati rather than Cutchi at home and with their peers. The situation seems to be similar to that in the most sophisticated and affluent parts of the Panjabi population in urban Panjab and in Delhi, and with virtually all sectors in Karachi, Pakistan: though they are native speakers of Panjabi, they don't really like to speak it except in their innermost circle or with Panjabis who do not know Urdu; but they want their children to speak Urdu rather than Panjabi, the former being the more prestigious language. In East Africa, Gujarati is the literate Asian language, and there are few or no Cutchis left in East Africa who do not speak, read, and write Gujarati. Cutchi, of course, can be and is written in Gujarati characters, but writing in Cutchi is regarded as either folkloristic or as slightly lowbrow ("women sometimes do it").

Culture change on the caste level, then, is linguistic rather than anything else. In the first place, social intercourse no longer moves along caste lines in East Africa as it does in rural or marginally urban India. People meet and communicate on the basis of common language. Although virtually all Asians in East Africa speak and understand Hindi, not much corporate feeling exists among speakers of different vernacular languages. The Gujarati speaker may have his "best friend" among the Panjabis, but there is no intensive social mixing except on linguistic lines. The Panjabis would mix with each other socially, quite regardless of their caste, and a Panjabi Banya would be more comfortable with a Panjabi Muslim than with a Gujarati Banya. Concededly, socializing is not of prime relevance for the study of social structure: the Panjabi Banya (by caste—that is, an Aggarwal, Mittal, Goyal, or the like) may socialize with a Panjabi Muslim, but he will not choose a Panjabi Muslim as a mate for his son or daughter; neither would he choose a Gujarati Banya. These are not considerations of sociability, but of structural conformity. If, however, culture change is viewed in a wider anthropological sense, linguistic rather than caste socializing assumes much greater importance. Young people rebel against the stricture, and many Panjabi Hindu boys court, overtly or clandestinely, Panjabi Muslim girls.[15]

What has just been said leads into a final point, also on the linguistic level, and pertinent for the younger generation that is now

---

[15]Of course, those who do would date Khoja Ishmaili girls too, but I have a hunch that they do so by somewhat subtle psychocultural transference: we get along better with Muslims than with our own Hindus, they would argue, hence, on a noncognitive level, with Panjabi Muslims, due to the basic linguistic cohesion discussed just now. But then, because Muslims are seen as a separate cultural unit and as a different unit of interpersonal communication, Khoja Ishmailis (who are Gujarati speakers) are often included in this pattern; a further reason is that the latter are "freer," that is, more emancipated (in the general Asian image at least) than the other communities, and hence more likely objects of romance and courtship.

coming to the fore. Diffusely among all caste and religious groups, a sizable number of people under thirty use English as their medium of communication. Even among the older, the domestic use of English, however poor from a stylistic angle, has been considered prestige-giving. Among the young, of the medium-affluent to affluent sectors of the Asian population, English has become the common tongue. Young Panjabis, both Sikhs and Hindus, as well as Muslims; young Gujarati and Cutchi speakers, and all Goans, converse in English. And when such intimate processes as courtship or other interpersonally crucial discourse are pursued, English has become, and is increasingly becoming, the sole medium. This fact is bound to relax the interpersonal and intercaste situation toward a greater rapprochement and, most of all, toward a much larger degree of intercaste marriage, which alone affects and changes social structure in the long run. This tendency has been underrated by most anthropologists working in the Indian field. Though everyone in the diaspora drives cars and takes a walk with a transistor radio slung across his shoulder, these practices do not affect culture change in any but a trivial and anthropologically irrelevant sense. But premarital courtship does, and where premarital courtship across caste lines is made easier or possible through the use of a linguistic intercaste medium, culture change must ensue in structure and in content. There has always been a tendency in middle-class India to use English terms and phrases for critical communication (Bharati 1963), but in East Africa this syndrome is considerably more important. Where a Hindu Panjabi boy can and does ask a Gujarati-speaking Khoja Ishmaili girl for a date at the Rendezvous,[16] he does so in English; there would hardly be any other language in which he could or would do so, for neither of them know Hindi well enough to communicate such a suggestion. Also, to all Asians, romantic discourse in the vernacular is somehow felt to be improper or embarrassing; not so in English. Here, supported by English and American movies and by some amount of "popular" reading matter, a very large percentage of the adolescents and young adults feel at ease; the less than $\frac{1}{2}$ per cent of intercaste marriages among Asians in East Africa (the figure did not exceed this proportion in 1964) all came about through courtship conducted in English.

The kind of discourse that is inceptively apt to challenge funda-

---

[16]An Italian-owned restaurant-cum-coffeehouse in downtown Nairobi.

mentals, be they religious or ideological in the wider sense, is conducted almost exclusively in English. The reason is not so much that Asians feel shy about using their own language for discursive points, but rather that the Indian vernaculars, as spoken by the East African Asians, have not developed the style of critical or romantic discourse. Given the exigencies of Hinduism or Islam, the strictures of the caste system, the traditional rules, ritual, and ceremonial adherence, all juxtaposed with modernity, such discourse is just not conducted by Asians who speak only their vernacular (as the small dukawalas in the bush, or the *fundi*. It is conducted, if at all, by those who handle the English medium. By extension, therefore, English also aids cultural criticism, germinally at least, and it is almost certain that caste ideology in East Africa, as in India, would not have changed without the English language as a linguistic lever.

The Ideology and Content of Caste

The third and final part of this paper considers the ideology and content of caste in the more important Asian communities in East Africa and will cover well over 95 per cent of the settlers. I cannot include such small, though fairly influential groups as the Marathis, who number well over 500 in Dar es Salaam and other places; the Kerala Nayers and Christians, who are diffusely present in Tanganyika and to a lesser degree in the other East African countries; and the Bengalis, who number roughly 400 in East Africa. All of these are civil servants or people in clerical jobs in the middle and upper echelons of service. There are less than 100 Ceylonese families in Dar es Salaam, where they have a Buddhist temple quite close to the Kerala Kala Mandalam, the Malayalee service society. All of these are bound to leave East Africa in the not too distant future, as they had been hired on terminable contracts.

Let us start with the most numerous and economically strongest communities, the Gujarati and Cutchi Hindus and Jains. Among the Hindus, the most highly evident groups are the Patels, Lohanas, and the Shahs who, although they are mostly Jain by religion, are hardly distinct in matters of cultural behavior from the Gujarati Hindu groups, yet sufficiently distinct to be treated separately when caste is concerned.

When Gujarati and Cutchi speakers use the word 'Hindu' for a person or a group, they *always* mean Gujarati and Cutchi speakers *only*. It requires some directive prodding to make them agree (which they do with some amazement) that Panjabi or Maharashtrian Hindus are Hindus, too. Thus they take Gujarati together with Cutchi as the most general denominator of identification. The religio-ideological superstructure of Gujarati Hinduism or Hindu-hood serves as the test of identity. The Patels, Lohanas, the few Gujarati Brahmins, and perhaps the small castes (Sutarias, Darzis, Muchis, and other *fundi* castes) are culturally close and share the identical ideological content: a highly ritualistic, puritanical, largely anthropomorphical theology, in addition to social selectivity and segregation from other communities, both Hindu and non-Hindu. Unlike the Panjabis, who socialize on purely linguistic lines with other Panjabi speakers, regardless of their being Hindu, Sikh, or Muslim, the Gujarati Hindus do not relate to the Khoja Ishmailis, Bohras, and Ithna-Ashari although these three Muslim groups are Gujarati and/or Cutchi speakers like themselves.

"Socializing" here means a good deal more than just meeting for business or pleasure on the 'sundowner' or similar levels. Rather, in any Asian context, it implies constant or at least regular commensality (though not conjugality except within the constituent endogamous group) and cooperation and participation on the level of religious institutions. For instance, the various parochial service societies, though theoretically open to all Asians, actually include only Hindus by Gujarati usage: the Lohana Mandals all over East Africa have 95 per cent Lohana members, the rest being Patels and other Gujarati Hindus; the Patel Societies have 90 per cent Patels, the rest being other Hindus or Jains who share in the ideological pattern of the Gujarati Hindus despite the very radical theological differences between the Hindu and the Jain doctrines; the Visa Oshwal (Jain) organizations have about 80 per cent Jain members, the rest being other Hindus.[17]

---

[17] A high executive, even a president or secretary, frequently belongs to one of the other constituent castes—thus a Lohana institution in an East African city has a Patel or a Jain secretary or treasurer for a while. However, none of these would contemplate electing a Gujarati-speaking Muslim to any office, although he may and does participate in occasional functions as a guest or even as a speaker.

Continuing with the Patels proper, then. There are two sections of the Gujarati Patels in East Africa, the Kharwa from the western sectors of the Gujarati-speaking areas in the present State of Gujarat and the Lewa from the central and eastern regions.[18] Over 85 per cent of the East African Patels are Lewa. In the Gujarati caste ranking, Lewa ranked slightly above Kharwa and there was no inter-marriage in India, perhaps largely because of geographical separation of the two subgroups. In East Africa, Lewa and Kharwa Patels do not intermarry as a rule, and the very few exceptions (there are only three Lewa-Kharwa couples to my knowledge) were viewed by their elders as having married outside their caste. The feeling seems to have been that if a boy selects a girl himself, he does so with a view to flout caste rules. In one case out of the three Lewa-Kharwa liaisons known to me, the father insisted that his son had married outside their caste. When I demonstrated that his daughter-in-law was a Patel after all, he said "we do not regard those people [meaning Kharwa Patels] as Patels; they were different from us in India."

There are approximately half a dozen caste surnames among the East Africa Patels, *Patel* and *Amin* being the most frequent. There is no doubt that among the Gujarati-speaking Hindus, the Patels are the most highly sophisticated in an over-all view. Their service societies are proportionately as numerous as other group's societies, but their active fellowship devolves on lines of differential modernization and sophistication. Thus, in Nairobi and some other large cities, there are two ideologically opposed Patel sections institutionalized by distinct associations. These two are called the Patel Brotherhood and the Patel Club; they have different designations in other cities. In the self-image of the interested members of these organizations, the Brotherhood stands for orthodox, conservative behavior, the Club for "advanced," modernized attitudes and their implementation. Thus, the Patel Brotherhood recommends the continuation of vegetarian diet and abstention from alcoholic beverage. The Patel Club not only permits drinking but the large, rather elegant Club building in Nairobi has a well-equipped bar where male

---

[18]The descendants from the "six towns" near Ahmedabad (Satgaon), though Lewa, regard themselves, and are tacitly regarded by others, as slightly superior to the other Lewas, most of whom hail from the Charottar district in the Gujarat less than 50 miles from Ahmedabad.

club members meet and drink hard liquor almost every evening. The fact that the terms "advanced" or "modern" almost always imply the drinking of alcohol in East African Asian parlance is one reason why the more conventional view these terms with suspicion, whatever their beneficial implications.

The dichotomy between the Club and the Brotherhood and their respective equivalents does not mean that there are no Club members who are vegetarian and teetotalers. First, women do not drink as a rule, and those who do—this holds for all Asian communities—do so privately, except some of the very young and very sophisticated. Second, among Gujarati Hindus, well over 90 per cent are strict vegetarian—they do not touch meat, fish, and eggs. The membership of their husbands in the Brotherhood and the Club respectively has no bearing whatever on female traditional behavior.

In religious matters, the Patels show a great degree of "great-tradition" venturesomeness. Their connection with the Aurobindo movement in Pondicherry, South India, has already been pointed out as the main paradigm of religio-ideological experimentation. Among the "small Patel" (an East African Gujarati term covering in an overlapping fashion the less affluent and the less modern, that is, those who do not handle English as their intellectual medium) the most frequent religious "great-tradition" adherence is to the Swami-narayani cult (Bharati 1964). The image of the "small Patels," incidentally, affords an interesting sidelight on intragroup evaluation. Terms such as "small" often mean poor (the dukawalas of the smaller cities and the bush would refer to themselves as "small" and be referred to as such, even if some of them had acquired considerable wealth). "Small" when used to refer to the ego or the nos is frequently a protective device in an economically competitive society of a strongly conservative sort.

As would be expected in any Indian setting, the trade and employment preferences proceed on kin and caste lines. This statement, however, holds true entirely only for the "small" Patels as for other "small" parallel sections. At the top echelons of Asian trade in East Africa, as well as at the executive level in service and business, it cannot be said with fairness that employment and business preference is given to kin and caste mates—not at least during the past four decades or so. No doubt the Gujarati Hindus give preference to the

Gujarati Hindu, but here the standard-average-Gujarati, if we may borrow the term from Whorf, seems to have become the unit of selection. The seven or eight top industrialist families in East Africa employ Patels and other Gujaratis, even though they are Lohanas and Shahs. Where the joint family is large enough, and there are several sons to take over the different branches of the industry, the directors' jobs go to them. But where sons or relatives are lacking there has been a change toward wider selection.

In the alter-image of the other Gujarati speakers, the Patels are the most clannish and most self-centered, exhibiting singular arrogance. Apparently the Patels do not really object to this image.

The Lohanas are the other large Gujarati Hindu high-caste community. 'High-caste' here is used in a purely Gujarati context. In the all-Hindu caste ranking, both Patels and Lohanas would rank well below the Rajputs and other Kshatriyas, and perhaps would be on a par with the caste-merchants, the Banyas or Vaishyas of the varna classification. Upcasting one's own group is an age-old Indian custom quite as pervasive in East Africa as in the homeland. The Lohanas seem to have the strongest trend toward upcasting and their leaders go to considerable efforts to prove Rajput or other Kshatriya descent. One of the leading intellectuals of the community, a highly artistic and learned woman of about forty, who belongs to one of the economically most powerful Lohana families in Uganda, has spent quite a lot of money and energy to trace Kshatriya genealogy for the Lohanas. She has come to the conclusion that their ancestors were indeed Rajputs who fought Chingiz Khan (*sic*) and were settled in the Gujarat and in Cutch as warriors to defend the local kingdoms. Objectively, however, the Lohanas belong to the upper Sudra groups. They were not entitled to wear the sacred thread of the "twice-born" but many of them have taken to it, largely under the influence of the Ayra Samaj. This organization, though numerically strong and politically important only in the Panjab, has most of its Gujarati followers among the Lohanas in East Africa. Thus, paradoxical only to the casual observer, most high-caste Hindus among the Asians no longer wear the sacred cord although they are supposed to do so all the time, whereas many Lohanas, who are not ritually entitled to it, have taken to wearing it in East Africa.

The Patels rank a bit higher than the Lohanas in the Gujarati caste ranking. They were landholders (Patidars), and landholding over many generations tends to create ascriptive Kshatriya-hood; again, the function of the Kshatriya being, among other things, the holding of land and the farming out of rural work to laborers of lower caste status, the Gujarati Patels have assumed, so to speak, a "twice-born" status. Within East Africa, validity for the Patels being ranked slightly above the Lohanas is found in marital patterns. Among a dozen intercaste marriages between Lohanas and Patels, 10 are male Patel and female Lohana spouses; male-oriented hypergamy being quite frequent in most parts of India, this fact furnishes some sort of corroboration.

In the ideological approach of Lohanas and Patels toward non-Hindus, (in the Gujarati sense of East African parlance discussed earlier), Gujarati Muslims are not officially acceptable as partners. When asked whether or not they would look for Khoja Muslim business and social associates, several Lohanas and Patels, independently of each other, answered to the effect, "Why should we? We do not have to seek them out."

From other communities' alter-image of the Lohanas, several interesting points emerge. There is a strongly positive aesthetic appreciation by all, mingled with a sort of negative moral corollary typical for the contemporary Indian ideology: the Lohanas are handsome people; their women are the only really good-looking Gujarati speakers apart from the Ishmailis (who are good-looking *because* they are nothing but Lohanas converted to Shia Islam a couple of hundred years ago); but because the Lohanas are handsome, their morals are seen as tending to be loose. Many Lohanas are alleged to be unhappy in their married life, and most of the women who committed suicide during the past fifty years in East Africa were Lohanas who either could not get along with their mothers-in-law or whose husbands were unfaithful beyond toleration. This latter notion is frequently pronounced by Patels about Lohanas, but Lohanas, with the same frequency and certainty, reciprocate with equivalent statements about Patel women: most of the female suicides, they aver, are being committed among Patel women.

In intracaste relations, the Lohanas in East Africa are somewhat less rigid and conservative than the Patels—if the same ratio of modernization and its consequent abandonment of conventional ideological items be assumed. Although there is a large number of subcastes among the Lohanas, and though their sister community in western India preserves village exogamy, none of these seem to have any bearing on the community in East Africa. Among one hundred parents who had arranged marriages for their sons and daughters within the prescribed Lohana fold, village exogamy had been considered in two cases only and subcaste endogamy only once. The matches were not intentionally made in conventionally undesirable subcastes; rather, concern for arranging most of them within the conventionally permissible subgroups had not entered in the negotiations. The main reason for this comparative lenience in juxtaposition with the Patels seems to be that the Lohanas do not have a geographically reinforced dichotomy of the sort the Patels have, that is, between Lewa and Kharwa. All Lohanas were originally Cutchi speakers, and the fact that most of the younger Lohanas in East Africa now prefer Gujarati proper to Cutchi results from prestige and modernity considerations indicated earlier. Still, most Lohanas over forty speak Cutchi with their peers, though they speak Gujarati with their descendants and other young Lohanas. About one-third of the East African Lohanas hail from Gujarati-speaking areas proper, but the precise linguistic provenience—from a Cutchi or a Gujarati background—is in no way functional in intracaste matters and appears to be completely neutral.

On the other hand, there is more cohesion among the Lohanas as a whole than among the Patels, probably because of the relative lack of factions among the former. There is a head of the East African Lohana community, whose status is not disputed once he has been elected. He coordinates the religious, cultural, and educational activities of the Lohanas in all the territories for a period of office lasting five years. There is a tendency to reelect a senior, well-respected person. Thus, of the strictly Hindu communities (the Jains, who are even more tightly organized, are not strictly Hindu), the Lohanas are the most highly federated and intracaste communication seems to be smooth and almost perfect.

Whereas the Banyas, that is, people belonging to the merchant or Vaishya caste in India, are identified and thought to be coextensive with Gujarati traders in India, this identification is not the

case in East Africa. As was pointed out earlier, there is an identification of all Gujarati speakers with Banyas on a functional basis.
However, there is a considerable number of Banyas-by-caste in East
Africa. Though I could not obtain any exact figures, I would think
they form about 5 per cent of the Hindu Gujaratis. However, they
do not form any power block in the area and are not as conspicuous
a community as the Lohanas and Patels. Using wealth as a criterion
and taking the community as a whole, they would stand somewhere
between the Jain Shahs and the Lohanas. Culturally, they are strictly
endogamous; their ritual is the Gujarati type of bhakti, and formal
worship centers on Vishnu in his various forms and of the Mother
Deity (Jagadamba). As might be expected, they share what I have
called standard-average-Gujarati culture. In the all-India caste ranking, they stand above both the Patels and the Lohanas. They are
entitled to wear the sacred thread, though few if any of them still
do so in East Africa.

The Brahmins, though they form only slightly less than 1 per
cent of the total Asian population in East Africa, are a well-con-
tained community and respected as a whole, probably more than in
contemporary urban India. Their organization is the Brahmā
Samāj,[19] which is found in all the larger East African cities. The
majority of Brahmins belong to the Audich section of Gujarati
Brahmins.[20] Other Brahmin sections in the Gujarat are thought to
have been local, and their status is lower than that of the Audich
Brahmins, following the all-Hindu pattern in which Brahmins with
actual or legendary descent from relatively more northern regions
have higher ritualistic status than local Brahmins in relatively southern regions.

It goes without saying that a very small fraction of the East
African Brahmins are professional ritualists. Almost all purohitas

---

[19]*Brahmā-Samāj* in Gujarati simply means the organization of Brahmins.
The term has absolutely nothing to do with the *Brahma Samāj* (which
has a short "a" meaning "the Brahman principle" in Bengali)—the famous
and influential reform movement and church of the Hindu Renaissance,
founded by Ram Mohan Roy in nineteenth-century Bengal.

[20]*Audich* is derived from the Sanskrit *Udic* (north), and their legend
goes to say that the Gurjara kings of medieval times asked their ancestors to
come to improve the ritual and the pronunciation of the Vedic texts; they
claim to have Northern and even Kashmere provenience.

(professional priests) among the Gujaratis in East Africa are Audichs, and they are entirely in charge of the nitya and naimittika ceremonies —such regular life-cycle rites as marriage, initiation of boys (which happens usually a few days before marriage to save the double expense of two functions at different times), birth and death ritual, and the occasional rituals connected with healings, house warming, special blessings, and the like. One of the main functions of the purohita, in East Africa quite as much as in India (with absolutely no diminution in the "modern" setting of Nairobi, Dar es Salaam, and Kampala), is that of soothsaying, horoscope casting, predictions, divinations, and the whole gamut of predictory and valedictory offices so intimately tied up with the Brahminical lore. Although non-Brahmins perform healing and valedictory magic all over East Africa, the status of the jyotisi—the great-tradition astrologer—is reserved for the Brahmin exclusively.

Though it might be more logical to deal with the Panjabi Brahmins in our section on the Panjabi castes, a few remarks about them are appropriate at this point.[21] The Panjabi Brahmins, like most of the Gujarati Brahmins, follow the professions of the other settlers, except that the former tend to be in clerical and governmental services rather than in straight business, the Panjabi community being more service- than business-oriented. The number of purohitas (professional priests) among the Panjabis is less than a dozen in the big cities, and about another dozen in the smaller locations. No Gujarati ever hires a Panjabi Brahmin for any ceremonial work, nor does any Panjabi ever hire a Gujarati Brahmin for these offices. It is for this reason that the few Panjabi priests have full-time jobs, whereas the Gujarati purohitas usually do some trading themselves to supplement the somewhat meager income from sacerdotal work.

Temple priests, however, are usually hired for a definite period and brought over from India. They usually support the local pandit in the annual yajnas—the large-scale sacrifices sponsored by the various ritualistic groups—and they perform the daily ceremonies in the temples, of which there are well over one hundred in East Africa.

---

[21]The taxonomical arrangement in this book is that of caste rather than regional grouping; also, the number of Brahmins among the Panjabis (about 0.75 per cent) is even less, proportionately, than amongst the Gujaratis.

Brahmins, both Gujarati and Panjabi, tend to be stricter about food avoidances, though they seem to enjoy alcoholic beverages quite as much as other castes. Their women do not eat meat or drink liquor, but then few Asian women in East Africa do.

The self-image of the Brahmins is no doubt that of an elite group and contains the idea of greater ritualistic purity by birth. To the Indologist, there is nothing astonishing about the fact that hardly any Brahmins follow the great-tradition movements of the Hindu Renaissance (Aurobindo, Shivananda, or the like) since all these movements in India are antisacerdotal and their main ideological tenets comprise the doctrine of Brahminhood by temperament and spiritual achievement rather than by birth. The Brahmin-by-caste is accepted as a necessary residue of old times and as the only eligible functionary at the traditional rituals, especially marriage. For whatever claim to Brahminhood-by-spirituality the modern renaissance Hindu (in India and East Africa) may make, the idea of taking care of the ritual does not occur to him, chiefly perhaps because it would necessitate the rote learning of Sanskrit texts and of complicated rituals that require the hired specialist.

The attitude of the various Hindu communities toward the Brahmins in general and to their respective group's sacerdotal specialists differs in certain points from that in the Indian sister communities. In the first place, there is none of the minutely graded attitude pattern which we find in India, ranging from extreme disdain to quasidivine adulation of the Brahmin. The Asian population in East Africa being a congeries of just a few castes and groups, it seems logical that only a few attitudes are prevalent. To be exact, we can specify three attitudes toward the East African Brahmin. (1) the semiliterate small dukawala respects the Brahmin as the sole ritualistic functionary, as the source of supernatural knowledge (including that of the future) through his astrological and kindred qualifications, and as a person exalted by birth. He tends to connive at most of the nonsacerdotal caste Brahmins' indulgence in things not proper for the Brahmin by traditional standards, although he would censure these indulgences in his speech. (2) The literate and modern Asian, who is not specifically interested in religion and who has no active part in the Hindu Renaissance, tolerates the Brahmin with a shrug, as it were. He is deemed necessary for the rituals which cannot be dispensed with, and he is potentially an astrologer. Virtually all Asians in East Africa, Hindu, Sikh, and Muslim alike, believe in astrology as a possible science and over 60 per cent have hired the services of an astrologer at least once in their lives. (3) Lastly, the literate and religion-involved Asian who follows one or more of the great-tradition themes of the Hindu Renaissance (the Ramakrishna-Vivekananda movement, the Aurobindo cult, or the like) is systematically antagonistic to the ritual specialist. He tends to minimize the ritual in his home, unless it is of a new type created within his own special modern brand of great-tradition Hinduism. He claims as part of his ideology that persons are what they are not by virtue of their jati, but by virtue of their capacities, deeds, attitudes, and spiritual qualifications. For this view he has the support of the official culture of modern India as propounded by Vivekananda and Gandhi. They stressed those passages of the Hindu scripture where qualifications rather than birth are said to entitle a man to Brahminhood, Kshatriyahood, or other status.

These three attitudes exhaust the East African Hindu image of the Brahmin. Asian society in the area is simply not sufficiently stratified nor ideologically diversified to create and sustain the multiple attitude pattern Hindus in India project with regard to the Brahmins.

There is hardly any feeling of belonging together between the Gujarati and the Panjabi Brahmins: caste status as such does not bear significantly upon interpersonal relations in East Africa. The Gujarati Brahmin mixes with Gujarati Hindus and Jains, the Panjabi Brahmin with Panjabi speakers including Muslims. And on the sun-down level, all of them mix freely with all, including non-Asians, with no palpably greater degree of warmth between Gujarati and Panjabi speaker than between, say, Gujarati and native English speaker. All Indian groups have strong reservations about Goans and the latter lean toward Whites in their social contacts.

The "small castes" among the Gujarati speakers are about as conservative as the Indian sister communities in matters of trade, craft devolution, and socializing. The numerous mavericks among them do not conform. Those who have emerged from the craftman's circle have done extremely well. Men who belong to the Sutaria (Carpenter), Muchi or Mochi (Cobbler), or Darzi (Tailor) castes and who have entered the professions tend to avoid caste mates who

abide within their trade circle except for marriage and ritual, identifying themselves ideologically with the upper-caste Hindu and Jain
Gujarati rather than with their own caste-mates. They are also accepted as equals by Patels, Lohanas, and Brahmins in all social matters
except ritual and kinship. Marriages between these *fundi* castes (the
use of the Swahili word as a generic term for the "small" jatis is
pervasive) and other Gujarati castes are much rarer than those between Patels and Lohanas.

The Jains in East Africa are, next perhaps only to the Ishmailis,
the most highly organized and self-conscious group. The majority
of Jains belong to the Visa Oshwal[22] section. This is an intriguing
group. Jainism forbids the practice of agriculture, as it makes the
taking of microbic and other life inevitable. In India, Jains are
usually identified with Banyas (Traders) and indeed the great
majority of Jains in India are Banya by caste, who intermarry freely
with parallel Hindu Banya groups, both in the Gujarat and in Ra-
jasthan: the term 'marwari' in its caste connotation in India covers
Hindus and Jains. The Visa Oshwal and the numerically much
smaller Navnit Vanik[23] Jains hail from the Jamnagar region in
Gujarat, bordering on Cutchi-speaking areas. In India, they form
about 10 per cent of the total Jain population, which is roughly 15
million. But as it was Visa Oshwal and Navnit Vanik Jains who
settled in East Africa, the Asian image of the Jains in East Africa is
one of former farmers, in contrast to the alter-image in India, where
the Jains are identified with the merchants and often simply referred
to as Banyas. The most frequent caste name of both the Visa Oshwal
and the Navnit Vanik Jains is *Shah,* so much so that in East Africa
the term "a Shah" has become tantamount to "a Jain." The common
notion that they are the richest community is probably objectively
true. Perhaps the most thrifty of all Gujaratis, they also have a strong
organizational backing in India, a statement that cannot be made
about the other caste and parochial groups among the Asian Hindu

---

[22]The etymology of *Visa Oshwal* was not known to any of the informants
I asked; it is probably a medieval Gujarati development of *Visa-ujjvala* =
"excellent, illustrious, among the vaisya, or among the gentry, in general."

[23]The etymology of this caste designation is perfectly clear: it simply
means "Butter Vendors," by extension cattle breeders and cattle tending
agriculturists, similar to the Ahir in northern India.

settlers. Most of the communities in India publish a monthly organ whose title usually means "wellwisher of the x-community" or "news of the y-community" *(Lohana Sandesh, Patidar Hitaishi,* or the like) but only the Jains have a similar publication in East Africa itself. The Khoja Ishmaili papers are not strictly sectarian; Ishmailis own many secular newspapers and publications. But the Jain community sees to it that its cohesion is continuously reinforced by local publications.

In matters of religious practice and discipline, as well as in ritualistic organizations, the Jains rank next only to the Khoja Ishmailis. They have elaborate temples in Tanganyika and Kenya, where they are most numerous, and some of them contain exquisite works of art. Thus, the new Jain temple in Mombasa, an exact yet most tasteful replica of the Dilwara shrine in the Gujarat, is one of the few genuine architectural sights in East Africa. Sculptors were invited from India, as was the architect, but they in turn trained local Jains who have since become highly expert iconofactors in their own turn.

We now proceed to the Panjabi groups. The majority of the Panjabis are Sikhs, and among them over 90 per cent belong to the Ramgarhia caste, which has low caste ranking in the Panjab. In East Africa, they are identified as *fundi,* and indeed they were artisans, carpenters, contractors, masons, and the like from the beginning. They are known as the best craftsmen in East Africa; the fact is not challenged either by Europeans or by Africans. The Ramgarhias have their own gurdvaras (Sikh shrines) in almost every location, and attendance on Sunday (in emulation of the British Sunday as a regularized holiday) is complete. Some Ramgarhias have gone into the professions since the turn of the century, and at least two of them are among the most outstanding and highly respected Asians in East Africa, holding high and responsible government positions in independent East Africa. Most of these emancipated Ramgarhias do not like to be identified with the Ramgarhias by outsiders. Some of the most vociferous spokesmen for African and Asian integration who belong to this caste tend to become vehement whenever the topic of caste provenience is brought up. This vehemence follows a general tendency in India to deny the relevance of caste where one's own cannot be upcasted because its ranking is universally known. Patels,

Lohanas, Brahmins, Jains, Khattri, and Jats among the Panjabis tend to upcaste their group because their status is not exactly known except to the ritualistic specialist and, of course, to the interested anthropologist. There is a trend to deny caste any importance of functionality on the part of members of the low jatis (Sutarias, Muchis, Darzis, and the like) from Gujarat and the modernized Ramgarhias among the Panjabis in East Africa.

The minority group among the Sikhs are the Jats, the traditional farmers. They are wealthier than the Ramgarhias as a group in proportion. The Singh Sabha is their parochial institution in East Africa and its main sacerdotal commitment is the creation and organization of the gurdvaras (shrines) of the Singh Sabha, which are always separate from the gurdvaras of the Ramgarhias. They tend to be larger in size and more impressive in appearance, though the green cupolas of the Ramgarhia gurdvaras have an attraction of their own. The Singh Sabha Gurdvara in Nairobi, recently built, is a landmark and a structure of fine architectural design. It accommodates over 5000 persons quite easily. The Nairobi Ramgarhia temple, which is much older and much smaller in size, is packed with devotees on Sundays, whereas the attendance in the Singh Sabha Gurdvara is not as corporate and active.

The non-modernized Ramgarhias do not object to their appellation as *fundi;* in fact, they refer to themselves as such when speaking to non-Asians. In speaking with Asians they refer to themselves as Sikhs, or as Panjabis when they have shaved off their beards. Over 10 per cent of the East African Ramgarhias are "mechanized," the jocular North Indian term for a Sikh who have shaved off his beard. The Jats, though in a way more emancipated as a group, tend to be more conservative in appearance: hardly 3 per cent of the East African Jats have shaved their beards. Their sartorial conservatism is being reinforced during this period by the fact that quite a few of them have bought large tracts of wheat and sugar land in the former White highlands from white settlers who left for Britain or South Africa, thus reverting to their traditional work. Some Jats have bought up as much as 3,000 acres of wheat and/or cane land, and they grow their crops with the most up-to-date equipment. They are keenly aware of their special position as the only agriculturists among the Asians, and theirs is indeed a unique position: in the

African's image, the Asian is a tight-fisted, money-grabbing, uncivil, cold, and impolite petty merchant. There is no doubt that on the whole the Africans have been less hostile to the European settlers, because the latter were farmers and did something close to the Africans' heart albeit on an uncomfortably larger scale. That Indians in India are fundamentally agriculturists is not known to the average African, nor is he interested in what Asians do in India. The Jat families that have been on the land again for the past few years have indeed altered the surrounding Africans' picture of the Asians. But as this is a strictly regional situation, limited to the highlands around Eldoret and the cane-growing lowlands at Kibos near Kisumu, both of which are in Kenya, the image of the Asians as farmers (Narain Singh 1963) is not too likely to diffuse to the bulk of the East African indigenous population.

There is little intermarriage between Jats and Ramgarhias. Three Jat youths married outside their community during the ten years 1954-1964: one of them to an English girl, the other two to Panjabi Hindus. Less than half a dozen noncaste marriages among the Ramgarhias were reported over the same period. Only one Jat-Ramgarhia marriage is known to me and this was contracted between 1961 and 1964.

Socially, of course, the Jats and Ramgarhias are completely at ease with one another and almost so with Panjabi Hindus, most of whom are Khattri by caste. The Khattri, in India as in East Africa, upcaste themselves systematically: the etymological relation of the term *khattri* with the Sanskrit *ksattriya* is harnessed toward declaring the Khattris to be Rajputs, therefore members of the second varna. In the actual Indian caste ranking, they are nothing of the sort. Their status, ritualistically, is somewhat below the Panjabi Rajput or actual Kshatriya, and slightly above that of the Panjabi Banya (Aggarwal, Mittal, Goyal, or the like). Due to the strong Arya Samaj influence on the Khattris in addition to the numerally few Panjabi Banyas in East Africa, the original ritualistic gradation is blurred. In India, some Khattri gotras, especially those belonging to the Dhaighar group around Delhi, used to wear, and still do wear, the sacred cord. Though most other Khattris do not, pious Panjabi Banyas usually wear the cord. In East Africa, neither the Panjabi Banya nor the Khattri wear it except for their weddings.

Lastly we shall survey the Muslim groups. Here, more patently perhaps than in India and Pakistan where there is enormous complexity to Muslim society, the Muslims are enumerable in castes or jatis, that is, in strictly endogamous units. Whereas the sheer numbers of Muslim sects and jatis tend to obliterate mutual demarcations in northern India and in Pakistan, Muslim jatis come into relief in East Africa.

The most prominent and conspicuous Muslim group are the Shia Khoja Ishmailis, the followers of the Aga Khan. They form about 15 per cent of the total Asian population. Without exception, they were Lohanas by caste, converted to Shiism about 200 years ago (Picklay 1940). Historical accident perhaps more than anything else has made them into a unit that somehow stands out as separate from all other Asian groups, both in their self-image and in the alter-image of the other Asians, the Africans, and the Whites. The late Aga Khan, grandfather of the present young Aga Khan who is a Harvard graduate, passed a set of *firmans* (ex-cathedra injunctions) which altered the cultural physiognomy and the appearance of the Ishmailis. The women wear western dress as a result of one *firman* and they wear the saree only on formal occasions and in the evenings at parties, especially now that the saree has become known in international sartorial judgment as the most alluring garment.

The Ishmailis have their own places of congregation which they and the other Asians call the *Jamathkhana,* quite literally "assembly house," and they do not want it to be referred to as a mosque. In their ritualistic and religious behavior as well as in their inter-Asian and non-Asian relations they differ from the other Asians in almost every way. Although the most modern in their own eyes and in the minds of all other Asian groups ("modern" again being equated with mixing more freely, with more liberty between men and women, and with more indulgence in tobacco, drink, and the like), they are as strictly endogamous as the other groups. Only one intermarriage into another Gujarati Muslim group has been reported. Quite a few Ishmaili boys, however, have married English and other European women as a result of their stay in Europe or elsewhere abroad. Somehow, there seems to be less opprobrium on such a match than on an Ishmaili-non-Ishmaili Asian liaison. Over one hundred Ishmaili men have married white women, though only two Ishmaili girls married aliens; these latter live abroad and would hardly be accepted in their parental society. Again, a feeling of relative propriety of a hypergamous liaison might be the basis: Whites are automatically the lowest in the all-Indian caste-ranking, and Indian men have always married "down" though of course not to so radical a degree.

The other prominent Gujarati-speaking groups, not quite so affluent, are the Khoja Ithna-Asharis, followers of the eleventh Imam, and the Vohras or Bohras. The Ithna-Ashari Muslims are the most conservative among East African Gujarati Muslims. Unlike the Ishmailis, they do not believe in higher education for women, in line with the official Indian culture of modern times, as sending them to college might "spoil" them ("spoiling" means "conniving at flirtatious behavior," and nothing else). Although the Ithna-Ashari do not believe in a living Imam who is available to the congregation as the Aga Khan is to the Ishmailis, they believe in a hidden message accessible to the select and pious. They have a federated organization with its headquarters in Arusha, Tanzania, where they publish the Gujarati periodical *Federation*. It follows in every respect the published organs of the various Indian castes mentioned earlier. It coordinates religious and educational activities in the community and issues edifying tracts of Shia Islamic pertinence. The maulvis (the ministers) are usually non-Gujaratis and are invited from India and Pakistan. The idea is that a minister for the Ithna-Ashari should be a Khwaja himself, that is, a linear descendant of Imam Hussain, martyred in Yemen in the thirteenth century. Although the direct statement is not made even by the maulvis themselves, most of whom are native Panjabi or Urdu speakers, the implication seems to be that North Indians are most likely descendants from the Imam.

The Ithna-Ashari were also Lohanas previous to their conversion to Shia Islam, though it appears that some Ithna-Ashari have "small" jatis as their background. They are strictly endogamous and no intercaste liaison has been reported for the ten years 1954-1964. The Ithna-Asharis constitute about 3 per cent of the total Asian population.

The Vohra (or Bohra) Muslims are Brahmins by descent, and they are both aware and proud of this fact. Although endogamous and commensal to a greater degree than other Muslim groups in East Africa, they have largely given up the onion-shaped turban, the typical Bohra dress their men wear in India and Pakistan. The spiritual center of the Vohras is and remains Bombay, where their head, who bears the illustrious title *Dai-ul-mutlaq* (representative of divine communication) has his seat. He is supposed to have communication with the living Imam who is thought to live in hiding, and some pious Bohras believe that the Dai may at times be the Imam himself. Though not as affluent, as a group, as the Ishmailis, there is considerable wealth among the Vohras. The Karimji Jivanji family, the richest and most powerful in Tanzania, is Bohra.

The Panjabi Muslims in East Africa are partly Sunni and partly Ahmaddiya. But these are sectarian designations with no one-to-one caste equivalence, hence they should not be treated in a study of caste.

We are now at the end of our study. It is possible, even likely, that many of the caste-originating structures will disappear in East Africa, provided the Asian community continues to stay on there, which is doubtful. Yet, if the basic definition of jati is that of an endogamus group, then jati will last in East Africa about as long as in metropolitan and urban India. Prophecy is not the anthropologist's job; the fact that about 1 per cent of the Asians in East Africa have married across caste lines during the long period of their settlement weigh heavier than the enthusiastic forecasts of modern Asians that caste is vanishing in East Africa.

REFERENCES

BHARATI, AGEHANANDA
1963 "Kinship term avoidance and substitution in North Indian middle class milieux." *Sociologus* XIII:2:112-120.
1965 "A social survey of the Indians in East Africa." in *The Indians of East Africa,* D. P. Ghai, ed. Cambridge: Cambridge University Press.
HSU, FRANCIS L. K.
1959 "Structure, function, content, and process." *American Anthropologist* 61: 790-805.
1963 *Clan, caste, and club.* Princeton: D. Van Nostrand Co.
KLASS, MORTON
1961 *East Indians in Trinidad.* New York: Columbia University Press.
KUPER, HILDA
1960 *Indian people in Natal.* Natal: Natal University Press.

320   AGEHANANDA BHARATI

MAYER, ADRIAN C.
1963   *Indians in Fiji.* London: Oxford University Press.

NARAIN SINGH, ED.
1963   "The Asian as farmer." In *Kenya independence day souvenir.* Nairobi: Kenya Indian Congress.

NIEHOFF, ARTHUR, and JUANITA NIEHOFF
1960   *East Indians in the West Indies.* Milwaukee Public Museum: Publications in Anthropology, No. 6.

PICKLAY, A. S.
1940   *History of the Ishmailis.* Bombay: Popular Printing Press.

SHILS, E.
1959   *The intellectual between tradition and modernity: the Indian situation.* The Hague: Mouton & Co.

SRINIVAS, M. N.
1956   "A note on Sanskritization and Westernization." *Far Eastern Quarterly* XV:4:481-505.

STAAL, J. F.
1963   "Sanskrit and Sanskritization." *Journal of Asian Studies* XXII: 3:261-275.

STEWARD, JULIAN H.
1955   *Theory of culture change.* Urbana: University of Illinois Press.

GLOSSARY

apad dharma   Rules of conduct which may be applied during emergency situations when normal rules cannot be followed.

Arya Samaj   Modern reformist Hindu sect which advocates return to the Vedas. Founded by Swami Dayananda in 1875.

apanjat   Slogan used during the 1961 general election in Guyana in an effort to gain unity based on Indian culture.

atma   Universal soul or spirit.

babuji   Honorific title or term of respect.

bhagwat   Hindu ritual usually involving some religious instruction by reading and interpreting sacred texts.

baitka   Generic term applied to Hindu socioreligious associations; a meeting place.

bamboo wedding   Traditional and orthodox form of Hindu wedding. Frequently referred to as "under the bamboo" among overseas Indians.

Bhagavan   Term used to refer to the Universal Being by Hindus.

bhajan   Adoration, worship.

bhakti   Devotion and love of God.

Bharat Sadhu Samaj   A modern religious and political organization of holy men (sadhus) in India.

Brahmo Samaj   A nineteenth-century religious movement devoted to restoring a "pure" Hinduism. It makes use of the Upanishads for their authority.

Brahman   The Supreme Being; ultimate and absolute reality.

Chattri   Term used by overseas Indians to refer to those of the Kshatriya varna.

chela   Godchildren.

321

chowdree   Headmen of a panchayat or village organization.

creolization   A process of culture change present in East Indian groups over-seas and especially in the Caribbean area, resulting in the modification of traditional Indian culture and greater sharing among diverse cultural groups coexisting in the same area.

dakshina   Gifts made to Brahmins; ritual payments.
deota   Village godlings.
dharma   Duty as prescribed by the sacred scriptures; the proper way of life; righteousness.
dhoti   Article of clothing covering the lower part of the body. Usually tied to give the appearance of full-draped trousers.
Divali   Festival devoted to the goddess Lakshmi. Sometimes depicted as the festival of lights.
driver   Overseer; a position that characterized indentured systems on the sugar estates.
duka   A house or shop, frequently of a temporary nature and/or one that is located in the rural areas; a temporary structure used for shading in wooded and field areas.
dukawala   Shopkeeper; one who uses or inhabits the duka.
Durga Jhandi   Ritual devoted to the goddess Durga.

eye-pass   Offenses and disputes regarding prestige that occur on Guyanese plantations.

fire-pass   (fire-walking) A south Indian ritual which involves walking barefoot across hot coals, usually in fulfillment of a vow.
fundi   Swahili term for skilled artisans. The word *fundi* has been incor-porated into the Indian languages spoken in East Africa.

Gentoo   Corruption of the word Hindu. Used extensively by migration officials in recording the caste of indentured migrants.
ghee, ghi   Clarified butter.
Gita, Bhagavadgita   Sacred scriptures of Hinduism.
gotra   Clan. Usually exogamous.
guayap   System of reciprocal exchange of labor in rural Trinidad.
guru   Teacher; spiritual preceptor.

Hanuman   A Hindu deity, the monkey hero who was deified because of the aid he rendered to Rama in his recovery of Sita; sometimes referred to as Mahavira or Mahavira Swami. The object of frequent ritual.
Harijan   Unclean or so-called "scheduled castes" in India.
Hindu raj   Hindu rule or government.
hur   Reciprocal exchange of labor in Trinidad.

jajman   Patron.

jajmani system   System of economic exchange among castes in rural India.

jandhi, jhandi, jhandhi   A religious ceremony; in Guyana, a flag associated with a ritual.

janeo, janeu, janao, jeneo   Sacred thread which can be taken only by the "twice-born" castes.

jati   The effective, endogamous unit in the caste system; often translated as *nation*, especially by overseas Indians.

ji   Honorific suffix.

jumby   Spirit which is widespread in the Caribbean.

Kabir Panth   The religious sect devoted to the teachings of Kabir, a fourteenth-century Muslim weaver whose doctrines attempted to combine elements of Hinduism and Islam.

Kali Mai   Religious healing ceremony in Guyana; a shrine devoted to the Hindu goddess Kali.

karma   The law of action and causality. Closely linked to the Hindu concept of reincarnation.

mandir   Hindu temple.

maraj   Name of Brahmin caste; surname of Brahmins; title of honor given to those Brahmins in Guyana who lead a respectable life. Also *maraz* in Mauritius.

mati   A term used in Guyana to indicate persons of equal social status and power.

maya   Illusion.

moksha   Release from the cycle of birth and death; salvation.

nation   Jati; the effective endogamous unit in the caste system.

obeah   Sorcery; magical curing. Widespread in the Caribbean.

padhan   Vice-head of a panchayat.

panchayat   Council, either village or caste.

pandit   A scholar or learned man. Frequently applied to Brahmins and especially Brahmin priests.

papa, pap   Sin.

passing   Process of changing caste status. Held to be relatively common practice among indentured migrants.

pattal   Leaf plate.

puja   Generic term for Hindu ritual, usually involving the worship of an image of a Hindu deity.

pujari   Temple caretaker.

punul   Tamil word for sacred-thread ceremony, *janeo*.

purohita   Priest.

purdah   Muslim practice of seclusion of females. Extended to Hindus, especially in north India.

Ramayana   Hindu epic relating the incarnation of Vishnu as Rama; also *Ramayan*.

Ravana   The devil or king of the demons; major character in the Hindu epic, the *Ramayana*.

Ravidas   Term used to refer to members of the Chamar caste.

roti   Flat bread.

sadhu   A holy man.

samanvaya   Reconciliation of opposing views about the same matter.

samsara   Reincarnation.

sanatan dharma   The eternal way.

Sanatan Dharma Maha Sabha   Hindu socioreligious organization. Depicted as the most orthodox of the Hindu sects.

sandhya puja   The daily prayers of the "twice-born" Hindus.

sanskritization   Process of culture change which involves raising caste status and emulation of Brahminical behavior.

sannyasi, sannyasin   An ascetic; one who has renounced the material world.

Seunerini   A member of the Siva Narayani Hindu sect.

siddha   Uncooked food; reward, gift, or ritual payment made to Brahmins.

sirdar   Overseer.

Siva Narayani   Hindu religious sect.

sruti   Revealed scriptures. Most frequently associated with the Vedas.

Sunni   A person who belongs to one of the two major sects of Islam; the orthodox sect of Islam.

twice-born   The members of the three highest varnas.

upanyana   Sanskrit for the sacred-thread ceremony (janeo) of the "twice-born."

varna   Classification of Hindu society which places all castes into five major categories—Brahmin, Kshatriya, Vaishya, Sudra, and Untouchables. The first three are the "twice-born" and the fifth is outside the caste system.

Vedas   Basic scriptures of Hinduism; revealed (sruti) texts.

Vishnu   A major Hindu deity; identified as the second member of the Hindu Triad which is composed of Brahma, the first and primary member, Vishnu, the second member, and Siva, the third member.

yag   Reading and exposition of the scriptures.

yajna   Annual sacrifices.

INDEX

Date Due

OCT 14 '81			
MAR 0 1 2001			